THE POLITICS OF PROTEST:
THE ISRAELI PEACE MOVEMENT AND
THE PALESTINIAN INTIFADA

T0367232

For Dafna

The Politics of Protest

The Israeli Peace Movement and the Palestinian Intifada

Reuven Kaminer

sussex
ACADEMIC
PRESS

First published 1996 by

SUSSEX ACADEMIC PRESS
18 Chichester Place
Brighton BN2 1FF, United Kingdom

Distributed in the United States by
International Specialized Book Services, Inc.
5804 N.E. Hassalo St.
Portland, Oregon 97213-3644
USA

British Library Cataloguing in Publication Data
A CIP catalogue record for this book is available from the British Library.

ISBN 1–898723 28 1 (hardcover)
ISBN 1–898723 29 X (paperback)

Copy-edited and typeset in 10 on 12 Palatino
by Grahame & Grahame Editorial, Brighton, East Sussex
Printed and bound in Great Britain by
Biddles Ltd, Guildford and King's Lynn

Contents

Preface

The Palestinian Intifada, which broke out in December 1987, continued for more than three years. In a matter of months it destabilized Israel's twenty-year long effective control of the occupied territories. Naturally, world public opinion and the media focused mainly on the direct clashes between the Palestinian community and the Israeli Defense Forces. However, the main goals of the Intifada were basically political, and in order for these goals to be realized it was important that the Intifada influence the thinking and the political behavior of the Israeli establishment. The message of the Intifada for the Israelis was that the Palestinian question was not going to disappear and that without a solution for the Palestinians there could be no peace or quiet in the area.

The Israeli peace movement had consistently rejected the carefully cultivated belief that the occupation had created a new and irreversible status quo and that the Palestinian question was fading into the historical past. It was the first political force in Israel which understood the meaning of the Intifada and perceived that the uprising could serve as a starting point for a new approach to the Israeli-Arab and the Israeli-Palestinian conflict.

The emergence of a strong protest movement in Israel against the repression of the Intifada was yet another indicator that the status quo in the occupied territories was crumbling. The peace movement was ready and able to suggest viable alternatives to the occupation which had long before lost any semblence of being "liberal" – an illusion that Israel tried to foster in the first years after the June 1967 war. Although the voices of moderation in Israel's parliament filled a vital role in criticizing the policies of the Likud–Labor, national unity government, it was the protest movement, through its many, highly diverse components, which kept up the pressure on the government and convinced much of the public that Israel had to change its policies. This book describes the emergence and the growth of the protest movement in Israel in response to the new circumstances created by the Palestinian Intifada, and concentrates on its political content and impact.

I believe that many observers – because of the emphasis that protest groups place on action as opposed to ideology – tend to underestimate the role of the political thinking devoted to issues of policy and strategy in the activity of protest formations. Drawing on the Israeli experience, I have attempted to show that the new organizational forms, developed by the Israeli peace movement, have a rich political life of their own. However, instead of choosing between alternative theoretical options (each claiming to be the sole "correct line"), protesters and protest formations create new political syntheses designed to attract potential activists and mobilize part of the public. In so doing, protest politics and activity pave the way for the emergence of new strategies and forms of political struggle.

Defining the Israeli Peace Movement

The Israeli peace movement is the sum of all the organized political forces which attributed a major degree of responsibility to Israel for the emergence and the continuation of the Israel-Arab conflict. Activists and supporters of the peace movement came from that section of the public which rejected the simplistic, widely-held belief that the absence of peace and the ever present danger of war stemmed from a single source, i.e., the refusal of the Arab world to recognize the legitimacy of the Zionist presence in the region. Of course, there were widely different approaches in the peace movement regarding exactly how much blame to attribute to each side: militants considered Israeli policy as the decisive, if not exclusive source of the conflict; moderates underlined the responsibility of both sides while stressing the value of greater and more sincere Israeli efforts to overcome the dangerous deadlock. "The Politics of Protest" attempts to tell the story of the entire peace movement and its main component forces as they battle against the policy of their own government; at the same time attention is devoted to the differences between the two main sections of the peace movement, between moderates and militants.

While it is still too early to measure the precise influence of the Israeli peace movement on the shift in official Israeli policy which led to mutual recognition between Israel and the PLO in the Oslo Agreement of September 1993, the Israeli peace movement's response to the Intifada deserves special attention for two central reasons. Firstly, the peace movement created a unprecedented diversity of new, autonomous protest formations and provided a wealth of experience regarding political activization in a period otherwise characterized by growing alienation between citizens and the political process. Secondly, the depth and the scope of protest activity involved an unprecedented level of cooperation and solidarity between Israelis and Palestinians in the occupied territories. One would like to hope that the links that were forged between Israelis and Palestinians in the battle against the occupation may play an important role in building and strengthening peace. It is these two unique phenomena which justify a highly-focused inquiry on the peace movement during an intensive period of activity in highly specific circumstances: the Palestinian Intifada. I have no doubt that the experience accumulated in this period is of importance for both observers of the Middle East scene and for students of political action and protest in other spheres.

I do not claim to be neutral regarding the subject under discussion in these pages. In addition to identifying with the broad goals of the peace movement in Israel, I personally participated in many of the events portrayed here. Despite this involvement, I sincerely believe that I have presented a fair and accurate account of the Israeli peace movement's response to the Palestinian Intifada. I would like to stress that this is, as far as I know, the first comprehensive effort to tell the story of protest in Israel during the period of the Intifada; it makes no claim to be exhaustive. Unfortunately, I have not been able to mention all the groups active during the relevant period. The subject under discussion is worthy of many interpretations and there are certainly additional aspects of protest action that deserve further treatment.

In writing this book, I have enjoyed the counsel and support of many colleagues and friends. Prof. Joel Beinin, Prof. Stanley Cohen, Ruth Cohen, Judy Blanc, Dafna Kaminer, Randy Freidman and Sheldon Klimist read and commented on the whole or significant parts of the manuscript. Prof. Linda Gordon, Prof. Gordon Fellman and Prof. Baruch Fishhoff offered welcome encouragement. Needless to say that the book's many limitations and weaknesses, are the sole responsibility of the author.

Glossary of Political Parties and Groups

The purpose of the following list (in alphabetical order) of political organizations – parliamentary parties, the smaller extra-parliamentary radical groups and protest formations – is to assist readers unfamiliar with Israeli politics in following the thread of events that had a direct bearing on the development of the Israeli peace movement.

Ad Kan (Up to Here) – Group of academicians at Tel Aviv University which developed a militant line against the occupation and conducted intensive activity on campus. Ad Kan worked with the radical section of the peace movement on a regular basis.

Ahdut Ha'avodah (Unity of Labor) – Ahdut Ha'avodah, established after a split with MAPAI in 1944, was a militant Socialist-Zionist party which combined militancy on social issues with extreme militarism and expansionism. Based on the Kibbutz Ha'meukhad federation of kibbutzim, the party formed an Alignment with MAPAI in 1965 after years of bitter rivalry and merged with that party to create the Labor Party in 1968.

Association of Israeli and Palestinian Physicians for Human Rights – The Association monitored violation of human rights in the medical field resulting from repressive acts by the occupation authorities and extended assistance to Palestinian physicians working in extremely difficult conditions.

B'tselem, Israeli Information Center for Human Rights in the Occupied Territories – B'tselem was established by human rights activists in the various Zionist parties and quickly earned the respect of the media and political circles by issuing a steady stream of

xiv

accurate reports exposing the scope of human rights violations by the Israeli Defence Forces.

Citizen's Rights Movement (CRM) – Stressing individual and human rights, supporting the citizen against bureaucratic inflexibility, the CRM founded in 1973 by Shulamit Aloni grew, over the years, progressively closer to the two-state solution. The CRM gained three seats in the 1984 elections and was later joined by MK Yossi Sarid who left the Labor Party in protest against its decision to form a national unity coalition with the Likud. The CRM, MAPAM and Shinui joined together to form MERETZ, which received 10 percent of the national vote (12 seats) in the June 1992 Knesset elections.

Committee Against the War in Lebanon (CAWL) – Established within hours of the Israeli incursion into Lebanon on June 5, 1982 and basing itself on the organizational structures developed by the CSBZU, CAWL spearheaded the movement of growing opposition to the war.

Committee for Solidarity with Bir Zeit University (CSBZU) – Established in November 1981 in response to the closure of the Palestinian university by the military authorities, the CSBZU was the focus of militant action and educational activity by a broad assortment of radical individuals and groups against the occupation.

Committee of Jewish and Arab Creative Artists (Va'ad Ha'yotzrim) – The group, which came into existence before the Intifada, went on to achieve an impressive level of Palestinian – Israeli cooperation while attracting many Israeli artists who were identified as supporters of the Zionist-left.

Communist Party of Israel (CPI) – The CPI, the strongest force on the non-Zionist left, was highly orthodox in its support for the Soviet Union. From 1945, the Palestinian Communist Party (the forerunner of the CPI) held that both Jews and Arabs have an equal right to national self-determination in Palestine. A major split occurred in the CPI (1965) resulting in the emergence of rival groups both claiming to represent Israeli communism. The Mikunis-Sneh faction revised its opposition to Zionism and merged with various left-Zionist groupings; the Vilner-Toubi faction, known also as Rakah, the New Communist List, maintained the CPI's traditional line. (See also: Democratic Front for Peace and Equality – DFPE.)

Dai La' kibush (End the Occupation) – Dai La'kibush, formed immediately after the outbreak of the Intifada, December 1987, was a coalition of left-wing groups and individuals and a pace-setting force during the first year of the Intifada.

Democratic Front for Peace and Equality (DFPE) – The establishment of the DFPE by Rakah (New Communist List) in 1977 was an attempt to broaden the Communist party's appeal. However, the public and the media, and even party supporters, never actually distinguished between the Front and the party.

Imut, Mental Health Workers for the Advancement of Peace – The organization enjoyed considerable support from members of the profession and was able to synthesize professional concerns with a forceful statement against the corrupting influence of the occupation. It organized a series of annual national conferences to examine the ramified psychological effects arising from the Intifada and its massive repression.

Israeli Committee Against Torture – The Committee specialized in documenting and reporting the wide use of torture by the Israeli SHABAKH (General Security Services).

Israeli Council for Israeli-Palestinian Peace – The Council, founded in 1975, was led by a group of prominent Israelis who stressed their Zionist credentials while pioneering contacts with the leadership of the Palestinian Liberation Organization.

Israeli Labor Party – Direct continuation of MAPAI from 1968, the Israeli Labor Party participated in electoral battles on its own or together with additional Socialist-Zionist parties in the framework of the Alignment (Ma'arakh). Both MAPAI and its successor, the Labor Party, encompassed a full range of conflicting approaches to relations with Palestinians and the Arab world, from militaristic nationalism ("activism") to realistic moderation.

Kav L'oved (Workers' Hot Line) – Kav L'oved was a human rights organization which specialized in protecting the rights of Palestinian workers from the territories who sought their livelihood in Israel.

MAPAI (later known as the Labor Party) – MAPAI (Party of the Workers of Eretz-Yisrael), headed by Ben-Gurion, was the dominant party in the pre-state Jewish community in Palestine (the Yishuv) and during the first three decades of Israeli independence. MAPAI combined a right-wing Social Democratic philosophy with a pragmatic approach that gained it a central role in Zionist construction and politics.

MAPAM (United Workers' Party) – MAPAM, historically the

most militant and internationalist party of the Socialist-Zionist movement, called for reaching understanding with the Arabs. MAPAM was the political arm of a major kibbutz federation, KIBBUTZ ARTZI, which was in turn the historical project of the HASHOMER HATZAIR Zionist Youth movement. MAPAM, became, over the years, a consistent supporter of Peace Now.

Matzpen, Israeli Socialist Organization – Matzpen, established in 1962 by a group expelled from the CPI for criticizing conservative and bureaucratic distortions in the Soviet Union and the international communist movement, went on to develop a critique of Zionism as colonialism and Israel as a settler society. Towards the beginning of the seventies, clashes between different Trotskyist, Maoist and independent Marxist tendencies weakened the organization which had attracted national and international attention on the basis of its radical critique of Israel and its role in the region.

Minute Before the War (MBTW) – An ad hoc formation of academicians and intellectuals which promoted an initiative designed to defuse the Persian Gulf crisis. The group suggested that Israel offer to negotiate withdrawal from the occupied territories in return from Iraq's willingness to leave Kuwait.

Mo'ked – A Left-Zionist election bloc created in 1973 by a combination composed of former MAPAM members, many of whom had been active in SIAH, and the pro-Zionist section of the CPI. The Mo'ked list, headed by Meir Pa'il, gained one seat in the 1973 Knesset elections and later became a constituent part of the coalition that created SHELI in 1976.

Movement for Peace and Security (Ha'tnuah Le'shalom ve'bitakhon) – Established by professors and students at the Hebrew University in 1968 in order to counter propaganda for the annexation of the occupied territories, the Movement for Peace and Security argued that annexation and the occupation would endanger both the Jewish and the democratic character of Israel.

Nitzotz (Derech Ha'nitzotz) – Nitzotz, one of the Matzpen splinter-groups, was active in and around various militant sections of the peace movement. Nitzotz suffered from repression by the authorities for alleged membership in the Democratic Front for the Liberation of Palestine.

Peace Now – Formed by Israeli Defense Force reservists in 1977, and defining itself as a mainstream Zionist force, Peace Now expressed the readiness for compromise and moderation in broad sections of the electorate. Peace Now managed to mobilize peace-loving supporters of the major central and left Zionist parties and built up a cadre of activists who preferred working in Peace Now, in a protest movement framework, to the alternative of participating in less attractive and effective party organizations. Peace Now always saw itself as part of the national consensus on questions of security and stressed its desire to exert practical influence on day-to-day decisions. Peace Now's ability to rally tens and occasionally hundreds of thousands of demonstrators in critical periods underlined its pivotal role in Israeli protest activity.

Progressive List for Peace – Parliamentary list, headed by Mohammed Miari and Mattityahu Peled, gained two seats in the 1984 elections on the basis of a program calling for full Israeli withdrawal from the occupied territories. The party failed to receive the one percent minimum required for representation in the 1988 elections.

Rabbinic Human Rights Watch – The group protested against human rights violations, stressing the contradictions between Israel's behavior as an occupying power and the precepts of Judaism, while seeking to promote dialogue with Moslem and Christian Palestinian clergy.

Revolutionary Communist League (RCL or Le'kam) – Le'kam, developed as a Trotskyist faction (linked to the Fourth International) within Matzpen. From the late 1970s, despite its ideological proximity to the rejectionist currents in the PLO which denied Israel's legitimacy, Le'kam members participated in militant peace groups which fought against the occupation and favored the two-state solution.

SHANI (Israeli Women Against Occupation) – SHANI was a Jerusalem-based women's group which firmly supported the two-state solution. SHANI stressed the importance of political and educational work, while participating in Women In Black and other coalitions of the women's peace movement.

SHASI – Israeli Socialist Left – Independent Marxist, non-Zionist group formed in 1975, chiefly by members of the left-wing of SIAH. SHASI actively built and participated in various peace coalitions supporting the "two-state solution."

SHELI – An election bloc formed in 1976 and based on a coalition headed by Lova Eliav, former Secretary-General of the Labor Party, SHELI ran for the Knesset in 1977 and won two seats on a platform supporting Palestinian self-determination and negotiations with the PLO. SHELI included Mo'ked, Uri Avneri's group MERI, and a splinter of the Israeli Black Panther group (which appeared in the early 1970s to challenge discrimination against Israel's Sephardic poor). Internal dissension weakened the group which failed to pass the one percent threshold in the next elections in 1981.

Shinui (Change) – A liberal grouping with strong dove tendencies established in 1976 as part of the Democratic Movement for Change which gained 15 seats in the 1977 Knesset elections. Shinui, headed by law professor, Amnon Rubenstein, survived the demise of the Democratic Movement for Change established in 1977, continued to receive about two seats in subsequent elections and expressed dove sentiment and sensitivity to constitutional issues in sections of the public which had no links with the various Socialist-Zionist parties.

SIAH **(New Israeli Left)** – Based on ideas drawn from the student rebellions of the 1960s, adapted to Israeli conditions, SIAH, formed in 1968, introduced active confrontational tactics in the fight against annexation and settlement. SIAH was the major force of the student left in the 1968–73 period, but split on the eve of the elections in 1973, when the Zionist sections in the movement chose to join the Mo'ked list.

The Twenty-first Year – The Twenty-first Year, established in January 1988, organized around a manifesto exposing the cancerous effects of the occupation on Israeli society. The group sought to present a radical alternative to Peace Now and called for readiness to pay a serious price for opposition to the occupation.

Women and Peace – Women and Peace was a coalition of the more radical sections of the women's peace movement.

Women In Black – Created by Israeli women in direct response to increased Israeli violence and repression against the Palestinian Intifada, Women In Black maintained weekly vigils denouncing the occupation, thus becoming a symbol of perseverance in the fight for peace. In its strongest phase, Women In Black conducted tens of vigils all over Israel and could mobilize thousands of women for national actions. The movement evoked considerable international interest and solidarity in the women's movement abroad.

Women for Women Political Prisoners (WWPP) – Women for Women Political Prisoners based itself on activists from the anti-Zionist left and individuals who wished to combine human rights actions with deep feminist concerns.

Women's Peace Network (Reshet) – Formed in the wake of a meeting between Israeli and Palestinian women in Brussels in 1989, the Network (known as the Reshet) represented a broad coalition of women activists, including women active in the Labor Party. The Reshet's policies and strategy opened the way for cooperation between women from mainstream organizations and the more militant sections of the women's peace movement.

Yesh Gvul (There is a Limit) – Movement of Israeli Defence Forces reservists, established in the fall of 1982, which called for refusal to serve in an unjust war and mobilized support for those who went to jail instead of serving in Lebanon. Yesh Gvul censured the Shamir government for turning its back on the rights of the Palestinians and squandering chances for peace and decided to extend its policy of refusal to the occupied territories in March 1986. Many opponents of Yesh Gvul in the peace camp who considered refusal politically unwise paid tribute to the integrity and moral example of the "refusenicks."

Basic Ideological Approaches to Peace and the Arab Question in Israeli Politics

The following sketch is designed to assist readers unacquainted with Israeli politics. The four main classic "core" positions relating to Jewish demands regarding Palestine are presented - from right to left - in telegraphic brevity. Despite their conciseness, they may be helpful to readers who have not had the opportunity to acquaint themselves with the Zionist foundations of Israeli politics. Inevitably, there are important nuances that are obscured in this kind of presentation.

Right-Wing Nationalist Zionism – Right-wing, nationalist Zionism holds that all historical Palestine belongs to the Jewish people. The demand for Jewish sovereignty in all Western Palestine is an ideological article of faith and not negotiable. On the basis of the above principle, nationalist tendencies have designed various solutions to the problem of the Palestinian Arabs ranging from the extremist position supporting expulsion to more moderate positions which recognize the civil, though not national, rights of "indigenous" Arabs. In fact, all right-wing Zionists, by rejecting demands for national equality between Israelis and Palestinians, perpetuate the need for the active repression of the Palestinian Arabs in Israel and the occupied territories.

Mainstream Zionism – Mainstream Zionism holds that all historical Palestine belongs to the Jewish people. The source of the Arab-Israeli conflict, according to the mainstream approach, is the the refusal of the Arab world to recognize any Jewish rights in Palestine and its war on the Zionist project. These have forced Israel to concentrate primarily on security and military preparedness, while building strategic alliances with the major Western powers which dominate the region. Mainstream Zionism insists that its more pragmatic approach is the effective, step-by-step method to maximize the gains of the Zionist movement in terms of territory and military security. Thus, territorial compromise with the Palestinians may be considered, but political benefits and strategic superiority are prerequisites for any compromise designed to end the conflict.

The non-Zionist Left and Sections of the Zionist Left in Israel – The militant left holds that, as a result of historical circumstances, Palestine has become the homeland of two peoples, the Palestinians and the Jews in Palestine. Thus, both peoples have the right to national self-determination. Given present-day realities and the decisions of international organizations, a logical and realistic solution of the Israeli-Palestinian conflict, which is the heart of the Israeli-Arab conflict, would be the establishment of an independent Palestinian state alongside of Israel. The non-Zionist left stresses the principle of national equality, while the Zionist left stresses the importance of establishing separate national identities.

The Anti-Colonialist and Anti-Zionist Position – Palestine is an Arab country and the homeland of the Palestinian Arab people. The rise of Israel stems from the exploitation of Jewish suffering to launch Zionism which was and remains an essentially colonialist project. Zionism entered the region on the basis of imperialist sponsorship and operates in the region as a foreign body. Just peace is possible only on the basis of the elimination of Israel as a sovereign entity. The rights of Jews can and should be recognized either on a civil or a national basis, within the framework of the democratic transformation of the country and the region.

Introduction:
The Roots of Protest in Israel

Cracks in the Hegemony of the Party System

The prominence of the role of political parties and the party system in Israel during the first years of the country's existence cannot be exaggerated. Political parties were much more than instruments for registering mass sentiment in the electoral process and the subsequent formation of a government and a parliamentary opposition. Broad sections of the citizenry held strong ideological convictions and members and supporters of a particular party considered it the embodiment of their own personal world outlook. Most parties enjoyed the support of a large and devoted membership. Most of the members could be classified as "cadres" – activists who combined deep ideological conviction with day-to-day activity on behalf of the party and readiness to defend the party and its interests.

Because of the particular circumstances which existed during the first decade of Israel's existence, the political parties provided, in addition to their traditional role, a variety of social services in areas such as employment, housing and health services. These arrangements further strengthened the links between the ideologically-committed party member and the party. As a rule, the social institutions which offered such services were managed and controlled by party members who saw their work as part of their party duty and mission. It is almost superfluous to point out that in such circumstances politics invariably meant party politics. The only venues of political activity were the parties, and they were the exclusive source of political influence.[1]

Despite the sway of the party system during the first decade of

Israel's existence, there were a number of attempts at conducting political activity beyond the confines of the party system. A number of single-issue groups were formed and operated as protest groups. The relative success or failure of these new formations depended highly on their interaction with the party system. In the long run, the rise of independent political activity depended in no small measure on weakening the monopoly of the party organizations on public life. Therefore, the appearance and the highly limited success of these attempts – first attempts at political action formally outside of the party system – were highly significant for tracing the development of political protest in Israel.

Va'ad Ha'shalom Ha'yisraeli (the Israeli Peace Committee – IPC) was active during the 1950s, especially regarding issues linked to the Cold War. The IPC was actually the product of an inter-party agreement between three Israeli parties, each of which wished to maintain its affiliations with the World Peace Congress. The three parties were the Communist Party of Israel (CPI), MAPAM (the United Workers Party), and Ahdut Ha'avodah. The IPC was ostensibly interested in attracting the support of independent public figures, especially intellectuals. Usually, the non-party figures who were prominent or active in the organization were known as non-party supporters of one of the parties that jointly conducted the activity of the IPC. These "independents" had little or no impact on the politics and the work of the Committee. The politics, organization, and funding were all part of the exclusive domain of inter-party coordination. It was the relationship between the parties and their ability to work out a joint political line which was decisive in the organization's existence.[2]

Despite these limitations, the creation of the IPC brought forth appreciation by the public and the party apparatuses that there were other legitimate forms of organization. The committee format in Israel was probably modelled on that of a European sister-organization, which could boast of the active participation of large numbers of prominent, non-party figures, especially among the intelligentsia. However, in Israel, due, among other reasons, to the heavy-handed control by the various party centers, the participation of prestigious but unaffiliated personages was meager. The IPC floundered and disappeared when relations between the IPC and the other left-Zionist parties deteriorated in the wake of Cold-War tensions affecting the Middle East.

In another group, the Movement against Religious Coercion,

active during the 1950s and the early 1960s, the independent intellectuals fared better. Hebrew University professor Uzi Ornan and geneticist Dr. Ram Moav were recognized leaders of the organization and probably shaped much of its public image. Neither of them were known as supporters of a particular party. However, the strength of the organization depended largely on two parties, MAPAM (the United Workers Party) and the liberal Progressive Party. It was these parties which funded the Movement and brought out the bulk of participants in key demonstrations. However, the anti-clericalist motivation of these and other secularist parties faded when these parties were forced, because of coalition considerations, to enter long term agreements with the religious Orthodox and Ultra-Orthodox parties. Unaffiliated activists found it impossible to maintain an effective independent organization.

One historically significant group which was active in the field of Arab-Jewish relations had no conventional party support, direct or indirect. Ihud (Unity) formed in the early 1940s was composed of prominent intellectual figures such as Martin Buber, Hugo Bergman, Judah Leib Magnes, and other eminent Zionists who believed that the achievement of Arab-Jewish understanding was a precondition for the success of the Zionist venture. This belief was the basis for their support for the proposal of a "bi-national state" in Palestine. The "bi-national state" proposal which was also supported by Hashomer Hatzair before 1947, endeavored to prevent a confrontation between the Jews and Arabs in Palestine by providing for the self-determination of both communities in a single polity. However, in the absence of any kind of party backing, Ihud's voice of peace literally became a voice crying in the political wilderness. Despite its distinguished past and the individual prestige of most of its leadership, Ihud was never able to command any serious public support. Over the years, the group became more and more marginalized and dropped out of the public eye.[3]

"Death of Ideology" in Israel

From the late 1950s, the party structures underwent a slow, steady transformation. The intensity of rank and file identification and participation in regular party life began to wane. Similar processes emerged in other countries where day-to-day participation in party life had previously been the rule rather than the exception. The diminishing role of the political party in Israel prepared the ground for a new phenomenon: the emergence of single-issue political formations composed of activists acting outside the party system. Political life began to witness more and more exceptions to the party system's monopoly on political activity and influence and there were more and more politically active people who owed no allegiance, organizationally or ideologically to a political party.

There is a clear parallel between the gradual decline of the "mass cadre" party and the declining role of ideology in Israeli political life. Party membership during the era of the mass-cadre party had been based mainly on ideological grounds. The sharp drop in the number of ideologically-committed and motivated members reflected a growing social distrust and uneasiness about any kind of ideological commitment. The rise of an ethos based on individual taste and choice made ideological commitment appear as some sort of a weakness – a mental crutch for the immature and the dependent. In addition, the "death of ideology" was linked to the accelerated expansion of higher education in Israel and the resulting increase in independent academicians. This new generation of academicians, many of whom were trained in the United States, tended to see ideological commitment and party membership as being inconsistent with the style and the substance of free and independent inquiry.

The Israeli parties which had some sort of socialist orientation were hit particularly hard by the series of crises which seized international communism from the exposure of Stalin's cult of the personality at the Twentieth Congress of the Soviet Communist Party in 1956 and onwards. At first it appeared that the anti-Communist social-democratic parties would profit from a moral victory over their historical Marxist adversaries. However, in fact, the collapse of communism undermined the stature and prestige of all ideology related to the vision of social reconstruction. Israel's Marxist left was in retreat (mainly because of international factors), while the strong social-democratic traditions in the country were cracking under the impact of neo-capitalist influence and pressure. Israel's vaunted experiment in social reconstruction began to appear as just another impractical theory. The workers' parties, which had served as the moral and intellectual mainstay of the Zionist movement, entered a long period of ideological disarray.

Many rue the demise of a strong party system and the social role of ideological commitment and see in this development a serious threat to democratic processes. However, it is difficult if not impossible to defend the party system after immense doses of corruption and antiquated phraseology have convinced most citizens that the parties are devoid of principle and honor. Independent political action, outside the sphere of the party system is, at any rate, one of the more positive responses to the vacuum created by the retreat of the party system.

The changes in the forms of political organization and expression created new tools and political space which enabled more and more citizens to grapple with critical issues such as the Israeli-Arab conflict, which had become a matter of life and death for Israeli society. The protest movement against the occupation and for Israeli-Arab peace became an important political force over the years because it had something very relevant to say about these questions and was successful, in certain critical periods, in shaping the political process.

Crisis at the Heart of the Party System

MAPAI (Miflaget Poelei Eretz-Yisrael – Party of the Workers in the Land of Israel – later known as the Israeli Labor Party) led by the Israeli Prime Minister, Ben-Gurion, was the hegemonic party and the prototype of the entire system. It was not accidental that the first major crisis in that system was a crisis within that party over Ben-Gurion's absolutist tendencies.

The inner-party crisis gave birth to the first important extra-parliamentary movement which took shape and developed outside the traditional party structure. During 1960 and 1961, a group of prominent Israeli intellectuals established the Movement for the Defense of Democracy in response to Ben-Gurion's conduct during the "Lavon affair."[4] Ben-Gurion, as Prime Minister and leader of the party, had issued an ultimatum to the party demanding that Lavon be dismissed from the key post of General Secretary of the Histadrut (General Federation of Labor).

Lavon's "crime" was his untiring battle to clear his name regarding a spying fiasco in 1954, when Lavon was Minister of Defense. The difficulty was that Lavon's exoneration would have been seen as an indictment against Ben-Gurion, who maintained decisive influence in the Ministry of Defense, even after he had retired to

Sadeh Boker. Many considered Ben-Gurion's demand that Lavon be fired from his post as the General-Secretary of the Histadrut a dictatorial act which endangered the foundations of Israeli democracy. Despite Lavon's many defenders in party circles, and the strong support for him among intellectual and student circles on campus, Ben Gurion did succeed in forcing Lavon out of his post as General Secretary of the Histadrut. The powerful party apparatus had to pacify Ben-Gurion or face the wrath of its historical leader and a possible split. Public opinion was appalled at Ben-Gurion's unabashed abuse of power in defense of his own personal interests. Public concern crystallized in the formation of a non-parliamentary movement for the defense of democracy centered at the Hebrew University.

Lavon, it turned out, had political allies and personal friends among professors at the Hebrew University. Nathan Rotenstreich (and others) had been active with Lavon in building an important Zionist youth movement in Europe, Gordonia. Rotenstreich mobilized Yakov Talmon, Yehoshua Arieli and other academicians who had close connections with MAPAI and the labor movement. The professors – in no way dependent on the party or its bureaucracy for their livelihood – initiated contacts with student groups which formed a broad coalition under the name of Students for the Defense of Democracy. The student coalition was built mainly on cooperation between student party cells, but succeeded in attracting many unaffiliated students. Eventually, these professors and Lavon's supporters in the party established a group called Min Hayasod (From the Foundations), which attracted a young novelist, Amos Oz, then a member of Kibbutz Hulda, one of the settlement projects of the Gordonia youth movement.

Less Votes Than Half a Transit Camp

It was hard for the party bureaucracy to evaluate the meaning of the events. The party apparatus and vote-getters did not seem worried. When the party faced an unprecedented ferment on Israeli campuses during a critical stage in the "Lavon affair," Joseph Almogi, a leading Ben-Gurion loyalist in the MAPAI apparatus, commented – in what came to be considered a classic example of dangerously underestimating the political strength of Israeli intellectuals – that the professors commanded less votes than the party could obtain easily in one half of a ma'abarah (immigrant transit camp).

Though campus-centered protest activity could not save Lavon, it did help to create the public climate which lead to Ben-Gurion's eventual fall from the MAPAI leadership in 1963. The movement for the defense of democracy was an important element in the government crises that brought down the government in 1961. While most of the leading figures in the protest movement, which was a combination of student political groups and unaffiliated students and professors, identified with the labor Zionist movement, the mechanics of protest were new. Israel had not seen independent political action on such a scope. And this time, protest was against the leadership of Israel's strongest political party. Political analysts came to the conclusion that intellectuals in academia were a political fact that deserved serious attention.

Most of the protest activity was coordinated on campus and an independent group of professors played the central role in forming and executing policy. Professors and their students appeared as an independent force, outside the party structure. An independent political protest formation had a serious impact on national politics. The movement was university-based, and it was the first but not the last time that the university served as a focus of political protest.

Accidental Empire, Inadvertent Occupier

The formation of an independent peace movement received tremendous impetus from the circumstances that developed in the aftermath of Israel's victory in the June 1967 war. As a result of the war which had been, according to the official version, forced on it, Israel conquered large stretches of Arab territory: the heavily populated West Bank and the Gaza strip, the Golan Heights and the vast Sinai desert. Approximately one and a half million Palestinians came under control of the Israeli army. The valid criticism coming from the CPI and a small group of militant intellectuals to the effect that it was really Israel which had commenced hostilities – while diplomatic efforts to head off the war were still going on – was easily drowned by the clamor of victory. Israeli society rejoiced euphorically over the overwhelming victory which came after a long period of pre-war tension, during which most Israelis had considered themselves face to face with a serious threat to their very existence. Victory, and especially its swiftness, was portrayed as a miracle of deliverance.

Even so, there were some disquieting features in the new set up. Liberals, including devoted supporters of the government, began to discern that Israel was getting into a situation that had the makings of becoming a real mess; Israel had become an occupying power and more than one and a half million Palestinian Arabs came under its direct military rule. Liberals were quick to express the fervent hope that it would be a liberal and hopefully short occupation. But the contours of this new reality meant very different things to different kinds of Israelis.

The right-wing of the Zionist movement saw the essence of the Zionist project in the reconquest and settlement of what they termed "Greater Israel" (Eretz Yisrael Ha'shlema). Literally, this is "the complete Eretz Yisrael" or the "complete land of Israel." Though there are a number of variations on the exact geographical boundaries of this vision, it is absolutely clear that the borders of "Greater Israel" extend, according to right-wing doctrine, well beyond the occupied territories, which were heavily populated by the Palestinians. It followed that no Israeli government had the right to forfeit sovereignty over this sacred territory, under any circumstances. This approach was common to the secular nationalist and religious right. Moreover, there was an important section of the Labor-Zionist movement, linked historically to Kibbutz Ha'meuchad (one of the major kibbutz federations) and its political arm, Ahdut Ha'avodah) which had a similar ideological and doctrinal approach to the question of the land of Israel. Thus, Israeli irredentism had its roots in religious and secular nationalist approaches, all of which were totally and irrevocably committed to the goal of undivided Israeli sovereignty over (at the least) all of the heavily populated West Bank.

For most other thinking Zionists, the territories were a mixed blessing. The strategic advantages were important. But the political entity that was emerging was far from the idea of a Jewish state: three million Jews dominating the lives of over one and a half million Arabs living under military rule, in addition to more than a half a million Israeli Arab Palestinians, formally citizens of Israel. It was just too far removed from the simple and classical goal of Zionism, the Jewish state, to be acceptable as a permanent situation.

The reigning Prime Minister, Levi Eshkol (and Ben-Gurion's successor as the head of MAPAI) issued a compromise formula regarding the fate of the territories: Israel had no territorial designs on the territories; the territories would be considered a "deposit" to be held until the Arab countries agreed to enter negotiations on peace with Israel. This was a demand that the Arab's agree to negotiate on the basis of the "new status quo" – and practically it meant that Israel had plenty of time at its disposal. In the meanwhile, Israel as a liberal democracy would have to organize and impose a "liberal occupation" on the occupied territories and their inhabitants.

A Not-So-Jewish, Jewish State

It was not long before the annexationist groups decided to force the government's hand by sponsoring unofficial settlement initiatives. The growing fear that settlement plans were receiving aid and assistance from inside the government prompted a large concentration of professors and intellectuals – mainly at the Hebrew University – to express their concern. Their response took the form of A Call for Peace and Security issued at the beginning of 1969. The essence of the call was to reject dangerous illusions involved in the drift towards a Greater Israel. The call cautioned against the dangerous dynamics inherent in the new situation and warned against any permanent arrangement which would create a political entity almost half of whose inhabitants would be Palestinian Arabs. In these circumstances, if the state would be democratic, it could not be a Jewish state, and if it was "Jewish" it could not be democratic.

The professors represented the heart and the brains of the academic establishment. Ya'akov Talmon, Nathan Rotenstreich, Yehushoa Arieli, Ya'akov Katz, S. N. Eisenstat, among others, were both prominent in their academic disciplines and closely associated with the political establishment. Though there were leading academicians who supported Israeli militarism and annexation of the territories, it was somehow clear to the public and the media that those associated with the Call for Peace and Security were the most authoritative voice of the professoriate. Many of the prominent figures who launched the Call for Peace and Security had been associated with those forces in MAPAI which successfully rebuffed Ben-Gurion's dictatorial tendencies and led to his eventual fall from power. That previous success enhanced the political status of the professors. It should be appreciated that the sponsors of the Call for Peace and Security were very far from seeing themselves as an opposition to the regime and its policies, nor were they ready to think about any confrontation with the government. They saw their role as advisors and counsellors whose warnings could be ignored only at great cost.

The professors' argumentation was Zionist to the core. Israel had Zionist reasons for divesting itself of the territories and the only ratio for holding them was to trade them off in exchange for security considerations. Any attempt to legitimize the new status quo by annexing the territories would doom the idea of a Zionist state. Expulsion of the local population was unthinkable, granting citizenship to the occupied populace would, by virtue of the demographic shift, cancel the Jewish nature of the state and prolonged rule over an entire people without rights would be the end of Israeli democracy. Permanent Israeli presence in the territories was unacceptable and unworkable. This was a sober assessment of the new realities that sounded a somber warning to those in power and to many Israelis who had forgotten their principles in the postwar atmosphere of unbridled euphoria.

Colonialism Materialized – Radicalism in the Student Left

The emergence of the occupation served to confirm, in the eyes of the student left, the correctness of the orthodox Marxist view which held that the Zionist project was inherently colonialist. The student left can be defined in this context as the members and supporters of the parties to the left of MAPAI. During the 1950s and early 1960s, Communist student cells, organizing Jewish and Arab activists, had considerably greater political presence on campus than in the general population. It should be noted that after the 1967 war there was a considerable influx of young student immigrants from Latin America, Europe and the United States to Israel – many of whom had participated actively in the radical student movement before coming to the country. The spiritual climate and the prestige of the New Left also had a deep influence on those organized in the ranks of the Zionist youth movements abroad.

The circumstances in which Israel achieved independence seemed to render the classical Marxist critique of Zionism implausible. In fact, Israel was born in a conflict with colonialist Britain and enjoyed the support of the Soviet Union in the period of its formation as a state. The plausibility of this critique was thus considerably reduced during the late 1940s and the first half of the 1950s. The 1956 Suez war – when Israel teamed up with England and France against the new nationalist regime in Egypt led by Nasser – was the first unequivocal example of the strategic alliance between Israel and the West against radical Arab nationalism.

The emergence of a similar alliance in 1967 – Israel, enjoying Western support against the pro-Soviet regimes in Egypt and Syria (considered by many the root cause for the outbreak of the June 1967 war) – gave a new impetus to this critique. Then, when Israel became the new lord and master of the Palestinians under occupation, many Israelis on the left, Zionist and non-Zionists, were quick to discern the manifest colonialist character of the new situation. It seemed that Israel had no real hesitation about doing almost everything possible to confirm the worst fears of its critics by assuming a new posture which had to draw fire from all opponents of colonialism.

The student struggle in Israel against the new reality, Israel as an occupying power, received added inspiration from the ideological and social ferment in the universities in the West. However, it drew its main strength from a growing local determination to fight the right-wing drive for settlement of the newly-occupied territories and to expose the complicity of the Israeli government which repeatedly succumbed to pressures to establish new settlements, often in the heart of the Palestinian population. While their professors were concerned that Israel was going to deviate from the goal of establishing a Jewish state and end up a mixed half Jewish / half Arab state, the students on the left were beginning to challenge the colonial role and function of their own country. This was a role startlingly similar to that of their colleagues, the students in the United States and Europe who were battling against the crimes of their own country: colonial war and colonization.

The classical approach held that whatever the specific circumstances that attended the rise of the Zionist movement, the real dynamic was that of colonization and domination of the indigenous population by European based and European financed settlers. Even among many in the Zionist left who rejected this classical definition of Zionism as a colonialist movement, there was a growing willingness to admit that the vicissitudes of the conflict and the nefarious policies of the government, after the victory in the Six Day War, were creating a neo-colonialist reality. The development of the student protest movement against the settlements and the annexationist policies of the government was inspired by both these approaches to Israel's role in the region. Almost any vantage point from the left led to the conclusion that the occupation was the realization of all the negative and dangerous elements of Zionist politics.[5]

Given the period, the latter half of the 1960s, the student struggle in Israel against the new reality of occupation was inspired by the ideological and social ferment in the universities of the West. However, it drew its main strength from determination to fight the drive for settlement and annexation spearheaded by the right, and aided and abetted by the government's consistent surrender to settler pressures. Expropriation and settlement, under the protection of superior military power, were an all too familiar historical pattern.

Internationalist Perspective

The emergence of radical groups in the Israeli student body was linked to the development of two groups: Matzpen, the Israeli Socialist Organization and SIAH (New Israeli Left). Both groups had their roots in the regular left-wing party structures, but were unique in that much of their style and tactics were molded in response to their social base in the student sector and ideas current in the New Left abroad. The long series of crises that hurt Israeli Communists from the Soviet Twentieth Congress in 1956 up to a ferocious split in the Israeli CP in 1965 helped both new left formations to utilize new opportunities for development and organization.

Matzpen had its origins in the CPI from which it split in 1962. Starting from issues linked to the lack of inner party democracy in the CPI, the group developed a critique of Zionism as the key to understanding current Israeli politics. While the CPI accepted Israel as a legitimate expression of national self-determination, Matzpen came to the conclusion that the colonialist essence of Zionist colonization had made an indelible mark on Israeli society.

Matzpen's analysis of Israel as a colonialist society appeared to receive stark confirmation by the June 1967 war and its aftermath. Israel was settling into its role of direct military rule over the Palestinians in the occupied territories. While Matzpen's actual membership never exceeded forty or fifty members, its radical and total negation of official discourse was of lasting influence on many young radicals. The Matzpen message was that politics had a wider horizon than the limited confrontation between the ruling government and the loyal opposition – there was also a possibility of a total and sweeping negation: the definition of Israeli society as a Western implant designed to perpetuate foreign rule over the Arab peoples.

Matzpen eventually broke up into three smaller factions, none of which matched the achievements of the parent organization.[6] However, the boldness of Matzpen's thinking and its radical life-style molded the politics and the sensitivities of many individuals who would make important contributions, in one capacity or another, to protest politics in the country.

SIAH, the New Israeli Left, had even a greater impact on the university scene. While Matzpen was a theoretical variant in the broader field of orthodox Marxist thinking, SIAH bore most of the markings of a new left formation. It ignored the need for traditional political tools such as programs, membership and elected bodies, and in their stead worked on the principal of spontaneity. Whoever was in the room that evening, usually a university classroom, was a "member" and fully entitled to participate in the decision-making process. There was a heady sense of a new participatory style of organization and how good it was to do politics far from the eye and the control of any party bureaucracy – benevolent or otherwise. Spontaneity as an organizational principle had reached Israel.

SIAH, was actually a combination of two groups based at Tel Aviv University and at the Hebrew University in Jerusalem. SIAH very pointedly refrained from working on any program. Each local group was naturally autonomous and national action was launched by a coordinating committee. The idea was that "ideology disunites" but "action unites." Accordingly, the goal was to launch and coordinate activity against settlement and the governments indifference to peace, and this is how SIAH did make its mark. SIAH emerged as a public force through a series of actions during the 1968/69 academic year. SIAH at its peak could mobilize hundreds of activists and demonstrators. It was far from having the strength or the resources of a parliamentary faction, but it had the kind of energy and enthusiasm which demanded public attention. Moreover, though it never made any conscious decision to opt for illegal demonstrations, SIAH and its members had a feeling for the politics of direct action and confrontation.

SIAH began inauspiciously enough with the formation of two

independent discussion groups at the above mentioned universities. Meetings became more regular during the 1968/69 academic year. The groups succeeded in ignoring the elections to the Histadrut and the Knesset that took place in the fall of 1969, where the peace forces appeared in three separate lists. In February 1970, the Jerusalem group held its first action, an attempt to picket the "illegal" Jewish settlement in Hebron. At the beginning of April, the Goldman affair "broke." After Nahum Goldman, the dovish President of the influential World Jewish Congress, was discreetly invited to Egypt for talks with Nasser, Prime Minister Golda Meir squashed the entire initiative and ordered Goldman to stay away. To protest Meir's refusal to explore a real possibility for negotiations with Egypt, SIAH led hundreds of students into the streets of Jerusalem in a militant demonstration which was dispersed violently by the police. The very same month about sixty high-school seniors wrote to the prime minister expressing doubts about their ability to serve in the IDF in the light of the government's refusal to sanction the Goldman–Nasser meeting. The very idea that political opposition (perfectly acceptable according to the rules of the game) could lead to doubts about military service (totally unacceptable) sent shock waves and warning signals through the establishment.[7]

Shortly afterwards, SIAH sent hundreds of marchers to Hebron; when the army blocked their path, the marchers returned to Jerusalem and attempted to meet with Golda Meir, setting off a fierce confrontation with the police. This and other actions made this unorganized and spontaneous grouping a focal point for opposition to government policy. It was in April 1969 that Nasser officially abrogated the 1967 cease-fire. The war of attrition between Israeli and Egyptian forces stationed along the Suez Canal intensified and casualties rose. Even the most phenomenal of victories could not guarantee breathing space between one war and the next. SIAH expressed a level of anxiety and despair among large sections of students and young kibbutz people hitherto unknown in Israeli society. There was too much evidence that Israel cared more about keeping territories and establishing settlements than it cared about peace.

Neither SIAH or Matzpen, or for that matter the more mainstream intellectuals organized in "Peace and Security", ever accumulated sufficient influence to challenge existing party structures. Matzpen, and the different groups which it sired, had a longer political career than SIAH, which never really survived a split in 1973 when the majority of its members opted to participate in electoral politics by joining in the establishment of the Mo'ked list. As a rule the Matzpen groups had deep disdain for typical Israeli electoral politics, and concentrated their efforts to build a mass constituency in Israel's Arab sector. Here and there some of the Matzpen groups succeeded in attracting Arab cadres who felt that the CPI (Communist Party of Israel) was being absorbed into the system. Their ability to outflank the CPI on the question of Israeli legitimacy – by stressing the colonialist essence of Israel – gave them an advantage for contact with some of the more radical nationalist trends in that sector. Even so, at no stage were any of the groups able to organize more than tens of activists.

SIAH, as we have seen, disappeared in 1973 for all practical purposes when most of its leaders and activists fell prey to the attraction of parliamentary politics and decided to participate in the establishment of a new left-wing formation, Mo'ked.[8] Matzpen, under the impact of tensions and splits in the European extra-parliamentary left, split into three different groups. Former activists from the Movement for Peace and Security were the core of a group which launched the formation of the NESS (Miracle) peace list in 1969 elections. The original conception was to present a list headed by prominent academicians such as Professors Yaakov Talmon and Yehoshua Arieli. The two leading academicians refused to head the list – actually sealing its fate. The list, headed by Dr. Gadi Yatziv, received approximately 5,000 votes and failed to gain a seat. The appearance of the various peace groups did add a new important dimension to Israeli politics; however, when it became increasingly clear that all efforts by the various peace groups to build a permanent organizational base were fruitless, small groups of activists found their way to electoral politics and participated in the formation of several new parliamentary lists.

The euphoria of the 1967 victory was going up in the smoke of the increasingly frequent clashes along the Suez Canal; casualties were mounting during the war of attrition, which raged between Egypt and Israel for two years from the middle of 1968. The Arabs had suffered total defeat in 1967, but peace was still far off, and the government appeared to many of the country's young men and women less and less interested in peace. The intellectuals saw the government fall more and more under the influence of hawks and settler forces. The universities witnessed the beginning of student ferment echoing that in the West. Anti-war satire found more and more cultural outlets.[9] Despite the ebb and flow of protest, the appearance of the first peace groups after the 1967 war meant that the existence of an independent peace movement, outside the boundaries of the party system, was on the way to becoming a regular feature of the political scene.[10]

1

From Miracle to Débâcle

The first real crisis in the belief system that kept Israelis loyal to their government occurred during the October 1973 (Yom Kippur) war when the Egyptian army smashed its way over the Suez Canal in a surprise attack that caught the Israeli Defense Forces totally off guard. Before it was over, more than two thousand Israeli soldiers were dead and many thousands wounded in a war that most Israelis were convinced should never have taken place against an opponent who was supposedly incapable of attacking. There is good reason to believe that Israel could have prevented the war by agreeing to a partial retreat from the Suez Canal, thus alleviating Egypt's humiliation at having the Israeli Defense Forces positioned on the opposite shore of the Canal. Friendly diplomatic sources did their best to convince the Israeli leadership that no Egyptian regime could tolerate Israeli presence on the bank of the Suez canal. However, Israel remained indifferent to the warnings.

Most Israelis were unaware that Israeli intransigence made the war practicably inevitable.[1] Justly so or not, most of the young people who carried the burden of the country's defense, as well as the public at large, were still willing to accept the official version to the effect that the absence of peace was due solely to Arab refusal to recognize the very existence of Israel. Hence, until the Arabs were willing to take that step, Israel had no real alternative but to rely on its military strength and superiority. Military intelligence was, of course, a central component of that superiority.

The blow to the prevailing belief system fell at its most sensitive point. Though the Egyptian army was under constant surveillance, Egypt managed to launch a surprise attack on Yom Kippur, October 6, 1973. The attack almost opened the floodgates of military defeat and possible annihilation. After Israel repelled the onslaught in the Canal Area and on the Golan Heights, it became clear that the haphazard thinking and negligence at the top echelons of the military and security sector had been the immediate cause for thousands of needless deaths and injuries. Israel had moved in seven short years from the Six Day War miracle to the Yom Kippur War débâcle.

The fact that the IDF eventually pushed the Egyptians back and rebuffed the Syrian attack in the north only served to convince the Israeli public that if Israel had acted with caution and called up the reserves in time, the Egyptians would have been unable to mount the attack, or the attack would have been rebuffed with a minimum of casualties; 2,500 Israeli soldiers were dead and no one – including the most devoted supporters of Israeli policy along the years – could understand how Israel had allowed itself to fall into such a trap.

Thus, it was a new war that created a far reaching crisis in the Israeli political system, though it was not government policy as such that came under fire. The issue that caused so much pain and anguish was the refusal of anyone in the government to assume responsibility for the fateful miscalculation by the Israeli security apparatus. The demand for accountability, which in the circumstances meant ministerial or governmental responsibility, was inscribed on the flag of a rapidly-growing protest movement composed of Israeli soldiers. After the cease-fire, hundreds and then thousands of reservists stopped off in Jerusalem on their way home from the front to vent their anger against the government.

Accountability – Where Does the Buck Stop?

By February 1974, as the demobilization of the reserve units pro- ceeded, a new protest movement had emerged. The movement focused its activity at a site opposite the Prime Minister's Office where a lone protester, Motti Ashkenazi, was the first to take up a vigil demanding the immediate dismissal of Defense Minister, Moshe Dayan. After their discharge, entire reserve units joined other reservists who were maintaining a permanent demonstration site opposite the Prime Minister's Office in Jerusalem, even before the soldiers went to their homes. A series of demonstrations during February and March in which thousands of reservists participated elicited nation-wide support and sympathy.

This movement consistently avoided any discussion of basic policy questions. There was a common desire to ensure the movement's
unity and this meant that it was necessary to narrow the focus of the
issues that the soldiers could raise. Therefore, "political" questions,
such as whether the government policy had sincerely attempted to
avoid a new war, were "off-limits". This abstinence came naturally,
since the movement wanted to stress its non-partisan character and
very few, if any, of the participants were aware, at any rate, of the
connection between the immediate issue of accountability and the
basic questions of policy.

When the government refused any concessions to their demands,
thousands of reservists came to the capital to demand the government's resignation. With all their bitterness, they could not be
described as a dangerous crowd. First of all they observed the
legal guidelines for demonstrations and went out of their way to
cooperate with the police. More important, their complaint was
utterly respectable and really quite modest. The officers and the
soldiers wanted to know who was responsible for this mammoth
failure – which had caused the death and suffering of so many of
their comrades-in-arms.

They wanted heads to roll in the army and, no less important,
they wanted the issue of ministerial responsibility determined objec-
tively. In truth most of them wanted the resignation of Minister of
Defense, Moshe Dayan and maybe even that of his boss, Prime
Minister Golda Meir. The movement, which enjoyed tremendous
public support, succeeded in placing the entire government on the
defensive.

The movement seemed to have been deflected from its goals
with the publication of the report by the Agranat Commission
on April 1, 1974. The report of the Commission which had been
established a few weeks after the end of the war in November 1973
to determine responsibility for the "mekhdal" (best translated as
a 'grave act of omission') limited responsibility for the "mekhdal"
to the military level. The government was more than pleased by
the report and hoped that it would be able to ride out the storm
of public criticism. However, support for the protest movement
which demanded implementation of the principle of ministerial
responsibility continued unabated. Prime Minister Golda Meir was
forced to resign at the end of May and Moshe Dayan was excluded
from the Rabin government formed a few days later.

Though the implications of the "mekhdal" affair were debatable regarding basic policy orientations, the dismal failure of the security establishment expanded the limits of public discourse on questions of peace and war. The public had learned "the hard way" that the Israeli military was not as it had believed – a preserve of efficiency and wisdom unaffected by the mounting social, political, and economic ills which had created a sense of malaise in the country. The Israeli Defense Forces and the generals turned politicians were subject to the same inefficiency and irresponsibility which seemed to be spreading in Israeli society. Though most Israelis still refused to entertain any thoughts to the effect that justice and wisdom demanded deeper consideration of the Arab and Palestinian case, they were forced to understand that it was actually dangerous to put excessive trust in the wisdom and the caution of their leaders. Security affairs and issues, which were supposed to be the "holy of holies" – a special province where objective and altruistic considerations reigned – were, alas, subject to political blindness and military blunders. Young Israelis, traditionally confident in the workings of the army and the security apparatuses, had to learn the lesson: Your's was not only to do or die – your's was to question why. At this stage, it was only logical to ask about the "next war" which seemed to be a perpetual element in the national agenda: Is this war necessary or inevitable?

Before and after the Yom Kippur War, settlement activity inspired by the fundamentalist religious right was growing. When the government wasn't actually sponsoring settlement activity, it found itself acquiescing to facts created by the settler right – which concentrated its efforts in strategic areas on the West Bank. Israel was on the way to becoming a state of colonizers and colonized. Warnings against the trend from large sections of the professoriate and other intellectuals were disregarded; the radicalization of small sections of the university left were of no practical, immediate concern to the establishment. Despite the shockwaves in the internal Israeli political arena in the wake of the Yom Kippur fiasco, the old stalemate between Israel and the Arab countries was coming back into force.

Two important shifts in Middle East politics were to undermine the stalemate. In June 1977, the Alignment lost the election to the Israeli right and Menahem Begin became prime minister. In November the same year, Anwar Sadaat came to Jerusalem. The Egyptian leader had become convinced that only by making peace with Israel could he reap the full rewards of Egypt's switch from the Soviet Union to the United States' side in the Cold War.

The Fall of Israel's Ancient Regime

The Yom Kippur war was a turning point. Israel had moved from the "Six Day" miracle in 1967 to the Yom Kippur débâcle in 1973 in seven short years, having also fought a bloody and inconclusive War of Attrition along the Canal zone, between the two major wars. The country's political and spiritual center, MAPAI at the head of the Labor movement, was unable to ward off a series of crises and mishaps that lead to its electoral downfall in 1977. For the first time, the Israeli labor movement had lost control of the regime and it lost the premiership to its sworn enemy, Menahem Begin. An accumulation of governmental arrogance, corruption and inefficiency paved the way for the change. It was an historical upheaval, the first of its kind. Moreover, there must have been many voters who concluded that if settlement of the occupied territories was the order of the day, there was no reason not to support the right for whom the project was clearly top priority.

A sense of despair and anguish descended on large sections of the population and particularly on vast sections of the country's developing new middle class with the ascent of Menahem Begin to power. One can sketch the character of this new middle class in broad strokes in the following terms: (a) It was an expanding section of population by virtue of new structural opportunities created by the recent growth of the country – especially in academia, education and the social services – during the 1950s and the 1960s; (b) this expanded social role did not involve decreased individual or collective identification, participation or responsibility for security and defense obligations. As a rule, this new middle class was and remained disproportionately overrepresented in the reserve officer corp and other sensitive security areas; (c) the overwhelming majority of this section of the population had, in one form or another, personal, social and psychological links with the leaders and the cadre of the deposed labor Zionist movement.

Sadat Finds Begin in Jerusalem

Anwar Sadat came to understand that his decision to switch sides in the Cold War was not sufficient and that Egypt could reap the full rewards of this change from Washington, if and when it ended the Egyptian-Israeli confrontation. Sadat had no real reason to believe that Begin was any different from Golda Meir or Yitzhak Rabin for this purpose. At any rate, he had to break the deadlock and for that purpose he came to Jerusalem to speak to the people of Israel from the rostrum of the Knesset. Begin, lionized by the Israeli street and market-place, but mistrusted by all sections of the "ancient regime" had been given an unprecedented opportunity to end the conflict.

The intellectuals, the professors and the students, the more politically-minded sections of the new, upwardly mobile, middle class and large sections of what can be termed as a neo-elite – were all watching him carefully. They did not believe in him or his ideology. For most of them this ingrained mistrust was one of the sole surviving components of a value system and world-outlook imparted to their generation by that of Israel's founding fathers. The progress of the negotiations that began after Sadat's visit, or rather the lack of such progress, fed that mistrust.

Prodding Begin to Camp David

When it seemed, after a particularly frustrating meeting between Sadat and Begin at Ismailaya in February 1978, that the talks were on the verge of failure, a group of reserve officers drafted a carefully worded letter to Begin. In a matter of days they managed, through mainly informal connections, to gather more than 350 signatures, before the letter was sent to Begin on March 7, 1978.[2] The letter, which came to be known as the "Officer's Letter," warns against choosing the borders of Greater Israel and settlement activity in the Occupied Territories instead of chances for a negotiated peace. It stressed the inevitable danger to Israeli democracy stemming from the domination over more than a million Arabs.

The letter's political message was therefore basically identical to the standard dove criticism of government policy but dared to stress the existence of a direct link between government policy and the morale of the Israeli Defense Forces. Political doubts and reservations about government policy could conceivably affect, the signers of the letter argued, the morale of the army and impaired morale could affect the fighting capacity of the Israeli Defense Forces. Begin's hard line policy was presented as a threat to the IDF's fighting capacity, since it would impair the identification of many in the IDF with Israel's basic path.

The organizers and the letter had found the appropriate method for dealing with the sensitive topic – the conditions in which one is willing to fight and die for one's country. Coupling political criticism with security considerations was the perfect formula for a constituency for whom thoughts of refusing or evading military responsibility were totally unacceptable. The letter, and the movement which grew up around it, was actually issuing a stern warning to the government: "Only a peace-seeking Israel which has exhausted all possible means for attaining peace will be able to stand firm and win any future war that may be forced upon her."[3]

The Officer's Letter

This letter is sent to you by citizens of Israel who serve as reserve officers and soldiers.

It is with a heavy heart that we write these words to you. In these days – when for the first time new vistas are opening up for the State of Israel, for a life of peace and cooperation in the region – we feel duty bound to call upon you to refrain from action which might become a source of grief for generations to come, for our people and for our state.

A sense of deep anxiety prompts us to address you. A government which would prefer Israel with the borders of a "Greater Israel" over Israel's peaceful existence on the basis of good relations with its neighbors arouses in us severe apprehension. A government which would prefer the establishment of settlements across the "green line" to achieving an end to the historic conflict and the establishment of normal relations, would disseminate doubt about the justice of our cause. Government policy leading to the domination over one million Arabs would probably impair the Jewish democratic character of the state and would make it difficult for us to identify with the fundamental path of the State of Israel.

We are fully aware of the State's security needs and of the difficulties on the path to peace. Nonetheless, we know that genuine security is possible only with the advent of peace. The strength of the Israel Defense Forces is in the identification of its soldiers with the fundamental path of the State of Israel.

We call upon you to choose the path of peace, and by this choice, to reinforce our faith in the justice of our cause.[4]

A campaign to win additional signatures on the letter served as the organizational impetus for the establishment of a national movement which came to be known as Peace Now, with local centers in different areas of the country. By the end of March, the organizers announced that 10,000 Israelis had signed the letter[5] and called for a series of demonstrations to tell Begin of their concern that greed for a "Greater Israel" could sabotage the chances for peace. On April 1, an unprecedented crowd of 40,000 participated in the first large Peace Now demonstration; the movement used the next months to build a mass base and shape its identity, launching over thirty activities, including smaller demonstrations, petition drives and happenings to keep its name and message before the public. In culmination of these efforts, on September 2, 1978 on the eve of Begin's trip to Camp David, Peace Now rallied approximately 100,000 Israelis in Tel Aviv.

The battle by Peace Now to ensure the success of the Sadat initiative was the first instance in Israeli politics where the intervention of an extra-parliamentary peace movement had a clear and decisive influence on the course of critical political developments. Begin, the great hope of the settlers and the annexationist elements, was pushed and pulled to Camp David by an irresistible combination of forces: United States interests in forging an Egyptian-Israeli alliance in the Middle East and an unprecedented surge of peace sentiment in Israel, inspired and mobilized by Peace Now.

Peace Now, aided and encouraged by its success in the campaigning for the Egyptian-Israeli Peace Accords, decided in December 1979 to remain on the political scene. It reoriented its main activity to efforts to block the settlement drive. In the long run, the right hoped to create conditions for the annexation of the territories. In the short run, every new settlement was the most effective way to turn the autonomy section of the Camp David Accords into a dead letter.

The main thrust of Peace Now activity after the Camp David Accords and the Egyptian-Israeli Peace Treaty was devoted to a running battle against Gush Emunim, the political arm of the settler movement, which used every means – legal and illegal to take over land in the territories. Peace Now was effective in building mass opposition to the settlement drive, but was unable to actually curtail settlement activity, which enjoyed the direct or indirect support of the government.

Towards the end of 1980 Peace Now faced one of the classic dilemmas of any protest movement: how to respond during the period when electoral politics take center stage. Despite the temptation to cash in on the prestige of Peace Now and its leadership, the movement decided to stay out of parliamentary politics. MK Shulamit Aloni, head of the Citizen's Rights Movement, succeeded in luring several key figures into her parliamentary list, the Citizen's Rights Movement.[6]

After trying, with negligible success as far as the Labor Party was concerned, to influence the programs of the parties of the Zionist left, the movement refused to endorse any single party. There is no doubt that Peace Now's refusal to be involved, as a movement, in electoral politics, especially in conditions where the dove vote was split between different contending lists, was a major contribution to its long-term survival. At any rate, the latter part of 1980 and the first months of 1981 were a dormant period in the history of the movement. Naturally enough, the voice of protest is hushed when electoral cannons are being fired.

PLO – Diplomacy of a Movement for National Liberation

It is generally accepted that the Palestinians emerged as an independent political and military entity in the wake of the Arab countries' miserable showing in the June 1967 war. From that point in time, the Palestinian Liberation Organization (PLO) began to act as the leadership of an independent national liberation movement. It was politically logical and perfectly acceptable for the leadership of a national liberation movement to maintain contact and cultivate political connections with peace movements which supported their right to self-determination. On this basis, in the early 1970s, representatives of the PLO met with representatives of the Communist Party of Israel (Rakah, the New Communist List) and with members of Matzpen. Meeting with radical opponents of the regime and the reigning Zionist ideology was hardly a problem for the PLO leadership.

These meetings did serve to sensitize parts of the Israeli public, especially informed observers, to the Palestinian cause and to the fact that there was an independent Palestinian voice interested in political contact with part of the Israeli community. However, the policy line of the PLO, which negated the existence of Israel and hence, any compromise which left Israel intact, made it almost impossible to mobilize support for an Israeli-Palestinian agreement in the Israeli public. The radical left did insist that changes in Israeli policy and a willingness to discuss the implementation of Palestinian self-determination could not fail to encourage realistic

and moderate forces in the PLO. Its argument was that Israel, as
the stronger of the two forces, could create a realistic option by an
initiative in the direction of recognizing the PLO.

Israeli Support for Palestinian Self-Determination

The radical left had always been a firm supporter of the principle
of Palestinian self-determination and saw this issue, historically, as
part of the anti-imperialist struggle in the region. In the framework
of Israeli politics, the Communist Party of Israel was from the inception of the state the chief advocate of Palestinian national rights. The
Communist Party of Israel, though it was one of the thoroughly
orthodox communist parties, and hence a fervent supporter of
Soviet policy in all of its aspects, had developed over the years its
own principled approach to the Israeli-Arab conflict. At the heart
of this approach was recognition of the right of both peoples, the
Jews and the Palestinian Arabs, to self-determination and mutual
recognition of these rights as the key to peace. However, since the
Israeli Communists were firm supporters of Soviet policy which
was considered as "pro-Arab and anti-Israeli," many observers
minimized the importance of their ideological commitment to the
just national rights of Israelis and Palestinians.

Matzpen, in its various versions, while accepting the principle
that both peoples had the right to self-determination, did not accept
the Communist Party's conclusion to the effect that Israel was
a legitimate national entity. Furthermore, it criticized the Communist Party of Israel for dulling its attack on Zionism in order
to pursue united front tactics with sections of the Zionist left.
The Matzpen criticism did find some support in parts of Israel's
Arab sector, especially among more educated youth. However,
in Israel's intensely patriotic majority Jewish population, it was
simply unfeasible to build a political organization of any scope
which denied the legitimacy of Israel's existence.

Changes in Palestinian Politics

Developments in the policies of the Palestinian national movement
had a crucial influence on the thinking of the Israeli peace movement. Initially, the PLO program saw as its mission the restoration
of the entire homeland to its rightful owners, the Palestinian people

and this meant, for all practical purposes, the elimination of Israel. At a later stage, the PLO adopted the call for the establishment of a secular democratic state, a call designed to refute the allegation that the Palestinians wanted to "throw the Jews of Israel into the sea." However, support for the establishment of a secular democratic state certainly did not include readiness to recognize Israel.

However, in 1974 the PLO adopted a resolution envisioning the establishment of Palestinian sovereignty over any part of Western Palestine liberated from Israeli control. This sounded very militant, but Palestinian critics of this new line were quick to point out that even the hypothetical coexistence of two sovereign entities might prepare the ground for a compromise and mutual recognition between the two entities – involving concessions to the Zionist state. Simultaneously, advocates of Palestinian self-determination in Israel were quick to point out that the PLO was indeed moving, though cautiously and step-by-step, towards a willingness to entertain the possibility of recognizing Israel.

Despite the ambiguity of its formulation, the 1974 resolution did in fact signal the emergence of a new political option – the possible establishment of a Palestinian state alongside Israel. This development created political "space" enabling Israelis to fight for the recognition of Palestinian national rights without having to answer accusations that they were forfeiting Israeli national rights. This option, after a period, came to be known as the "two-state solution" or the establishment of an independent, sovereign Palestinian state alongside Israel.

These major shifts in PLO policies, though they occurred slowly and over a long period of time, created new political possibilities in the Israeli left. While the support of the radical left for Palestinian national rights was a matter of principle and did not depend on the PLO willingness to recognize Israel's existence, it was clear that it was difficult if not totally impossible to convince members of the Israeli body politic to support any option that did not guarantee Israel's future.

In response to the Palestinian "feelers" designed to widen the PLO's contacts beyond the radical left, a group of prominent Israelis, acting on the fringes of the country's party structure, established the Israeli Council for Israeli-Palestinian Peace (1975). Uri Avneri, editor of a popular Israeli weekly, Ha'Olam Ha'zeh, Matti Peled, former member of the Israel Defense forces General-Staff, and Dr. Ya'akov Arnon, former Director-General of the Ministry of the Treasury were the kernel of the group which held a series of meetings with PLO emissaries in Europe, first with Said Hamammi, PLO representative in London and afterwards with Dr. Issam Sartawi. For the PLO the meetings were exploratory overtures. They wanted to know more about Israeli politics and to encourage new circles to support recognition of the PLO. At the same time, the PLO was interested in beginning an unofficial dialogue with the Israeli leadership. The Council explained to the PLO its view on the modifications and clarification required so as to impress Israeli public opinion and the government that the PLO was sincere about the possibility for an agreement between Israel and the PLO. The Council did not try to impress the Palestinians with its political clout back home, arguing that it was the responsibility of the PLO to convince Israeli public opinion that the PLO was indeed willing to establish a Palestinian state along side of Israel. In the meantime the Council was more than willing to serve as an intermediary between the Palestinians and the Israeli government. However, official Israeli reaction was either indifferent or hostile to the reports received on the content of the meetings.

Leading figures in the Council joined with members of the Moked (Focus) party in 1976 to establish SHELI (an acronym from the Hebrew, Shalom Le'Yisrael, Peace for Israel). MK Lova Eliav, who had earlier served as General-Secretary of the Labor Party, and left the party in anger over its hawkish stance under Golda Meir and Yitzhak Rabin, agreed to head the party's list in the 1977 elections. SHELI's electoral efforts were only partially successful – it gained two seats. Even so, it was the first time that an avowedly Zionist party in the Knesset called for direct negotiations with the PLO and the establishment of an independent Palestinian state. SHELI was highly instrumental in legitimizing the Palestinian orientation beyond the confines of the radical left. Thus, the Council for Israeli-Palestinian Peace and the adoption of its objectives as a vital component in the SHELI program served to broaden the base of an emerging current in the Israeli peace movement, which saw an agreement with the Palestinians as the main path to any settlement.

An additional advance in this direction occurred during the latter half of the 1970s at Israeli universities. Among other factors, a change in the organizational format of the radical wing of campus politics helped to popularize the ideas of Palestinian-Israeli understanding. The Communist Party of Israel opted for participation in local radical coalitions, abandoning its previous mode of operation as the student organization of the party on campus. Thus, student members of the Communist Party of Israel joined with independent activists from SHASI (Israeli Socialist Left), and SHELI to establish autonomous campus organizations based on joint Jewish-Arab participation. The two-state solution was the centerpiece of the movement's thinking on the Israeli-Arab conflict. The participation of activists from SHELI, officially a Zionist framework, broadened the appeal of these groups which could demonstrate Jewish-Arab cooperation on a day-to-day basis. It should be noted that while the left was largely isolated or marginal in Israeli society, this was not true on Israeli campuses, where the relative strength of the left made it a relevant factor in the ideological and electoral aspects of student politics.

Two Basically Different Conceptions in the Peace Movement

Peace Now certainly spoke for the broad base of dove opinion. It had become, in a short period of months, the symbol of a deep will and yearning for peace in the Israeli Jewish public. However, the politics of Peace Now were far from expressing the peace sentiments of all sections of the peace movement in the country. As we have seen, there was a distinct and relatively active minority of the overall dove constituency, which found the politics and strategy of Peace Now far from satisfactory. These groups and individuals, ranged to the left of Peace Now, criticized Peace Now on a number of accounts, chief of which was what they considered its opportunistic reluctance to take a principled position for the establishment of an independent Palestinian state.

There were, then, after the rise of Peace Now and the signing of the Camp David Accords, two basic conceptions in the peace movement. Peace Now spoke for those who felt that peace with the Arab countries, and it was really Jordan that seemed to be readying itself to follow the Egyptian example, was the key to solving the conflict. The different groups to the left of Peace Now insisted that the Palestinian question was the heart of the conflict and that conditions had been created for a dialogue between Israel and the PLO, which was the sole, authentic representative of the Palestinian people.

Peace Now, in its formative years, was extremely cautious about the Palestinian question. Its programmatic position was centered on peace with the existing Arab countries to be achieved on the basis of territorial compromise. Even after the breakdown of the autonomy talks between Israel and Egypt (1978–79), Peace Now had no clear stand on Palestinian self-determination.

> Israel paid a high price for peace with Egypt. The Palestinian issue is the next stage in the building of peace; a step in which any lack of progress might also harm the stability of the existing peace agreement with Egypt.
> Peace Now has never demanded a return to the border of '67 nor the creation of a Palestinian state. The Movement's main concern is the security of the State of Israel. We demanded and demand again of the Israeli Government not to close any option to peace, provided that it is not detrimental to the security of the State.[7]

The document proceeded to outline three options – the Jordanian option, a combined Jordanian-Palestinian option and the Palestinian option – and detailed a set of principles which should serve as the framework for negotiations on the Palestinian option. The identity of the negotiating partner was defined as "Palestinians prepared to recognize negotiation as the only way towards the resolution of the Middle East conflict," and the negotiations on the future of Jerusalem were premised on the fact that "Jerusalem the capital of Israel will not be redivided."

Though many of Peace Now's ideas and approaches on the Palestinian issue might have been considered progressive in the traditional Israeli context, it was clear that Peace Now was far from a growing current of thought in the peace movement that the Palestinian issue was the core of the entire Israeli-Arab conflict.[8]

It must be appreciated that the PLO, and Palestinian public opinion, rejected the Camp David Accords and the peace treaty signed between Egypt and Israel, and condemned them as a "separate peace." The almost unanimous feeling among the Palestinians was that Sadat had sold out the Palestinian cause, and betrayed Arab solidarity by agreeing to peace with Israel, in exchange for the return of Sinai to Egypt, without effectively guaranteeing Israeli withdrawal from the other conquered territories. The failure of the negotiations on autonomy and the resulting stalemate which continued until the Israeli attack on Lebanon reinforced Palestinian suspicions that, not only had they been excluded from the United States sponsored diplomatic process, but it was their interests which were sacrificed in order to cement the deal.

The Communist Party of Israel and the Democratic Front for Peace and Equality, which it dominated, found it both convenient and advantageous to be the main advocates of the Palestinian position in Israeli politics. The criticism of the US-sponsored Camp David Accords reflected both the Soviet position which the Communist Party of Israel supported without reservation and mass sentiment in the Israeli Arab sector, which understood and sympathized fully with the criticism of the PLO on the Egyptian gambit. On the other hand, almost all of the Zionist left supported, to one degree or another, the Camp David Accords. But, among this grouping, there was also disappointment and consternation over the stalemate on the Palestinian issue.

The breakdown of the talks on autonomy based on the Camp David Accords, the continuation of the settlement drive by Gush Emunim with the tacit support of the government and increased repression of different forms of Palestinian resistance, whether armed or clearly non-violent, tended to convince wider and wider sections of the dove constituency that the Palestinian question had to be addressed directly.

From Sadat's initiative (November 1977) up to the series of events that led to the Israeli invasion of Lebanon (from the fall of 1981 up to June 1982), Peace Now was the crowning achievement of the peace movement in Israel. Not only did Peace Now lead the fight for the Camp David Accords and the Israeli-Egyptian Peace Agreement; it maintained its centrality in the battle against settlement activity during this period. But Peace Now was either uninterested or unable to satisfy a growing feeling, based on gradual changes in the contours of the conflict, that the PLO was gaining international prestige and constantly expanding its influence in the territories themselves. More and more Israelis sensed that Palestinian self-determination was not just one of the aspects of the Israeli-Arab conflict but its very core. This approach found concrete expression in the establishment of the Committee for Solidarity with Bir Zeit University in December 1981, later transformed at the outbreak of the Lebanon war in June 1982, into the Committee Against the War In Lebanon (CAWL). The period of the "committees" added a new and dynamic dimension to the peace community. If this meant a semblance of competition for Peace Now which remained by far the larger and more respectable force in the peace movement, this was all for the best.

2

The Establishment of the Committee for Solidarity with Bir Zeit University

The creation of the Civilian Administration division of the Israel Defense Forces on November 1,1981 was designed to revamp the occupation mechanism by concentrating the mainly administrative functions of the occupying army such as municipal services, health, education and the like in a special command. The population correctly interpreted this change as a move towards a more permanent occupation-based "normalcy" and began to vent its opposition by every possible means at its disposal. One venue of meetings and demonstrations against the Civilian Administration was Bir Zeit University, the leading institution of higher learning on the West Bank. In response to protests on the campus, the Israel Defense Forces simply closed down the university, with its 3,000 students and 300 teachers, for two months.

A number of teachers at Bir Zeit University had decided, during the late 1970s, to develop private, informal contacts with Israeli peace activists. After a degree of mutual trust had been developed between the Israelis and the Palestinians, members of the Bir Zeit University group agreed, from time to time, to meet with Israeli intellectuals and political groups in the peace camp. This was an act of considerable daring on their part. Though, in retrospect, it is clear that they were putting the real intentions of Palestinian Liberation Organization policy into practice, contact with Israelis was subject to malicious distortions by opponents of the Palestinian Liberation Organization line. In the rarified, nationalist atmosphere prevailing in the Palestinian community, there was a justified anxiety that any contacts with Israelis – whatever the basis for such meetings – could be construed as collaboration. It was, at that time, something that "just wasn't done."[1]

The strong contacts and friendships that were forged between Palestinian academicians and Israeli activists created a special sensitivity on the Israeli side to the speciousness of collective punishment enforced against an entire university. The fact that many of the Israeli activists were affiliated as teachers or students with Israeli universities intensified their anger at the arbitrary behavior of the IDF and made resistance to the closure of Bir Zeit University a rallying point for the organization of a new and unique political formation. The strong personal links that had developed between young faculty members at Bir Zeit and Israeli peace activists posed a special challenge for the Israelis when the government cracked down on the university. Professor Daniel Amit, a physicist at the Hebrew University, played a pivotal role in the formation of the Committee, which was built around a coalition of left-wing groups.

The activity of the Committee for Solidarity with Bir Zeit University literally became front-page news during the months of November 1981–January 1982. This was a result of a series of demonstrations it held at Bir Zeit University and in Ramallah, the nearest West Bank town. Three days after the Bir Zeit University campus was closed, hundreds of Israelis sneaked into the grounds and held a symbolic re-opening ceremony before the eyes of the surprised Israeli Defense Forces detachment. Leaflets denouncing the closure were distributed in Bir Zeit and in Ramallah. Three weeks later, a demonstration by the Committee for Solidarity with Bir Zeit University was broken up in the center of Ramallah and fifty participants were arrested. A series of rallies against the closure took place in Israeli universities. It was no surprise when Bir Zeit University was closed for an additional two months, on February 16, 1982, just a few weeks after it had been permitted to reopen at the beginning of January. A few days later, the Committee for Solidarity with Bir Zeit University went to the streets and again clashed with Israeli Defense Forces soldiers in Ramallah. Not long after the Ramallah demonstration, a mass delegation of the Committee for Solidarity with Bir Zeit University participated in a stormy rally at Bethlehem University. The scope and the militancy of the various actions were unprecedented. Media coverage was abundant since the Committee's tactics were confrontational – and involved a hitherto unseen level of contacts and cooperation between Israeli activists and Palestinian leaders and institutions. The Committee for Solidarity with Bir Zeit University had found a formula of politics and tactics that made it an important factor in the Israeli peace movement up to and after the outbreak of the war in Lebanon in June 1982. The Committee's "two-state" line was important in keeping the coalition together, but it was the group's militancy that enabled it to dramatize the growing disgust for the occupation on the part of Israeli doves which was the secret of its success in the public eye.

A number of innovations increased the Committee's impact. No political party could claim any influence on the Committee which operated in a spirit of consensus and constant consultation. The Committee profited from the knowledge and experience of several Arab activists, most of whom had been active on campuses. They were members of the Communist Party of Israel, but never appeared as representatives of anybody but themselves. Amit sensed the importance of including Matzpen activists, who were willing to pay the price of membership in a "two-state" formation in order to break their isolation and play an important role where the action was taking place. A strong presence of members of a left-Zionist party, SHELI, gave the Committee for Solidarity with Bir Zeit University additional credibility. It was the widest and most unified combination of the forces to the left of Peace Now ever put together.

The strong wave of popular Palestinian resistance in the territories culminated in a series of bloody confrontations during February and March 1982. At the end of the month Peace Now brought tens of thousands of demonstrators to the streets in Tel Aviv to protest against the bloodshed, against annexation, and against the occupation. The Committee for Solidarity with Bir Zeit University and Peace Now, despite the understandable tensions between them, were working in tandem. Peace Now still had the confidence and support of broad sections of the dove community. The Committee for Solidarity with Bir Zeit University, for its part, had fired the imagination of a new wave of activists who felt themselves increasingly estranged from a society which wanted to keep up democratic pretensions while brutally oppressing another people.

War and Protest – From the Bir Zeit Closure to the War in Lebanon

On June 5, 1982, Israel invaded Lebanon. The official version was that this was a limited operation designed to restore peace to the

Galilee. Israel's real objectives became clear as the scope of the operation broadened and the Israeli Defense Forces were poised to enter Beirut. Israel was out to destroy the military and socioeconomic infrastructure which the Palestinians had created on Lebanese soil and this achievement was to be reinforced through a prominent Israeli role in putting an end to civil war in Lebanon. This was to be done by ensuring the ascendancy of those Christian forces willing to cooperate openly with Israel. One of the first complications in the war arose back home in the internal political arena. The war was met with opposition from the first day, and, what is even more important, opposition spread and deepened when the true nature of the operation became clear to the broad public.

The radical wing of the peace movement was in a state of mobilization before the war began. The Committee for Solidarity with Bir Zeit University had succeeded in drawing a crowd of some 5,000 in Tel Aviv for a march marking the fifteenth anniversary of the occupation – on the very day the Israeli Defense Forces invaded Lebanon. During a flurry of activity against the war which included hurried demonstrations in the streets and on the campuses, the Committee for Solidarity with Bir Zeit University decided to transform itself into the Committee Against the War in Lebanon.

The change facilitated the addition of new activists, especially in Tel Aviv, which also served as the focus point for a successful petition campaign against the war. When the Committee Against the War in Lebanon activists decided to call for a national demonstration against the war on June 26, 1982, it had a sense that it was far from being isolated in the public. Even so, the Committee was surprised when approximately 20,000 Israelis showed up to demand an immediate Israeli withdrawal. It was clear to all observers that opposition to the war was encompassing wider and wider circles – including many loyal supporters and adherents of Peace Now.

Peace Now had managed to express open doubts about the war after two weeks of fighting in an advertisement that posed the question of 'why are we killing and being killed in Lebanon?' It was quite a daring act for Peace Now, which hesitated about doing anything which would seem disloyal to the troops at the front. The success of the Committee Against the War in Lebanon demonstration, and the decrease in previous objections from Peace Now activists at the front who originally balked at the idea of opposition to the war when it was actually going on, opened the way for Peace Now to demonstrate on July 4, 1982. More than a hundred thousand participants at the Peace Now rally spelled out an unprecedented message in Israeli political life. Israel was waging war without the traditionally automatic political consensus that had been a bedrock asset of every government that had been involved in war – up to this point. The two sections of the peace movement had meshed gears and protest against the war became a central driving force in Israeli politics.

Complications at the front and the fact that what had been presented as a snap mopping-up operation was costing more and more Israeli casualties without there being an end in sight – not to talk of the confusing political signals regarding the exact nature of the war's objectives – fueled the protest movement, literally from day to day. Israeli Defense Forces' complicity in a mass pogrom by the Falangist forces against Palestinian civilians in the Sabra and Shatilla refugee camps on the outskirts of Beirut in September caused international outrage and convinced the public that the Israeli war machine was floundering in a political and military morass. Peace Now called the biggest ever demonstration in Tel Aviv in September. Peace Now and media reports put the crowd over the 400,000 mark.[2]

Yesh Gvul, Parents Against Silence

Over the summer months, members of a new group called Yesh Gvul[3] were successfully gathering signatures on a petition to the Prime Minister to "count them out" of the war. Political protest had been linked to army service in the past. Twelfth graders had announced as far back as 1970 their concern at having to fight wars that could be prevented. A group of twenty-seven twelfth graders announced their refusal to serve in the occupied territories in 1978; two members of SIAH, Yitzhak Laor and Yossi Coten, actually refused reserve duty and went to military jail in 1972; and of course, the officer's letter that served as the basis for the organization of Peace Now warned Begin that his policies might seriously impair the morale of the Israeli Defense Forces. The tone of letter by the Yesh Gvul activists to the Prime Minister and the Minister of Defense was accusatory and bitter, but more important it indicated that the government might face the problem of dealing with unprecedented numbers of "refusenicks." The signers blamed the government for trying to eliminate the Palestinian problem by destroying the PLO in Lebanon and went on to declare that their IDF oath to defend their country did not include participation in an unjust and unnecessary war:

Yesh Gvul's Call to Refuse Service in Lebanon

We, officers and soldiers in the reserves hereby request that you desist from sending us to Lebanon, because we cannot perform this duty! Too many have already killed and been killed in this war. We have conquered, demolished and destroyed too much. Why?

Today, it is clear to us: By means of this war, you are attempting to solve the Palestinian problem by military means. But there can be no military solution to the problem of a people. You are attempting to impose a "new order" on the ruins of Lebanon, to spill our blood and the blood of others for the Falangists. This is not the reason for which we joined the Israeli Defense Forces.

You lied to us. You talked about creating a line 40 kilometers into Lebanon, while you planned to reach 40 kilometers from Damascus and to enter Beirut. Again, we face a cycle of blood: occupation, resistance, repression. Instead of peace to the Galilee you started a war whose end is not in sight. There is no national consensus for this war, for these lies, for this occupation.

BRING THE BOYS HOME

We took an oath to defend the security and the welfare of the state of Israel. We are faithful to that oath. Therefore, we request you to permit us to perform our reserve duty within the borders of the state of Israel and not on the soil of Lebanon.

July 1982[4]

By the end of August, Yesh Gvul had gathered more than 250 signatures on the appeal. But even more important, there was a mounting roster of reservists who had actually refused to serve in Lebanon and been sentenced to military prison for their "refusal to carry out an order." In August, 1982 a press conference was held by "Soldiers Against Silence." The group, composed mainly of officers, met with the press after completing a stint of duty in Lebanon and added their authoritative voice to the growing dissent in the country, though they shunned the idea of actually refusing service. As the war dragged on Yesh Gvul was busy rendering moral and material support to a growing number of "refuseniks."

The report of a special commission of inquiry, the Kahan Commission, on the responsibility for the Sabra and Shatilla massacre, set off a new intensive round of demonstrations. The protest movement was growing all the time but the intense incitement against it by the government, and especially by Defense Minister Ariel Sharon, cited for gross negligence by the Commission, was felt in the streets. A hand grenade thrown in the dark at a Peace Now demonstration in Jerusalem on February 10, 1983, held to demand the implementation of the report's recommendations, killed movement activist Emil Gruenzweig and wounded five other demonstrators.

By the end of a year of war, more than forty soldiers had been sentenced to military prison for refusing to serve in Lebanon. There were reliable reports to the effect that the forty were only a tiny percentage of those who had actually refused. Many were accommodated by their reserve unit commanders who made efforts either to release them or find them alternative service within Israel while others who intended to refuse service were swayed by appeals to unit loyalty.

Thousands of parents of soldiers organized as "Parents Against Silence." Though the group stopped short of advocating refusal to serve in Lebanon, it did everything possible to express their opposition, as parents of the soldiers at the front, to the unnecessary war. There were instances of reservists demonstrating either before or after service in Lebanon. Peace Now and the Committee Against the War in Lebanon kept up with periodic activities and other smaller groups were formed to express disgust with the war. In September, 1983, Menahem Begin resigned, announcing only "I am unable to continue." Protest had "turned the country around" during the war. An Israeli retreat from Southern Lebanon was several months away but the majority of the public knew that it had been deceived at a terrible cost in life on both sides of Israel's northern border. The Israeli government – headed now by Yitzhak Shamir – consoled itself by stepping up settlement activity in the occupied territories and by taking repressive action against the local Palestinian leadership for attempting to organize resistance to the settlement drive.

Begin's muffled departure from the political scene signalled the beginning of the end of the coalition's slender majority. Protest continued on into the second year of the war until it became clear that new elections were inevitable. These elections did take place on July 23, 1984. The ruling Likud was hurt, but the Alignment was unable to build on its losses. There was a significant increase in the votes to the left of the Alignment, despite the fragmentation of the peace forces into different competing lists. The net result was that Israel was to have the dubious privilege of having a two-headed national unity government: Peres was to begin as Prime Minister and give up his post to Shamir after two years; Yitzhak Rabin was to act as Defense Minister for the entire four years.

Peres's premiership and the inclusion of the Alignment in the government were sufficient to dull the edge of protest, especially as the coalition agreement and subsequent decisions indicated that the government was going to retreat from Israel's main holding in Lebanon. The Committee Against the War in Lebanon and the Committee for Solidarity with Bir Zeit University got bogged down in arguments about strategy. It was an old story, almost a rule: as the spontaneous movement receded, factionalism increased. As the 600th Israeli soldier died in Lebanon in January 1985, it was mainly Yesh Gvul which remained active on the protest scene. The number of "refusenicks" was way past a hundred as the call-up orders that poured out of the military apparatus continued to force many Israelis to make the hard choice between serving in a war, clearly futile and dangerous, or taking the road of refusal. Refusal had even spread to the kibbutz movement. There it evoked firm opposition from the kibbutz establishment which had always sought to remind the general public of the disproportionate share of kibbutz youth among the dead and wounded in Israel's wars.

After Lebanon, there were few, even among the most conservative of commentators, who could ignore the potential impact of protest and the peace movement. Of course, the success of protest activity, or its failure for that matter, is always a product of a combination of circumstances. Short, neat and vividly successful military operations prevent the seeds of doubt and frustration from blossoming. Security policy and military operations seemed to the first generation of Israelis a part and parcel of the struggle for survival that dated back to Hitler's attempt to destroy the Jewish people. Israelis tended to rally around the flag like only those who have long been denied a flag and have recently gained one are wont to do. The open discussion of Israel's political and military options was presented as a luxury for a small people, remnants of the Holocaust, who still were fighting with their backs to the wall. Only that small section of the population guided by a firm ideological orientation on internationalism and anti-imperialism were immune from the dictates of consensual uniformity. However, when it became increasingly clear to more and more Israelis that superior military power and the unrestrained use of force and violence were unable to stabilize the region and ensure Israeli security, voices of doubt and criticism emerged and people created frameworks to challenge, in one form or another, the "received wisdom" of their leaders.

The vehicles of protest reflected differences of approach and the degree to which people were willing to challenge the basic precepts of their society. The differences gave rise to different slogans and tactics. Even so, the various currents of protest in Israel tended to complement each other. As a rule, peace activists were devoid of parliamentary ambitions. Nor were they locked in battle with those close to them on the political spectrum, a phenomenon known only too well on the Israeli parliamentary political and ideological left – where disunity and conflict were the rule rather than the exception. Looking back at critical stages in the development of the entire peace movement, one could see where the advantages of unity in diversity had made the critical difference. This is what happened during the zenith of opposition during the fateful months of March, 1982–September 1982, when people turned out to protest in greater and greater numbers first against the occupation and then against the war, which was conceived by its perpetrators as the best possible solution of the Palestinian problem. The war dwindled to its end. The Palestinian Liberation Organization was bruised but not destroyed. The Palestinians in the occupied territories tried vainly to turn back new waves of settlement and expropriation. Israel succeeded for the most part in destroying or banning incipient indigenous leadership. There were times when many observers saw the situation in the territories as a new 'status quo.' But the new 'status quo' never emerged.

3

Intifada! – December 1987

It should be appreciated that when the Intifada broke out in December 1987, it was not exactly clear what was happening. This confusion about the meaning of the events was certainly true as far as the occupation power and its military and intelligence arms was concerned. It even took some time before Palestinian political circles in the occupied territories began to understand that the sporadic outbursts were cascading into a rebellion. The picture was even cloudier in the Palestinian diaspora, and this held true for the PLO leadership whose distance from the territories had stilted its capacity to develop an effective strategy grounded in the day-to-day realities of Palestinian life under occupation. It was probably difficult for the leadership abroad to accept the fact that a major political breakthrough was transpiring without the supervision of the recognized national leadership.

Much has been written on the Intifada – quite naturally from differing, even opposing points of view. However, the following elements appear in almost all the accounts of the origins of the Intifada. The uprising was not planned ahead of time, no central or coordinating body determined the contours of the new stage in the struggle. When it broke out, its development was marked by an extraordinary level of grass-root participation and organization. Political coordination between the main political currents in the territories occupied by Israel developed and deepened as a result of the uprising. The acknowledged political leadership came together to further the Intifada and its aims after it had become a fact of life.

Since the uprising expressed itself through unfamiliar forms of struggle, it is not surprising that it took some time for the Israeli peace movement and the left to assimilate the importance of the events in the territories. Both moderates and militants in the Israeli peace community began to sense that the reports in the local and international media simply did not fit into the more familiar media "frames." This was not "terror," nor could the Israeli "information" apparatuses present it as such. It was not "armed struggle," nor could the Palestinian leadership pass it off as part of the military campaign to drive the Israelis out of the occupied territories. In a number of weeks, it became clear that an unprecedented, full-scale civilian uprising was underway, and the main weapon of this uprising was an unprecedented level of mass participation in every conceivable act of resistance: daily confrontations with the IDF and continuous demonstrations, strikes, road-blocks, boycotts.

The emerging Intifada was basically non-violent, though its spokespersons never adopted the philosophy or discourse of non-violent action. It was non-violent in the sense that an unarmed civilian population developed the capacity to confront an army of occupation and create, by virtue of internal cohesion and discipline, an alternative source of power. The Palestinians were proceeding to exercise that power in order to deny the occupier one of his most cherished assets: stability and all the semblances of normality that go with it.

This demanded organization, innovation and an astounding capacity for more and more sacrifices. The Palestinians had plenty of these qualities and they were demonstrating them for the whole world to see. The message was getting clearer and clearer: No price, no repression would move the Palestinians from the path to nationhood. The Palestinians had discovered and were exercising an unusual form of self-determination – under occupation – in order to undermine it.

Long before the Intifada, the main currents in the Israeli peace camp had come to an almost unanimous conclusion to the effect that the occupation was an ugly and degrading affair and a corrupting influence on Israeli society. Before the Intifada, Israeli officialdom had succeeded in convincing many observers that Israel was "digesting" the territories in a process that could continue indefinitely. The Intifada, when it came, made it clear to the Israelis and the international community that there just was not going to be a new status quo despite Israeli control of the territories for more than twenty odd years. These events and their meaning were not lost on the Israeli peace movement.

First Responses – The Organized Left

The first responses had their origins in the left wing of the political system. These responses naturally constituted an updated version of the traditional positions of the left on the Palestinian issue and incorporated the first lessons of the stormy events in the territories. The statements which came from the parties represented in the Knesset and the smaller radical groups were important in articulating and stressing the new elements in the political scene. A survey of these political groups is important for understanding future developments on the left and the emergence of the protest movement. Moreover, in many instances, members of the political parties or the smaller radical formations became key activists in the various protest groups.

The main feature of the parliamentary scene – determined by the results of the 1984 elections to the Knesset – on the eve of the Intifada was the dominant role of the national unity government composed of the Likud and the Alignment. This symbiotic formation resulted from the electoral deadlock that followed from the elections in July 1984. The National Unity agreement provided for the rotation of the premiership – Peres (Alignment) for the first two years and Shamir (Likud) for the last two years. A special slot was designed to allow Yitzhak Rabin to serve as Minister of Defense for the full four-year term. This government, which was almost a perfect mechanism for paralyzing any movement or initiative towards peace, was opposed by the following forces which made up the "left opposition" to the government and which served to express in the Knesset and the media the thinking of the peace movement.

The DFPE (Democratic Front for Peace and Equality) held four seats in the Knesset. The DFPE was still the strongest single political force in the Arab sector. But the main force in the DFPE, the Communist Party of Israel, was in the throes of a prolonged, enervating crisis, linked to the falling prestige and influence of the Soviet Union. The Communist Party of Israel had always been one of the more orthodox Communist parties and it considered support for Soviet policy as the loftiest expression of proletarian internationalism. Even in a period of growing demand among the cadre to examine the party's role, the veteran leadership, assisted by bevies of paid functionaries, had no difficulty in pushing any "revisionist" elements out of the party. As a result of ideological rigidity and the weakness of internal democracy, the party lost

ground among intellectuals and students, especially, but not only
in the Jewish sector. It commanded less and less respect beyond its
hard core of supporters.

Despite the crisis in the international movement, the Communist
Party of Israel and the Democratic Front for Peace and Equality continued to command widespread support among Israeli Palestinians
by virtue of their consistent advocacy of the two-state policy, which
included the demand that Israel return the territories conquered
in the June 1967 war and for recognition of the PLO as the sole
representative of the Palestinian people. Furthermore, in order
to counter-balance US domination of the region, the Democratic
Front for Peace and Equality demanded along with the PLO, the
convocation of an international peace conference on the assumption
that the Soviet Union was the most reliable pillar of support for
Palestinian national rights.

However, in the 1984 elections a new force appeared to challenge
the hegemony of the Democratic Front for Peace and Equality in
Israel's Palestinian sector. The Progressive Peace List was headed by
Muhammad Miari, a Haifa lawyer who had been affiliated with the
Democratic Front for Peace and Equality over the years and Matti
Peled who headed a modest sized circle of mainly Jewish activists
named "Alternativa." The Progressive Peace List succeeded, despite
bitter, almost vitriolic, attacks from the Democratic Front for Peace
and Equality, in electing Miaari and Peled to the Knesset.

The clash between the two parties was especially demoralizing to
the militant left because both parties had almost identical programs
regarding major current issues. The Progressive Peace List drove
the DPFE wild by suggesting that the Communists who led the
Democratic Front for Peace and Equality were "soft" on Zionism.
The DPFE, for its part, kept hinting that the Progressive Peace
List was created by "dark forces" to put a dent in the hegemony
of the Communist Party of Israel. Lacking any basis for genuine
disagreement on major current issues, each party made tremendous
efforts to convince the Palestinian Arab voters that it, and it alone,
had the backing of Arafat and the PLO.

The success of the Civil Rights Movement, which increased its
Knesset representation from one to three seats in the 1984 elections,
added two more seats to the representation of the parliamentary
doves. MK Shulamit Aloni, the founder and leader of the CRM, had
taken a firm stand against the previous national unity government
and its policies in the occupied territories and the CRM, which trans-

formed its traditional concern over human rights into a clear-cut negation of the occupation, earned heavy backing from activists and supporters from Peace Now, Yesh Gvul and dove-minded sections of the electorate. Not long after the formation of the new National Unity government, MK Yossi Sarid left the Alignment to join the CRM. Shinui, headed by Professor Amnon Rubenstein, also improved its showing and received three instead of two seats. Rubenstein, far from the left in every other aspect, was clearly in the dove camp. The overall picture was the emergence of a broad, though diverse, parliamentary grouping arraigned to the left of the national unity government, made up of the Democratic Front for Peace and Equality (four seats), the Progressive Peace List (two seats), the CRM (four seats) and Shinui (two seats). Another important left Zionist party, MAPAM (the United Worker's Party) was part of the Alignment, dominated by the Labor Party – but totally opposed to the Alignment's participation in the National Unity government.

The parliamentary opposition was a significant force, but its main components had become, in terms of the source of their electoral support, either Jewish or Arab parties. Jewish support for the Democratic Front for Peace and Equality and the Progressive Peace List was dismally small – less than 5 percent of the voters for the Democratic Front for Peace and Equality and the Progressive Peace List were Jewish. The dove vote in the Jewish sector went almost exclusively to parties on the Zionist left. The CRM and Shinui considered themselves an integral part of the Zionist movement and had no real roots in the Arab sector.[1]

Parties of the Zionist Left – the Zionist Peace Movement

Peace Now was at one and the same time both an integral part of the dove grouping in Zionism – represented in the Knesset by Mapam, the CRM and Shinui and by an important section of the Labor Party – and a totally independent movement. Peace Now never considered itself nor acted as the extra-parliamentary appendage of the Zionist left parties. Naturally enough, Peace Now leaders conferred regularly with dove-leaning MKs, but this was done without impairing Peace Now's autonomy which was in no small measure an important component of its own strength and prestige. Moreover, the various parties respected the fact that Peace Now could draw on a larger constituency and bring out a larger crowd than any of the parties, acting singly or together.

In the Israeli context, the pro-peace groupings and the forces of the "left" are considered identical. Since Shinui and the majority in the CRM considered themselves militant liberals and rejected any kind of socialist orientation, it would be incorrect, formally speaking, to consider these two parties part of the Zionist left. However, real-life politics seems to have decided that "left," in the Israeli context, means a principled readiness for compromise with the Palestinians and the Arab countries. Hence, it is the common practice in Israel to equate the peace movement in Israel with the left, though the peace movement contains groups and individuals whose social-economic philosophy had nothing in common with the positions of the left on social questions.

On the radical non-parliamentary left, there were four groups of importance. All of these were composed, at the most, of tens of activists and hundreds of sympathizers. SHASI, the Israeli Socialist Left, was the largest of the mini-left formations. It came into existence with the demise of SIAH after 1973 and strove to synthesize the main lessons of the experience of the old and "new left." SHASI, though close to the Democratic Front for Peace and Equality positions on the Israeli-Arab conflict, conducted a series of bitter disputes with the Communist Party of Israel, which according to SHASI, sought to dominate and manipulate any organization not already under the party's control. SHASI members were, over the years, key activists in CSBZU and CAWL and prided themselves on their ability to build and participate in broader formations.

Three different Matzpen groups were still on the scene at the end of 1987. One of the groupings, associated with the Maoist tendency in Israel, was smashed in 1973 when the leaders of one faction, the Red Front, Udi Adiv and Dan Vered, were accused and convicted of spying for Syrian intelligence. Rami Livneh and Meli Lerman, activists in a second faction, "Ma'avak "(Struggle) were sent to jail on lesser security offenses – essentially for refusing to report overtures made to them by illegal Palestinian organizations. The Maoist trend in the Israeli mini-left was effectively destroyed by these measures.

The Trotskyist, Revolutionary Communist League (LE'KAM) was the most active and stable of the Matzpen formations. Though its theoretical positions were close to the rejectionist position in the Palestinian camp, i.e. opposition to a compromise of any sort with Israel, the group opted to cooperate with peace groups which supported the two-state solution. It decided, as far back as 1981, with the establishment of the Committee for Solidarity with Bir Zeit University, that, in order to avoid political isolation in the Jewish sector, it would work loyally within the more militant "two-state" sections of the Israeli peace movement. This flexible strategy, implemented by the leading Revolutionary Communist League activist, Michael "Mikado" Warshavsky, Director of the Alternative Information Center, enabled RCL members and supporters – who were politically close to the rejectionist tendencies in the PLO – to become an integral part of the militant peace movement which supported the two-state solution.

The Tel Aviv branch of Matzpen, composed mainly of the veteran founders of the group, had opted to join Alternativa in 1984 in order to shape the development and the workings of the Progressive Peace List. A third group which had its roots in Matzpen was "Nitzotz" (the Spark). The group, which maintained a strict Leninist organizational structure, expressed on different occasions its esteem for the political role and work of the Democratic Front for the Liberation of Palestine (DFLP).

The various components of both the parliamentary and the extra-parliamentary left had lost much of their attractiveness for new social and political movements. The parliamentary parties were staffed by apparatuses of paid functionaries and peopled by small groups of devotees. The smaller radical groups were based on deep ideological and personal commitment – two central characteristics that were increasingly rare in Israeli society. New single-issue formations had much greater success in working with the public and attracting new activists.

There was a growing understanding in the peace constituency, which dated from the success of Peace Now, the CSBZU and Yesh Gvul, that if you wanted to advance your beliefs, the best idea was to join or build a single-issue group. Specialized formations, focusing on the issues of the day, were more democratic and more effective than the parties and radical organizations known for a mistrust of innovation. Moreover, single-issue groups, fresh on the scene, usually commanded more media attention.

Protest Profusion

By mid-February 1988, after approximately two months of Intifada, there were at least thirty different organizations which were active in Israel protesting the repression of the Intifada. Many of these groups went on to make a lasting impression on the protest scene and on Israeli politics. Still others disappeared early on in the campaign after making several timely statements on behalf of their members. Some groups, such as Peace Now and Yesh Gvul, were "veterans" of previous protest campaigns; they also represented polar opposites of protest philosophy and strategy. The women's movement which emerged at the beginning of the Intifada was a qualitatively and quantitatively new dimension. Those groups that organized along professional lines succeeded in creating personal paths for political intervention which were totally new. But the first impression that any observer received was that of the tremendous profusion of new groups, a profusion that provided convincing evidence that protest was on the rise:

> Not since the semblance of national consensus was shattered by guns firing past the 40-kilometer line in south Lebanon has the national peace camp been as mobilized as it was last week. Dozens of groups, both spontaneously organized and veterans of the anti-war effort, have sprung into action, each looking for a slogan that will draw the largest number of supporters, each jealously preserving the semantics that distinguish it from the others, and each searching for contact with other groups in the hope of forming a single mass movement.[2]

In many a sense this is where we begin our story. This is the story of those formations which took an early lead and became pace setters for the entire movement. This is a story of how the radical elements challenged the hegemony of the more moderate Peace Now in the protest movement and how that challenge was creatively met. This is the story of how women shaped an entirely new dimension of protest and protest politics. This is a story of endurance and frailty, of perseverance and submission. It is a story of the twists and turns in the search for unity, and unceasing attempts to intervene and shape the political process. In short, it is the story of those Israelis who refused to be against the Intifada because they understood that the Intifada was not against them.

4

"End the Occupation" – The Militants Make a Comeback

The outbreak of the Intifada was the background for a series of urgent consultations between veterans of the Israeli Committee for Solidarity with Bir Zeit University (CSBZU) and the Committee Against the War in Lebanon (CAWL). It will be recalled that these committees were the focus for militant peace activists in the period immediately before and during the war in Lebanon (1981–82). As a result of consultations in Tel Aviv and Jerusalem, in which the main political groups of the radical left were represented along with many unaffiliated activists, a group calling itself Dai La'kibush (DLK) was formed in each city. The name "Dai La'kibush," which can be translated either as "Enough of the Occupation" or "End the Occupation," was first used in June 1987 by a broad ad hoc coalition of intellectuals which called for a demonstration marking the twentieth anniversary of the occupation in June 1987 – almost a half year before the outbreak of the Intifada.

Activists from the Communist Party of Israel (CPI) were prominent in the Tel Aviv group and many of the unaffiliated independents involved had worked closely with them during the war in Lebanon. In Jerusalem there was a good "mix," composed of members of radical groups (the Revolutionary Communist League (Le'kam) and the Israeli Socialist Left (SHASI)), veteran peace activists and a new, fresh generation of unaffiliated activists. Shortly after the formation of the Jerusalem group, local CPI activists joined. Dai La'kibush in Jerusalem deserves special attention as it was certainly the most effective and dynamic group on the scene during the first year of the Intifada.

Project of the United Radical Left

The relative success of Dai La'kibush[2] stemmed from the fact that it created a framework which included almost every section of the organized left. It is important to point out that activists who were members of political groups did not operate in blocs or factions and made every effort to stress that they were participating as individuals and not as representatives of different factions. These efforts had a double purpose: first, to blunt possible tensions between the groups and to prevent the decision-making process from turning into tests of organizational influence; second, to assure unaffiliated individuals that they exercised as much influence on the proceedings as anyone else. Everything was done by the more experienced political cadres to create an organizational format which gave ample opportunities for democratic participation of unaffiliated individuals. The reason was clear. Experienced activists from the more seasoned groups understood all too well that it was the influx and mobilization of scores of new, unaffiliated activists which gave the group its vitality, enhanced its organizing capacity and broke down the wall of isolation which normally surrounded the militant left.

Even at the highest point of its activity, Dai La'kibush never became a formal organization.[1] It was composed of tens of activists, most of whom participated in a weekly decision-making forum as well as hundreds of people who participated in public activities of Dai La'kibush and considered themselves part of the movement even though they rarely participated in the weekly forum. Turnout for more routine activities in Jerusalem, probably the strongest Dai La'kibush group, such as weekly vigils, was about forty or fifty persons. Though it had no pretensions of being a mass movement, Dai La'kibush could honestly say during the first year of the Intifada that it was a growing force which set an example of intensive activity for other groups.

Action Agenda

Several weeks into the Intifada, Dai La'kibush had regular weekly vigils going in the major cities to protest the growing brutality involved in repressing the Intifada.[2] A flyer published by Dai La'kibush in Jerusalem in February 1988 revealed the range and scope of Dai La'kibush activity which included a weekly vigil at the Prime Minister's residence, regular dissemination of pamphlets at schools and theatres; a daily presence at the Prime Minister's residence to collect signatures and phone numbers for further contact; a weekly solidarity visit to the occupied territories; house meetings with Palestinian activists; and the central role in an emerging coalition of Jerusalem peace groups.[3]

The amount of contact between Israelis and Palestinians under the aegis of Dai La'kibush routine activity was impressive. The weekly visits to the villages, refugee camps or hospitals (!) in the territories drew a bus load or two of participants. The visits to the "heart of the Intifada" were an excellent way to bring home to those willing to learn and understand, the cruel realities of life under occupation and Palestinian readiness to make tremendous sacrifices in order to maintain the momentum of the Intifada. The visits became well known to broad sections of the peace community and many activists (as well as many tourists) made a point of joining one of the expeditions. By virtue of these regular weekly visits, Dai La'kibush brought many hundreds of Israelis (and no small number of tourists from abroad) into direct contact with local Palestinian leadership – and families of victims, killed, wounded or jailed as a result of skirmishes with the Israeli Defense Forces in meetings which centered on detailed accounts of local conditions and clashes.

The ability to chose the appropriate venue and to make appropriate contacts bore witness to Dai La'kibush's excellent contacts in the territories. In many instances, Arab students, activists in Dai La'kibush, served as "guides" and overcame complicated and sensitive aspects of journeys into the "interior" of the occupation. A circular distributed to each participant emphasized that the purpose was to conduct a quiet visit, and to avoid confrontation with the army, though, as a matter of principle, the sponsors were unwilling to attempt to coordinate the visits with the authorities. The organizers stressed that visitors were free to ask or say anything but sensitized participants to the fact that they would be talking to people living under severe repression, many of whom had suffered personally for their role in the Intifada.[4]

Coalition Building

Four months into the Intifada, Dai La'kibush was the central factor in building a Jerusalem-based coalition which sponsored a march by 500 participants through the center of the city.[5] The initiative was a joint project of Dai La'kibush, Yesh Gvul, Olim (New Immigrants) Against the Occupation, SHANI (Israeli Women Against the Occupation), The East for Peace[6] and a number of campus-based student organizations. The groups to the left of Peace Now, even together, had been unable to hope for anything like this number of participants in a Jerusalem activity since protest activity against the war in Lebanon (1982–83). It was a very respectable turnout for the militant left, and there were, for a change, many new faces.

The profusion of direct contacts and meetings between a broad spectrum of Palestinians on one hand, and a broad strata of concerned Israelis on the other hand, was a new feature on the protest scene. In addition to the trips over the Green Line, there were a series of house meetings where invited Palestinian activists would report on life under occupation. This pattern of contacts was a breakthrough, facilitated by the prominent role of Israeli Palestinian Arabs in Dai La'kibush. The breadth and depth of Israeli-Palestinian contacts was unprecedented and became a striking new feature of protest activity.

Auspicious Anniversary – Twenty-One Years of Occupation

The central role of Dai La'kibush in Israeli protest during the first years of the Intifada found expression in a mass demonstration in Tel Aviv on June 4, 1988. "Police estimates put the number of demonstrators at about 5,000, but organizers claimed over 10,000 people attended the march."[7] It was the kind of occasion on which the CPI could get out a considerable part of its own mass base. Moreover, in addition to traditional supporters from the left, there were large contingents of Women In Black and an impressive section of several hundred participants who marched under the banner of a new organization, "The Twenty-first Year."

The Politics of Dai La'kibush

Dai La'kibush politics centered on its support for the militant left's political program, known in political shorthand as the "two-state solution." Dai La'kibush written output usually featured the main principles of that position. A typical example, a leaflet distributed at the weekly vigil outside the Prime-Minister's residence, stressed the legitimate nature of the Intifada, and called for negotiations with the PLO on the establishment of an independent Palestinian state alongside of Israel.

"WHY ARE WE STANDING HERE?"

- The West Bank is burning. Gaza is in flames. Curfews, expulsions, killings.
- The iron fist has replaced the heavy hand.
- All this is perpetrated in our and your name. We are all responsible. The problems can no longer be ignored.
- We can no longer hide behind comforting formulas. These are not mere "disturbances", "a handful of inciters", "terror".
- This is a nation rising. A nation rising to fight for its rights. For freedom. For independence. For its life. For everything which we take for granted.
- We are part of this struggle. We don't want to be oppressors.
- Confronting this two-headed government of senselessness,[8] growing confusion and deception, we call for:
- Negotiations with the PLO, the sole legitimate representative of the Palestinian people.
- An independent Palestinian state alongside Israel.
- A peace settlement within the framework of an international conference.

END THE OCCUPATION, FEBRUARY 1988[9]

These political demands had been fixed elements of the left's program for many years. The militant section of the peace movement was distinguished from the more moderate sections in that it developed and maintained a clear "Palestinian" orientation, especially after 1967. The militants came to see the PLO as the main partner in solving the Palestinian problem and Palestinian self-determination as the path for implementing such a solution.

The stipulation that such a state be established alongside Israel was of major importance in differentiating this "pro-Palestinian" position from a different "pro-Palestinian" trend which considered Israel totally illegitimate and supported the establishment of a Palestinian state *"in place"* of Israel. The "two-staters" in Dai La'kibush considered the stipulation that the Palestinian state be *"alongside of Israel"* doubly vital since an important component in Dai La'kibush, members and sympathizers of the Revolutionary Communist League, had an ideological affinity to the school of thought which considered Israel, at least in its present form, an expression of colonialism, and not an expression of legitimate self-determination.

The demand for the convocation of an international conference, included in Dai La'kibush material, seemed to be a procedural matter. Technically, this was, of course, accurate. However, the point of the demand was to weaken United States diplomatic hegemony in the mediation of the conflict. Adding input from the Soviet Union and its allies, and from Europe with its greater sympathy to the Palestinian cause, was designed to neutralize United States partiality to Israeli positions. The Dai La'kibush position openly welcomed the Intifada as a means for freeing the Israelis from the yoke of being an oppressor nation. It is this kind of pathos which made Dai La'kibush attractive for many who felt that the Palestinians deserved respect for their daring and steadfastness.

A sharp debate took place in Dai La'Kibush in May 1988 on how the group should respond to the attack by an armed Palestinian unit in the Dimona region which resulted in the death of several Israeli civilians. Many in the organization felt that Dai La'kibush should clearly condemn the action and any form of terrorism directed against civilians, arguing that such a position was vital to rebuff allegations that the peace movement was insensitive to Israeli civilian casualties and unwilling to differentiate between legitimate protest by the Palestinians against the occupation and military action directed against all Israelis. However, there were many activists who maintained that it was simply not the task of Dai La'kibush to pass judgment on isolated Palestinian resistance activities, all of which stemmed, after all is said and done, from the occupation and the denial of Palestinian rights. In the absence of any consensus, the group refrained from taking a position on the matter. The argument about the response to terror was not a new one in the radical left. Advocates of the "two-state" solution tended to define any attacks on civilians as terror and considered such action a part of the attempts by the Palestinian rejectionists – who opposed the two-state solution in principle – to block any prospects for compromise. Those on the left who defined Israel as a colonialist project tended to see all manifestations of resistance as justified in principle. This debate anticipated differences which deepened at a later stage in the development of the group and which will be examined in the context of the crisis that affected the movement during the second year of the Intifada. With all of its importance, Dai La'kibush could not be considered a dramatic and new phase in the development of protest in the country. After all, most of the key activists in Dai La'kibush were repeating what they had been saying for more than a decade. Hopes for a new and significant stage in protest were centered on a new formation which called itself "The Twenty-first Year," because the organization was born during the twenty-first year of the occupation. The Intifada and the "The Twenty-first Year" were born during the same year.

From Protest to Resistance?

The Twenty-first Year emerged during the first weeks of the Intifada with a burst of energy. Hundreds of men and women of the younger intelligentsia attended house meetings devoted to the discussion of a new manifesto, the Covenant Against the Occupation, issued by the new group. The Covenant was largely the work of two young Israeli academicians, Adi Ophir and Hanan Hever, who had completed and circulated a first draft of the Covenant (interestingly enough) at least a month before the outbreak of the Intifada.

Hever and Ophir met after Ophir created a stir with an article in the June 1987 issue of "Politica," a periodical published by the Citizen's Rights Movement where he argued that failure to refuse to participate in the various aspects of the occupation is tantamount to actually collaborating with it. Ophir met Hever at a house meeting organized by Yesh Gvul and the two began a series of discussions, whose conclusions were eventually embodied in the Covenant.[10]

The drafters of the Covenant both had previous experience in the protest movement. Hever was a leading activist in Yesh Gvul and Ophir had been active in Peace Now and, at one time, a member of its national forum. In addition to the adaptation of universal concepts from protest theory, based on experience in different countries, Ophir and Hever drew two central lessons from their own previous experience. Both were convinced that the Yesh Gvul model could be extended beyond refusing military reserve service in the occupied territories. Furthermore, both firmly rejected the role of Peace Now as an effective tool of political protest. The admiration for Yesh Gvul and the reservations regarding Peace Now shaped the thrust of the Covenant.

Covenant Against Occupation – "The Twenty-first Year"

The Covenant begins by drawing attention to the fact that by virtue of the fact that "for more than half the years of its statehood,

Israel has been an occupying power," a new stage has begun in the relationship between the occupation and Israeli society. The occupation, which has become "the political and spiritual condition of Israeli society" is shown to have serious consequences for all aspects of Israeli society.[11]

Excerpts from the Covenant of "The Twenty-first Year"

The fortieth year of Israeli independence is also the twenty-first year of the Israeli occupation of the West Bank and the Gaza Strip. For more than half of its existence as an independent state, Israel has been an occupying power. Israel is losing its democratic character. The continued existence of the parliamentary regime within the "Green Line" cannot disguise the fact that Israel rules over a population – the Palestinian Arabs – which is deprived of all democratic rights. The occupation is not only a deplorable situation affecting the lives of the Palestinians; it has an equally pernicious effect on the very political and spiritual substance of Israeli society. The occupation has become an insidious fact of our lives. Its presence has not been confined to the Occupied Territories. It is among and within us. Its destructive effects are in evidence in every aspect of our lives . . . Expressions of protest against the occupation are circumscribed by the national consensus, protests do not transgress the boundaries deemed permissible by the occupation system. The "nice" Israeli expresses his or her anguish, remonstrates and demonstrates, but by accepting the term and norms of political conduct set by the regime implicitly collaborates with the occupation. The presence of the occupation is total. Our struggle against the occupation must, therefore, be total . . . The real moral and political question at issue today is not the price of peace but the price of the occupation. Against the all-embracing presence of the occupation, we posit a new framework for thought, for critical debate and for political action . . . we shall not be content with protesting yet another settlement, another shooting or killing . . . we shall resist the occupation wherever we can identify it. In our struggle against it, we shall be willing to play a personal price. We shall refuse to collaborate with the occupation . . . Refusal is the only morally and politically sound form of participation in Israeli society during the occupation. Refusal is a way out, a source of hope for our moral integrity as Israelis. Refusal is the form of our struggle until Israel will depart – by its actions, policies and daily contact – from the path of occupation and return to the road of justice and peace.[12]

Previously, Israeli protest movements usually satisfied themselves with the general observation that the "occupation corrupts," without drawing any specific conclusions regarding the possible structural implications of this process for Israeli society. The presentation of an integrated view of the occupation and its wider implications was more in the province of the "multi-issue," political and ideological groupings on the left. The Covenant of the The Twenty-first Year was a new departure in protest in that it presented a full-fledged, programmatic, revisionist analysis of Israeli society centering on a major redefinition of its nature and its government. The result was to define Israeli society as a "system of occupation," and to declare a "total struggle against the total presence" of the occupation.

A Cancer on Israel's Body

The Covenant lists the effects of the occupation on various sections of Israeli life such as security conceptions, economy, education, law, culture, language, political thinking and protest. The picture is one of growing, constant contamination, where the occupation is conceived as a cancer on Israeli society. Most indicative, for our inquiry, is the rejection of traditional, legal forms of protest: "the patterns of acceptable protests are limited by the consensus and limited to means deemed permissible by the 'system of occupation' . . . the nice Israeli shoots, cries, protests and continues to collaborate with the occupation system."[13]

This passage about the "nice Israeli" was an undisguised jibe at Peace Now which had been the subject of much satire, worded precisely in these terms. The criticism is based on the contradiction, either supposed or real according to one's outlook, between Peace Now's firm opposition to any reservations regarding military service, on the one hand, and its criticism, on the other hand, of much of what the Israeli army was doing in the territories. The specific object of ridicule, in the above passage, is the prototypical Israeli who, though a supporter of Peace Now, carries out orders to perform repressive actions in the territories and then demonstrates against the same actions as a civilian. This specific attack against Peace Now hypocrisy is launched on the basis of a broad critique of Israeli "moderates" which suggests that all protest activity conducted within the traditional bounds of Israeli parliamentary democracy is somehow counterproductive and morally tainted. This thesis negating legal protest activity could also be directed against the more militant sections of the peace movement (with the exception of Yesh Gvul), who usually preferred constraint to confrontation. The contention by The Twenty-first Year that legal protest was implicit collaboration was its way to prepare the ground to move from protest to resistance.

Arguing that the occupation had crippled the possibilities for genuine discussion and debate, and that most current rhetoric actually assisted in obscuring the emerging "colonialist reality" between Gaza and Tel Aviv, the Covenant called "for opening new options for personal and public response." These would demand "a readiness to pay a real personal price," and refusal to collaborate with the "occupation system" in any form including refusal "to participate in police actions and repression in the occupied territories."

Interpreting the Covenant

The full text of the Covenant appeared in full-page advertisements over the signatures of hundreds of supporters. Media interest was high and gave Ophir and Hever many opportunities to clarify the meaning of the text – which was certainly not a simple one.

Hever explained,

> . . . it is impossible to handle the occupation without taking into account its totality, which makes us all, really, its collaborators. The 'occupation system' requires for its existence, not only its own systems by which it organizes its activity; it also needs those with reservations and those who collaborate with it through limited protest. It is a very developed system of feedbacks. The occupation is always reproducing itself . . . We are proposing a new pattern of individual and political behavior which will demand of people perhaps more than they are willing to give. We are speaking explicitly about political work which will extract a price of political and social isolation and personal sacrifice.[14]

Hever was cautious about cutting all ties with Israeli society. "This is not the last step before returning our passport," he wrote "but an alternative to that act. We do not intend to abandon membership in Israeli society to the distorted discourse of the occupation."[15]

Hever discusses another aspect of this same problem in a series of articles on the Culture of Occupation: "Even so, we must remember, you can try and shatter it [the consensus] when you place yourself on its borders and refrain from taking a single superfluous step beyond it; when, on one hand, you refuse to cooperate with it while on the other hand you continue to be within it and continue to bear the moral responsibility that this situation imposes on you. This intermediate situation is a window of hope and a certain guarantee of the effectiveness of your actions. It is unnecessary to say that complete severance might sentence you to isolation without any influence." In the same article, Hever cites David Grossman's "Yellow Time" as an example of a seeming critique of the occupation which actually "reproduces its culture." [16]

There were, however, a number of serious questions and ambiguities about the Covenant which commentary by its authors failed to clarify. If the occupation were a totality, how could one fight it and stay in the consensus? And if one had to be ready to bear "isolation" as part of the price for fighting the occupation, how could one warn, at the same time, that isolation meant political impotence. There were serious questions that the Covenant simply avoided: why had Israel gone down the colonialist road and did total opposition mean a break with the Zionist ideology supported, up to that point, by the authors of the Covenant and most of those who signed it. The authors of the Covenant refrained from dealing with these highly relevant questions. Perhaps, they felt that they had already gone too far in attacking the ideological foundations of Israeli society.

The response to the Covenant was unprecedented. The Twenty-first Year initiative succeeded in mobilizing a considerable section of the liberal, Zionist wing of the dove community, despite the wording and the message of the Covenant which comprised a serious challenge to many principles of Israeli and Zionist cohesion. Hundreds of young Israelis, intellectuals, academicians and university students declared their support for the Covenant. Most were searching for a strong statement against the growing repression of the Intifada. Many may have not questioned the full ramifications of the document though it must have been clear to most that they were supporting a profoundly more radical path than that represented in their minds and in the public eye by Peace Now. In a matter of weeks the movement had an organizational structure of no small potential and began the challenging, complex project of turning its principles into a real social and political force.

A Promising Flurry of Activity

The first months of activity fully justified a sense that something new and significant had been added to the protest scene. Dai

La'kibush, with all of its initial achievements, did not come close to making a real dent in the liberal camp. The Twenty-first Year was enrolling and activizing people whose roots were clearly in that constituency.

In a few months, The Twenty-first Year had launched a number of projects, the sort of basic things that a group puts its mind to when it feels a surge of strength and increased interest from many on its natural periphery. The group could announce in a leaflet published in April/May 1988 that "1,250 individuals have signed the Covenant, including several prominent authors and jurists, a large number of academics." [17] It engaged in fund-raising and decided to organize youth who were "ultimately responsible for maintaining the occupation through their military service." [18]

The Twenty-first Year demonstrated a sense of innovation in five areas, expanding in one way or another, the traditional boundaries and methods of protest. These were: (a) Occupation Witnesses, composed of small units which hoped by their presence to be a moderating element; the Witnesses collected and distributed information; (b) a task force, composed of teachers, studied the influence of the occupation on Israeli public education and its manifestations in text books, maps and teaching aids, and curriculum; (c) a review of the judicial system and the legality of various routine military actions such as orders on when to shoot . . . and judicial inequities in the territories; (d) "planning an alternative Independence Day Celebration designed to emphasize that Israel will never truly be independent while the occupation continues; (e) the organization of a boycott of goods produced in Jewish settlements in the Occupied Territories.[19]

Not all of these projects were successful. The ambitious ideas about an alternative celebration of Independence Day proved impractical considering the time and resources available. The boycott never really got off the ground. The reasons are unclear; it may have been the lack of any previous use of the boycott technique, or it may have been the simple fact that it was hard to dramatize the idea as there were no prominent articles of consumption involved.

Radical Is As Radical Does

One of the most dramatic projects launched by The Twenty-first Year was a real test of their radical credentials. A very small group of Marxist militants, named Derech Ha'nitzotz (Path of the Spark), had, by virtue of its dedication and excellent connections in the territories, built its weekly, published in Hebrew and Arabic for a number of years, into an important source of information about the Intifada and its repression. The group, which grew out of one of the Matzpen splinters, had abandoned its Trotskyist orientation and developed excellent links with one of the pro-Soviet, Palestinian radical groups, the Democratic Front for the Liberation of Palestine (DFLP). In the spring of 1988, the group suffered from a series of severe repressive measures by the authorities, who "discovered" that the group had "illegal" links with the Democratic Front for the Liberation of Palestine – just a few months after the outbreak of the Intifada – precisely at the time that their weekly had increasing relevance in the media.

The newspaper, *Derech Ha'nitzotz* was closed by order of the Jerusalem District Commissioner at the beginning of March 1988 by virtue of his authority under British mandatory legislation, still in force in Israel. Six weeks later, April 15, 1988, after the *Nitzotz* editors put out three single, completely legal issues of the weekly under different names – the editors of the paper were arrested and held without access to counsel for over a month.[20] The government insisted that there was no connection between the closure of the *Nitzotz* weekly and the arrest of its entire editorial staff and released information that the editors were being interrogated in relation to serious crimes against state security. If there was really no connection, reasoned the activists in The Twenty-first Year, then the closure of the newspaper had to be seen as just one more act of repression against newspapers and journalists which had become so widespread during the Intifada.

The Twenty-first Year responded vigorously to these events, stating that the closure of the weekly, regardless of the "security" charges against its editors, was a dangerous precedent. The group decided to publish a special edition entitled "Shomer Ha'nitzotz" (Guardian of the Spark") as a protest and to provide a forum for those who were silenced by the closure of *Derech Ha'nitzotz*.[21]

The leaders of The Twenty-first Year wanted to avoid being identified too closely with the Nitzotz group, and stressed again and again that the issue was one of freedom of the press, par excellence. On the other hand, the editors of "Shomer Ha'nitzotz" had the courage to say, clearly and openly, that they wanted to provide a forum for those who were silenced – though they knew that the members of the Nitzotz group were political pariahs for most Israelis, including many who were an integral part of the liberal peace constituency.

The single issue of "Shomer Ha'nitzotz" was an impressive document. The editorial board comprised, in addition to the few Ha'nitzotz activists still at large (one of these – Assaf Adiv was arrested before the issue was circulated) and the leadership of the The Twenty-first Year, professors Asa Kasher, Nurit Gratz, Natan Zakh, Avishai Margalit, Zev Sternhal and Paul Mendes-Flor. The issue was devoted to the Nitzotz case and the wave of repression against newspapers and journalists in the territories since the outbreak of the Intifada. According to The Twenty-first Year, two thousand copies were sold within a day.[22]

Day-to-Day Work

Some of the more notable activities by The Twenty-first Year were the publication and circulation of materials specially designed for classroom discussion, a march by 300 supporters, in Jerusalem (August 1988), against expulsions, and a week long seminar (December 1988) for high-school students which centered on moral dilemmas linked to serving the occupation. During the first year of the Intifada, small units of The Twenty-first Year Witnesses reached the most remote corners of the occupied territories gathering information which often made its way into the media. Dr. Edith Doron, a linguist at the Hebrew University, told the press that she had visited the territories as a witness at least two dozen times since the beginning of the Intifada.[23]

Camping Near the Gate to Hell

The number of Palestinians in Israeli detention camps skyrocketed as the Intifada maintained its momentum, month after month. By its first anniversary (December 1988), 6,000 Palestinians had been arrested. Four thousand Palestinians had been tried, and only one out of twenty were acquitted; 2,000 were in custody, awaiting trial. Four thousand Palestinians had been jailed by administrative arrest, and 1,500 of them were still in jail.[24]

The peace movement had denounced the mass detentions and held several actions around the theme. The Twenty-first Year felt that more should be done and decided to launch an ambitious protest action outside Ansar prison, 200 kilometers south of Jerusalem in the Negev desert. The group was quite successful in its campaign to mobilize sponsors for a three-day camp out outside the Ansar prison. Ansar, a gigantic open-air desert prison, where prisoners were crowded into tents in dreadful climatic conditions and subjected to a highly-regimented depersonalized and dehumanized schedule, became a symbol of Palestinian defiance. A Palestinian writer who had been interred at Ansar told a Tel Aviv audience that "If there is a hell, Ansar is its gate."

The list of sponsors for the camp-out was successful in that it included the names of prominent artists, writers and entertainers, as well as names of people who do not usually support the more radical type of activities. The text of the call for participation was militant, but well within the bounds of a liberal response to an atrocious situation.[25] There was no hint in the text of a new way of looking at the Palestinian resistance, a promise made in the Covenant; the call condemned the brutality and the short-sightedness of the authorities, but it stopped far short of expressing any degree of identification or of even sympathy with the cause of those behind the barbed wire fence. The Twenty-first Year did not hesitate to abandon the strong language of the Covenant to attract the mainstream elements in the liberal section of the movement.

Participation involved spending considerable time at the site, three or four hours drive from the center of the country. Conditions were difficult. Even so, the site attracted about 500 participants during the three days, most of them on Saturday, the last day of the encampment. The event received a considerable amount of media coverage but the degree of success, even in the eyes of the organizers and participants, was open to different interpretations. One favorable report claimed, "Something is happening to Israeli society. Five hundred demonstrators on a cold rainy Shabbat at Ketzioth . . . is not an insignificant event. Dozens of demonstrators spent two nights in tents in torrents of rain . . . One must be very dedicated to an idea to do something like that."[26]

Even so, many participants and observers felt a sense of let down after the activity. Cynical observers noted pointedly that The Twenty-first Year tactics were no different than the way Peace Now would have run a similar activity. The logistics of setting up the camp site and running it involved negotiations with the army and police, and the organizers repeatedly warned the participants against any deviation from severe restrictions that resulted from compromises with the authorities. Suggestions from participants to march on Ansar were vigorously rejected by the organizers. The captions of a generally sympathetic account of the event captured this critical mood. "DO NOT STEP ON THE GRASS – The association with a picnic is, it seems, unavoidable and angers those present. 'Yes,' says one of the participants, 'we are soothing our conscience, that's also important.' Important, but not enough, says another demonstrator. We on the left continue to be pretty and nice and champions at holding symposia."[27] It appears that the bland tactics adopted by the organizers outside Ansar were a logical consequence of their initial strategy – to organize the activity in the name of a broad group of supporters many of whom were highly sensitive (like Peace Now) regarding any possible confrontation with the IDF, whatever the reason.

After a year of intensive activity, The Twenty-first Year could say that they had added an important new dimension to the style and substance of the protest movement. However, it was clear to all concerned that the group was still a long way from realizing its own set of ambitions. There was no sign that it had developed a strategy to implement its call for total opposition. The Covenant of the The Twenty-first Year had clearly suggested a radical departure from the traditional approach of the Zionist left. Since Israel was no longer a democratic society, one of the imperatives demanding that citizens obey laws even if they disapproved of them had been totally undermined. Here, it must be remarked that the The Twenty-first Year strategy was influenced by a type of revolutionary romanti-cism, which tended to see the apparatus of repression as a highly complex and [hence] vulnerable machine. The assumption was that there were pressure points that can cause, given sufficient devotion and understanding of the need for sacrifice, the machine to break down. In this case (as in others) there was a tendency to grossly underestimate the difficulty in finding the right pressure points and the amount of sacrifice and mass activity needed to cause such a break down.

The Twenty-first Year appeared as a rival to Peace Now, and the question of cooperation between the two organizations was simply not on the agenda. On the other hand, the The Twenty-first Year had to decide how to respond to initiatives from the left, primarily from Dai La'kibush, to work together. While on certain occasions The Twenty-first Year did join left-wing coalitions, it tended more and more to beg off when invited to joint actions. The reason given was that the group still needed to establish its own identity. In fact, the leadership feared that it might be "swallowed up" in a left coalition and stressed that this would narrow its appeal for the Peace Now constituency. This strategy, designed to preserve its appeal for the liberal section of the peace movement, was one of the many gaps between the group's radical rhetoric and its tactical caution.

While the The Twenty-first Year was struggling to find a way to totalize resistance to the occupation, Yesh Gvul, whose example had influenced it, found a clear and simple formula for dealing with the challenge of the Intifada. Service in Lebanon had been illegitimate because the war was unjust and unnecessary; participation in the effort to suppress the Intifada was just as unjust and unnecessary.

5

Yesh Gvul – Selective Refusal Extended from Lebanon to the Occupied Territories

Yesh Gvul, formed shortly after the outbreak of the war in Lebanon (1982), remained active after the war ended in 1983. Naturally, its main activity during the postwar period was extending support to the reservists who refused to serve in the "security zone" in Lebanon, kept by Israel after the Israeli Defense Forces retreated from their main hold in Lebanon. Discussions about extending the group's opposition to service in Lebanon to reserve duty in the occupied territories started long before the Intifada. It may be said of Yesh Gvul that even if the group had somehow known that the Intifada was on the way, it could not have prepared itself better.

Though the question of whether Yesh Gvul should take a stand against serving in the occupied territories appeared repeatedly on its agenda after the war, it was in March 1986 that Yesh Gvul came out with a clear stand on the issue. Several reservists were actually jailed during the period after the war in Lebanon for refusing to serve in the occupied territories. However, up to the adoption of the March 1986 position paper, these "refuseniks" were acting in an individual capacity and did not enjoy either official or material backing from Yesh Gvul – though they received moral support from most members of the group.

The March 1986 position paper which announced support for refusal to serve in the occupied territories also launched a new petition drive by Israel Defense Forces (IDF) reservists, in which the Prime Minister and the Minister of Defense were called on to "desist" from calling on them to serve in the territories. The text stressed that members of Yesh Gvul had fought for their country and were faithful to their oath to defend it. However, it had become clear to them and to many more Israelis that the occupation demonstrated that the government preferred territory to peace with the Palestinians. The signers cited the continuing deterioration in the territories as a challenge that must be countered with Yesh Gvul's strategy of selective refusal.[1]

Yesh Gvul Decides on Refusal to Serve in the Occupied Territories

We the undersigned serve, all of us, in the IDF reserves, and many of us have taken part in Israel's wars. We have different ideological outlooks . . . but we are united by our concern for the existence and the character of Israeli society.

The war in Lebanon, the settlements, and the acts of repression in the occupied territories express disregard for human life, values and a lack of realism. These blunders are an obstacle to the chances for peace with the Palestinian people and our other neighbors; they isolate Israel in the international arena and prove that the government prefers territory to peace . . . We have taken an oath to defend the welfare and the security of Israel and we remain faithful to that oath. Therefore, we request that you permit us to desist from participation in operations related to repression and the occupation in the territories."

Question: What has changed in the territories which we have occupied for nineteen years that has roused the members of the Yesh Gvul to focus their activity in this direction, precisely now?

Answer: There is no difference of opinion among us that we should have acted against the occupation more energetically from its very inception in 1967. Even so, it should be understood that a clear understanding of historical processes grows and broadens over the years. The war in Lebanon, the Jewish underground organization[2] and the dreadful intensification of the repression against the Palestinian people in the territories have demonstrated in clear and alarming ways the dangers imminent in continuing the occupation. More than ever before, there is a growing need for more radical and determined protest similar to political work conducted by Yesh Gvul.

Thus, when it became clearer to many of its members that the war in Lebanon and the repression in the occupied territories were expressions of a single policy – designed to prevent Palestinian self-determination – the group moved towards an explicit position against service in the occupied territories.

Patriotic Anti-Militarism

It is of cardinal importance to note that despite its being a powerful expression of anti-war and anti-militarist thinking and activity, Yesh

Gvul was not, in any sense, a movement of pacifists. It was proud of the fact that its members and supporters had served and fought for their country, and it was not averse to stressing this, especially in the face of accusations which impugned its loyalty. Yesh Gvul's explicit concern for Israel's genuine security problems and its willingness to take up arms in defense of Israel's existence enhanced the credibility of its argument that serving in the occupied territories had nothing in common with Israel's genuine security needs.

Double Challenge: Response to the Intifada and Repression at Home

Given its sensitivity to events in the occupied territories before the Intifada, it was no surprise that Yesh Gvul responded quickly and vigorously to its challenge. Yesh Gvul announced its decision to sharpen the tone of its previous petition (March 1986). At a press conference on December 31, 1987, just three weeks after the outbreak of the Intifada. In the new petition, 160 reservists announced their pledge to "refuse to participate in the suppression of the uprising in the occupied territories."[3] In June, less than six months later, Yesh Gvul, published a list of close to 500 reservists who had signed the petition. The list was published in a newspaper advertisement entitled, "There's a limit to oppression, there's a limit to obedience!," in which Yesh Gvul called on its supporters to participate in the united demonstration of the left marking the 21st year of "corrupting occupation."[4]

Yesh Gvul's Guide for the Perplexed

As reports of IDF brutality multiplied, Yesh Gvul published (February 1988) a slim booklet, similar in format to the official soldiers' service booklet (Pincas Sherut) and distributed it widely at soldiers' pick-up stations. It featured selections from the Geneva Conventions, court judgments and statements by eminent jurists explaining that soldiers who carried out orders to beat and victimize defenseless Palestinians in their custody were not legally protected by the claim that they were only carrying out orders.[5]

As it became clear that refusal to serve in the territories was gaining momentum, a clear tendency to probe the legality of Yesh

Gvul's various activities emerged somewhere in officialdom. The advocates of this approach believed that since the courts had been unequivocal in denouncing refusal to serve as a totally unjustified violation of the law, they could build a case against the group for inciting individual soldiers to refuse. According to press reports, it was the Attorney-General, Joseph Harish, who was determined to bring charges against the authors and the distributors of the booklet, pending the outcome of an investigation being conducted by the police.[6]

The Attorney-General and the Ministry of Justice tried to convince the public that they did not contemplate any steps against Yesh Gvul as an organization, but only against those responsible for composing the passages in the pamphlet which contained, on the face of it, incitement and solicitation in contravention of Articles 109, 110 of the Penal Code.[7] One observer noted that the Attorney-General spoke as if he were forced, against his will, to order the police to launch an intensive six-month long investigation of the leaders of Yesh Gvul responsible for the publication of 'Pincas Sherut,' – an investigation which included house searches, wire-tapping and mail censorship.[8]

When the government was forced to abandon the idea of prosecuting Yesh Gvul, the group issued a statement to the effect that: "Having learned the lessons of Lebanon, the authorities are well aware of the explosive potential of the refusal movement and have devoted much attention . . . to obstructing it."[9] The statement went on to emphasize that though the group had "abstained from any effort to persuade any individual to take this step, . . . this forbearance did not deter the Israeli government's legal advisor, (Attorney-General) Joseph Harish [acting at the instigation of the General Security Services – the "Shabak"] from ordering a police investigation of Yesh Gvul . . . [which] involved months of covert surveillance, included phone tapping and tampering with the group's mail. Early in January 1989, seven Yesh Gvul members were summoned to an interrogation; there was a search at the home of one member as well as a court order to scrutinize the group's bank account. These probes failed to uncover any proof of incitement . . . and the police recently recommended that the case be closed for lack of evidence."[10]

The weakness of the government's legal case certainly influenced the decision taken by the police to drop the whole case. However, it is more likely that the decision was influenced by a growing campaign of solidarity to defend the groups freedom of speech and association. The police harassment had convinced many leading doves who were also prominent critics of Yesh Gvul, including writers Amos Oz, A. B. Yehoshua and S. Yizhar that it was their democratic duty to come to the defense of the group. It was clear that there was a real danger, from the government point of view, that victimization of Yesh Gvul might evoke a great deal of sympathy for the group among a large public, which still considered the idea of refusal a serious moral and political mistake.

Throwing Away the Key

However, the greatest challenge to Yesh Gvul and its mission came from attempts in the IDF to "raise the ante." Normally, reservists who refused to serve were sent to military prison for about a month, a period similar in length to the scheduled reserve duty. In this case, the "refusenik" lost all compensation for reserve duty – which was usually equivalent to his civilian salary for the period. For many potential "refuseniks", the social stigma and possible complications (at work or in their family) were probably a bigger threat. Obviously, the potential impact of the sanctions involved in refusal were hard to measure and varied immensely from one individual to another. It should be noted that there were "refuseniks" who asked Yesh Gvul to desist from publishing their name and who succeeded in serving time in military prison without their names appearing in the media.

Many opponents of Yesh Gvul thought that the sanctions for refusal should be more severe. Ranking officers who wanted to raise the price the reservist would have to pay began to advocate and implement a rather simple solution: If a reservist wanted to refuse to do his reserve duty, he should be sent to prison, indefinitely, until he changed his mind. The legal situation was unclear; but the IDF could argue that the reservist could be remobilized after a prison sentence because he had not fulfilled the minimal quota that the IDF could demand of him. It may appear strange that so sensitive an issue was left to the private initiative of individual officers. But this was often the case; the IDF authorities decided to treat refusal as an isolated aberration of individual reservists and opted to allow the commanding officer (who often knew the potential offender personally) to handle the problem.

Rami Hason was a very unlikely candidate for victimization. Formerly a counselor for disadvantaged youth and the proprietor of a health institute, the soft-spoken Hason, a twenty-ninth generation Jerusalemite, was far, in every sense, from the radical left. His previous political activity had been limited to occasional participation in Peace Now demonstrations. But during the twelve months, April 1988 to March 1989, Hason served out three separate jail sentences in addition to a month of reserve duty. The "record" did not go unnoticed: "He is now serving his fourth [sentence]. When he is released late this month . . . Hason will have served 140 days in jail – the longest any Israeli soldier has been imprisoned for refusing duty . . . "[11]

This kind of victimization elicited a strong statement from a leader of the dove opposition, when MK Shulamit Aloni told the *Jerusalem Post*: "What they are trying to do is *to give him* life imprisonment."[12]

Hason's was, of course, an extreme case, but there were periods when almost all of those sentenced received a new call-up order upon their release from jail. As we have pointed out, policy in each case depended on the understanding of each unit commander. It was, indeed, difficult to discern any standard policy emanating from "above," though escalation in punishments did tend to come in waves. The extreme instances where a lone reservist fell into the clutches of a spiteful military bureaucracy, which intended to keep him in jail as long as possible, were clearly designed to warn those who might agonize over their decision in the future that refusal to serve might be a very costly proposition.

Often, "refuseniks" sought and received a transfer into Civil Defense units usually stationed within the Green Line. In other instances, reservists succeeded in snapping the 'sentence-after-sentence' chain by turning to the Medical Corp or even to the Mental Health Officer in order to request reclassification of their service profile or direct intervention against the results of excess pressure on the soldier. Many "refuseniks" often ended up with some sort of arrangement which spared them an annual confrontation with the apparatus.

The treatment of Rami Hason by the military was widely denounced. An impressive list of academicians, theater people and artists signed a call for his release which stressed that a "call-up order is not supposed to be used as a punishment and asked whether his commanding officers want to keep him in for life." The call was also signed by all the key leadership of Peace Now.[13]

In October 1989, the IDF eventually relented: "IDF authorities canceled the call-up order for reserve duty in the territories sent to Yesh Gvul member, Rami Hason. This is the fifth time that Hason has been summoned to serve in the territories after having served 140 days in prison for refusal. His call-up, for the fifth time, aroused intense protest and has been defined as abuse by the IDF against Hason."[14]

It is impossible to be certain that Yesh Gvul would have maintained its influence if the authorities had increased the sanctions against refusal to serve in the territories. However, in the light of Yesh Gvul's proven talent for marshalling support from the broad dove constituency, repressive measures against it may well have backfired. Yesh Gvul had been successful in repelling intimidation from the authorities because its sincerity and integrity aroused wide respect and prevented it from being isolated from broad, liberal sections of the peace community – despite the fact that Yesh Gvul was openly challenging a central article of faith in Israeli society.

How Yesh Gvul Works: Individual Choice – Collective Support

Membership in Yesh Gvul never exceeded tens of activists in Jerusalem and Tel Aviv and never involved a personal commitment to refuse to serve in Lebanon or the occupied territories. If, for any number of reasons, a member decided that, because of personal reasons, he had no option but to serve in the territories, or if he was simply not subject to such a call-up, he could still be an active, full-fledged member of the Yesh Gvul group whose goals were to legitimize refusal to serve in the territories and to grant support to those who decided to refuse such service. There was no such thing as a "collective" discussion or decision regarding each individual's own personal response to the dilemma of whether to serve or to suffer the consequences.

Member or not, if he decides to refuse, the reservist will receive the full support of the organization. First of all, Yesh Gvul can inform him of his rights, what the army can and cannot do to him, what to anticipate in prison, how to find alternative, but legal, routes to avoid serving – if the individual is so inclined. It can usually provide limited financial aid, when the consequences of refusal are especially damaging and legal counsel where this is necessary.

Paradoxically, many of those in military prison for refusal never had any previous connection with Yesh Gvul. At the same time, most Yesh Gvul activists were in no danger of having to do reserve duty by virtue of the fact that, as time passed, most of the activists had reached some sort of accommodation with their reserve units or had been transferred to reserve units which do not usually serve in the territories.

Part-time Soldiers – Full-Time Consciences

Yesh Gvul took root and developed, and probably could have only emerged within the framework of a particularly Israeli institution, the reserve units of the IDF. Yesh Gvul is essentially an organization which deals with the concerns of a specific constituency: reservists who have completed a full stint of military service between the ages of 18–21, as often as not in elite units of the IDF.

There have been important cases of selective refusal by young people drafted into the regular army, but these remained isolated cases of tiny groups or individuals who were unable to establish any permanent formation. The tremendous differences in circumstances attending regular, conscript duty as opposed to reserve duty go a long way in explaining the absence of a permanent protest formation dealing with refusal by conscripts. Conscripts do not have the ability to "come up for air" since the army for them is a long, uninterrupted three-year stint in a harsh and threatening environment. Compare this with the situation of the reservist who comes from a civilian setting and knows that he is about to return to civilian life in a few weeks.

The peculiar workings of reserve units in the IDF are very relevant here. Officers in charge of such units – usually reservists themselves – have a pronounced distaste for complications of any type – a sentiment often expressed in the comment: "Let's get through this thing without anybody getting hurt or into trouble."

The reserve unit acts as a highly specific kind of environment in which negotiations are held with the prospective resister and in which decisions are reached, in one direction or another. Even when the reservist is determined to say no, circumstances are rarely conducive to selective refusal. Often, effective social pressure against refusal can be exercised by a reservist's peers. The arguments may appeal to feelings of group loyalty and even to alternative ways of implementing the values and goals of the recalcitrant reservist in the most effective way. Sometimes the prospective "refusenik" is subjected to the appeal of like-thinking friends who ask him to come along and be on the spot in order to curb the appetite for violence that exists in some sections of the unit.

What Happens When You Say, "I Will Not Go"?

A variety of things can happen to the "average" reservist when he informs the commander of his unit that his decision to refuse to serve in the occupied territories is final. Almost invariably, the operative decision is taken on the local battalion level. The range of responses makes it difficult, most of the time, to discern any clear line of response emanating from "higher up."

The unit commander has a great deal of discretion. If he is determined to keep the reservists out of prison, he can usually, if not always find some way to avoid disciplinary action. The most common response is for the commander to sentence the "refusenik", during the period when the unit is organizing itself to assume its assignment, to a period in military prison roughly the same in length to the period that he would have served had he agreed to do his military service. This period is usually about a month, sometimes shorter but very rarely longer. The reservist is open, however, to further sanctions. Even after he has done his time in military prison, he is still subject to call-up for reserve duty, because he has not fulfilled his obligations under law. We have discussed the use of back-to-back call-ups. Yesh Gvul was unable to get a ruling against the use of this form of punishment despite the fact that the High Court of Justice, in rejecting a petition against the right of the army to imprison any "refusenik," did recommend that reservists receive an appropriate intermission between their sentence and a new call-up.

The act of defiance becomes "final, when the reservist refuses to get on the bus that takes his fellow reservists to their tour of duty in the occupied territories. The military trial is a uncomplicated affair and always turns on the simple question of "refusing to carry out an order." Anything that the "refusenik" might want to say in his defense is simply irrelevant to the local commander who will often explain that he has no alternative but to send the offender off to military jail, usually for a period of approximately 30 days. It is fraught with danger to appeal this kind of a sentence since any appeal tribunal would have the authority to impose even more severe sentences.

Charging the Ramparts of Respectability – Is Refusal Politically Wise?

Yesh Gvul was a focus of attention and maintained a high profile in the media because, in addition to the clashes with the authorities which stemmed from its goals, it was a constant source of political battles within the peace movement where mainstream forces considered Yesh Gvul highly counter-productive. Tension in the moderate section of the peace movement was on the rise as the Yesh Gvul "virus" was spreading. Many young men, from the heartland of the Zionist left, were getting tired of seeing their army service executed in the support of a cause whose basic immorality became clearer by the day. Avishai Grossman, a highly-respected educator in Kibbutz Artzi and Hashomer Hatzair, published a short note in the MAPAM daily, *Al Ha'mishmar*, identifying himself with others who supported Yesh Gvul and the idea of refusal. Grossman suggested changing traditional Hashomer Hatzair slogans such as "Always ready for an order," replacing them with, "Not always, not at any price" or "this far and no further."[15]

Opposition to Yesh Gvul in the dove community was spearheaded by Yossi Sarid. Sarid, MK for the CRM, and a close personal friend of Grossman, used Grossman's statement to warn Rabin that things were getting serious, i.e., there was a growing danger that many of the best of the country's youth might opt for refusal.

> I want Yitzhak Rabin to know . . . Service in the territories is something which many do not take for granted, and the number of those refusing is on the increase. It is only by tremendous efforts, that we manage to ensure the full mobilization of the annual age-groups, but who knows for how long we will succeed in this. In truth, I am not certain that Rabin understands what I am trying to explain to him.[16]

For Sarid, and others like him, including the Peace Now leadership, negation of refusal to obey call-up orders had deep political and ideological roots. But Rabin's instructions to the IDF for the brutal suppression of the Intifada were making it increasingly hard for Sarid to counter the influence of Yesh Gvul's ideas.

It was clear to Yesh Gvul and its members, that even in the new circumstances created by the Intifada, support from Peace Now and other moderate forces in the peace movement would be out of the question. As in the past, Yesh Gvul enjoyed the full support of the radical left and the militant wing of the peace movement. This support was important for Yesh Gvul, but nowhere sufficient to launch a serious campaign of widespread resistance to service in the territories. This goal required that Yesh Gvul somehow dent or crack the wall of respectability that separated it from the mass of potential candidates for refusal. This could be done when and if new forces, which generally owed their political allegiance to Peace Now, MAPAM, or the CRM, came to accept in full or in part the Yesh Gvul argument to the effect that there are limits to obedience and conformism.

Family Feud

It was Yesh Gvul's firm conviction that it was translating, by virtue of its supporters deep personal commitment, the ideals and the values of the entire peace movement into the sphere of concrete action. Yesh Gvul felt that most people in the peace movement should properly pursue the same line of behavior – refusal to serve in the occupied territories. Yesh Gvul did not see itself as the proponent of more militant political policies for the entire movement. Rather, it considered itself distinctive in that its path alone bridged the moral and ethical gap between thought and action. Yesh Gvul hoped to set a moral example for the entire peace constituency. The example was built on ideals of individual responsibility and moral consistency. People who really want peace and do not want to hide from the ugly truth of what the occupation is and does, should not bear arms in order to put down the Palestinian Intifada in the occupied territories.

The argument is simple enough, but it happens to go against the grain of basic tenets deeply rooted precisely in the broadest social-democratic and liberal sections of the population, i.e. the very constituency that provides the peace movement with its broad mass base. The Yesh Gvul "project" was to succeed or to fail to the degree that it made a dent or a crack in the liberal consensus and its ties with the national consensus. This was no small task as the organized political forces in the broad-based peace movement opposed the Yesh Gvul strategy on every plane: moral, ethical, political and practical.

From its very inception, Yesh Gvul had to deal with the fact that the moderate and liberal section of the peace movement was determined to reject, and even to denounce, the idea of refusing service. There is nothing surprising in this considering that Peace Now and other moderate formations considered themselves as part of a national ideological-political consensus and made every effort to cultivate their mainstream image.

Mordechai Bar-On, Peace Now's authoritative chronicler wrote:

> Yesh Gvul's call contradicted Peace Now's principles, which always insisted on adherence to the democratic rules of the game. The movement believed that the government had the authority to decide in matters of war and peace (especially, as in this case it received massive support in the Knesset) and its decision obligates the whole people. Peace Now expresses its opinion and its protest, legally and publicly, but refrains from transgressing the limits of the law – and demands that its supporters maintain military discipline despite political opposition to steps by the government. Moreover, Peace Now always held that Israel's political and strategic circumstances require that it must maintain an unchallenged military deterrence. The strength of the Israeli Defense Forces and its internal cohesiveness is, therefore, an absolute necessity for Israel. Even before [the war in Lebanon] Peace Now directed all its criticism and its attacks at the political hierarchy and was careful not to damage the stature of the Israeli Defense Forces or the fighting morale of its soldiers. Therefore, even though the members of Peace Now understood the motives of the members of Yesh Gvul, they opposed their actions and desisted from urging their supporters to refuse or disobey in any form.[17]

Moderates in the peace movement accepted the basic premise that political and ideological struggle must be conducted within the framework of the conventional definitions of Israeli national interest. This premise stemmed from their perception of two features of Israeli life. First, Israel was indeed under constant threat from the Arab world, which refused to accept its existence. Secondly, Israeli society was held together by a delicate fabric, and the political center and the left are historically responsible for maintaining national unity and national consensus. To whatever extent the right might act irresponsibly (it has a history of breaking ranks and withdrawing from national institutions) the dictates of political responsibility and good citizenship, requiring scrupulous observance of the law, are binding on the constructive forces in Zionism. Even when the right took power in Israel, the Zionist left imposed limits on its political behavior.

Moderates in the peace movement have always tended to see the fall of the labor movement, with which most of them identify, from power, as an exceptional or temporary state of affairs. In "normal" conditions, the moderate left sees itself as the natural rulers of the state, and ultimately responsible for its fate. Israel's liberals and social-democrats see themselves in a running, continuous battle for influence and hegemony in the Israeli Defense Forces. This being the case, the idea of challenging military discipline or being associated with any group which does so, was seen by much of the public as an abdication from civic responsibility. The whole idea of turning the best people of the younger generation into idealistic pacifists was simply unacceptable. Yesh Gvul protestations that it supported only a limited and qualified rejection of absolute loyalty to authority were rejected. Once law and legality are called into question, argued the moderates, who knows where the process stops?

Given the hold of these traditions on the vast majority of the peace community in Israel, the very existence of Yesh Gvul was remarkable. Even more remarkable was the fact that Yesh Gvul did seriously dent these ideological ramparts, even if it never breached them. Indeed, many of the ideologues of the Zionist left, such as Amos Oz and A. B. Yehoshua have admitted on different occasions that they too have their own "red line" which they will refuse to cross, whatever the legal ramifications. The common example cited was the moral obligation of the left to disregard the law in order to prevent mass expulsions of Palestinians from the territories. By this admission they revealed that many of their differences with Yesh Gvul were not as absolute as it seemed and were in many senses, more a question of strategy and tactics and less a matter of principle.

Limits of Protest and Limits of the Law

The attitude of the peace movement to law and legality deserves some attention. Peace Now represented that pole of thinking which held that the peace movement must adhere to the letter and the spirit of the law. Peace Now felt that any infraction of the law was counterproductive and would only help to push the movement, which prided itself on its mainstream image, to the margins. Peace Now was particularly cautious about any confrontation with the Israeli Defense Forces in the territories, even when it was clear to all concerned that the military was acting in a purely political capacity. Confrontation with the army or the police was to be avoided at almost any price. Tangling with Israeli soldiers in order to protest the occupation was simply bad politics, and not done whatever the circumstances. The single instance, where a Peace Now action ended in a not too serious confrontation, occurred in circumstances beyond the control of the Peace Now leadership.[18]

The radical section of the peace movement had a more complex approach. As a rule, the militant organizations preferred to operate within the law and without exception rejected the idea of direct, illegal support to the Intifada. On the other hand, the left waged a perpetual battle with the authorities about the ground rules of open political activity. There were numerous cases where the authorities arbitrarily ruled that completely orderly open air meetings were illegal assemblies and used unnecessary force to dispel them. The left would not hesitate to confront the police or the army over its right to demonstrate and protest – especially when it felt that it had a good case, regarding both the substantial issue involved and the circumstances in which its right to legitimate protest was curtailed.

Regarding political action in the territories, the left had a strong case against rank discrimination on the part of the authorities, who never took serious action against provocative actions and demonstrations by the settler right. The actions of the settler right were almost totally ignored by the IDF though many of them caused physical harm to Palestinians and their property, while everything was done to prevent the peace movement, and especially the Israeli left, from expressing itself politically against the occupation when and where the Palestinians might observe their protest.

A New Dimension to Israeli Political Culture

No protest group was as successful as Yesh Gvul in evoking an ongoing debate over the philosophical and theoretical implications of its ideas and aims. In order to create an intellectual atmosphere in which it would have some chance of a fair hearing, Yesh Gvul took serious steps to expand the horizons of political debate. The group issued a flow of publications: books and pamphlets which dealt with the historical, legal and moral aspects of the familiar dilemma – how should the individual respond when faced with the state-sanctioned demand for individual compliance in the perpetration of unjust collective action.

It should be appreciated that radical strategy in Israel had been dominated over the years by Marxism. Marxism, as known and practiced in Israel carefully avoided any challenge to the legal obligations connected with military service. The first and foremost reason for this abstention was undoubtedly linked to a justified fear that any organized challenge against military service would facilitate swift repression against the offending group. The Communist Party never suggested to members or sympathizers to avoid military service. One notable exception was the battle waged by the CPI and its sympathizers in the Druze community against conscription of Israeli Druze youth into the IDF, but this campaign was based on the argument that the Druze are Arabs.

Before Yesh Gvul took the initiative of publishing material on the subject, problems like personal responsibility and moral choice were known and studied, if at all, in purely academic settings. By introducing the Israeli reader to a wide spectrum of alternative political conceptions anchored in traditions spanning from liberal individualism to civil disobedience, Yesh Gvul expanded the scope and depth of political and philosophical discourse in the country. Of course, the effect of these initiatives was restricted to intellectual circles. However, Yesh Gvul understood that it had to contend with the political support of the liberal intelligentsia to Israel's national consensus. This was an obstacle which any serious anti-war or anti-militarist movement had to overcome. The relatively successful effort by Yesh Gvul to introduce new elements of critical thinking into Israeli politics was a political feat of no little importance.

A major expression of Yesh Gvul's efforts in this area was the publication and circulation, during the war in Lebanon, of a book of articles dealing with the "limits of obedience."[19] A second book was published during the Intifada in order to rekindle the previous debate and bring it up to date.[20] Yesh Gvul was also instrumental in the publication of a special brochure designed for use by teachers in high school, though the group decided, for tactical and technical reasons, to abstain from official sponsorship.[21]

Yesh Gvul managed to play a key role against repression of the Intifada by reformulating its basic ideas in new circumstances. Even though actual 'refusal' was never a mass phenomenon, the movement exerted tremendous moral influence by virtue of the integrity and the dedication of its adherents. Moreover, when measuring its effectiveness, Yesh Gvul argued convincingly that the absolute number of "refuseniks" sentenced was only a part of the picture – since hundreds more were successful in avoiding military service without ever coming to trial. We shall return to the examination of the relations between Yesh Gvul and the moderates in the peace movement later. Here, it is sufficient to note that Yesh Gvul demonstrated that assets acquired by the peace movement during one round of battle (protest against the war in Lebanon) would serve it again when the need arose. The appearance of the women's peace movement at the beginning of the Intifada showed that in addition to the reactivization of earlier protest groups, new and original dimensions of protest were in the offing.

6

The Formation of an Independent Women's Peace Movement

An autonomous women's peace movement, unprecedented in scope and creative force, appeared in Israel in direct response to the Intifada. Of course, Israeli women had a rich history of participation in politics as individuals in heterosexual organizations or as members of women's groups affiliated to – and usually controlled by – male-dominated parties. It was the modern, feminist movement that appeared in Israel in the early seventies, which laid the foundations for independent, militant women's organizations. However, the feminists shied away from dealing directly with the Israeli-Arab conflict, out of a fear that internal conflict on so highly charged an issue might endanger the existence of their new and delicate political formation. The new women's peace movement, unlike previous feminist initiatives, was aimed at protesting government policy regarding the Israeli-Arab conflict.[1] And unlike previously existing women's political groups, the new women's peace movement independently shaped its own political agenda and organizational formations.

A number of factors encouraged this radical development. The prestige of militant sections of the women's movement abroad – including the vivid example of groups such as the Mothers of Plaza De Mayo and the women from Greenham Common – inspired radical women in Israel. The strong women's response to the Intifada at the time also had much to do with the weakness of the more traditional protest formations, on both the moderate and radical left. Moreover, the intense cycle of violence and brutalization in the territories was a special dimension which evoked a specific response from women. It was Women In Black, which, more than any other group, expressed the resourcefulness and the stamina which went into the creation of the women's peace movement.

Women In Black – Politics as Ritual in the Street

Women In Black came on the protest scene sometime in January 1988 when a group of women, active in Dai La'Kibush decided, as part of the search for innovative forms of activity, to initiate a separate women's vigil. The group initiated a weekly vigil at different sites in Jerusalem and eventually decided on a fixed locality, Paris Square, a busy five-way intersection, five minutes from downtown Jerusalem, and a hundred yards from the Prime Minister's residence. Shortly afterwards, the women informed their colleagues in Dai La'kibush that the Women In Black vigil was a totally independent project and the participants in the vigil would make any necessary decisions regarding the group's activity. From that point, Women In Black disappeared from the agenda at the regular forums of Dai La'kibush.

From week to week, the number of participants grew and the vigil took on its permanent form. All the women wore black and each held a small sign, in the form of a hand, carrying a single slogan: Dai La'kibush (End the Occupation). One of the first press reports on Women In Black cited the decision of the group to dedicate a vigil to International Women's Day, March 1988. One of the organizers, Ruth Cohen, explained that black was associated with mourning, loss of morality and rational thought, and that the group intended to keep up the vigil as long as the violence and repression continued.[2]

Target of Provocation

As Women In Black grew, as the vigil became a landmark in Jerusalem and other cities, it became a target of provocation and counter-demonstrations by right-wing extremists. After all, "a bunch of women," just standing there, were an easy mark for those who wanted to prove their patriotism and their virility by insulting or intimidating them. In one of the many instances of insult and abuse, youths from the right-wing settlers' party, T'hiyah, mingled with the vigil and scattered powder from bottles labelled "pesticide against black widows." After scattering the "insecticide" in circles around the women demonstrators, the youngsters broke out in patriotic songs of Eretz-Yisrael and started up a stormy circle dance in the Square.[3]

The right-wing groups would often come with placards and flags and push their way into the vigil, usually cursing and pushing, in an attempt to push the women off the terrace. The women were also targets of objects thrown from passing buses and cars. But the most common expression of condemnation was an almost steady flow of invective from many of the drivers stopping at the intersection. As often as not, this abuse took the form of explicit sexist and racist vituperation. Anat Hoffman, Jerusalem City Councilwoman, listed ten such insults from different taxi drivers during a single vigil.[4]

The women invariably adopted non-violent tactics. Offers for assistance from concerned male sympathizers were politely declined, though the presence of male relatives and friends in the vigil area did tend to increase in periods of tension. When the pushing and shoving got serious or when some of the rightist trouble-makers got hot under the collar, women, with experience in dealing with such circumstances, managed to steer the offenders off to the side and calm them.

Many of the confrontations occurred over the right to use the Square. Despite the fact that Women In Black were the regular occupants of the square, the police claimed total neutrality over the issue, maintaining that the terrace belonged, by law, to whoever first occupied it. Thus, the early appearance of a small contingent of three or four rightists was considered sufficient reason to deny Women In Black the use of the terrace. When right-wingers did show up early in order to "occupy the square," the Women In Black strategy was to determinedly avoid any confrontation which could grow into a brawl. Usually, Women In Black would simply move the vigil to another corner, off the square, when and if the right-wing groups got to the terrace first.

In addition to their non-violent tactics, Women In Black frequently filed criminal complaints and insisted on active police protection. On occasion, Women In Black representatives initiated meetings with high-ranking police officers. Women In Black were also a permanent client of the Israeli Association for Civil Rights and impressed the police with the fact that they knew their rights and would not allow themselves to be intimidated or provoked. The size and the steadfastness of the Jerusalem vigil did eventually ensure a certain degree of impartiality from the police in that city.

In Tel Aviv and Haifa, which followed the Jerusalem lead in establishing permanent Women In Black vigils early in 1988, there was a general feeling that the police were less cooperative and managed somehow not to be around when violence erupted.[5] Full documentation of all the threats, provocations, and abuse against Women In Black – a project which might shed interesting light on the deeper connections between sexism and racism – demands separate treatment. There were often periods of relative quiet during which Women In Black could come to believe that more of the public had accepted their right to protest, and this was probably true. However, whenever Israelis were the victims of violence, there were always some citizens who considered it their patriotic duty to vent their rage . . . against Women In Black.

Of course, there were expressions of support, some of them moving. One Jerusalemite passed out roses, every week, to all the demonstrators, for as long as anyone can remember. Many drivers responded positively to the sign to "honk twice if you support us," until the police decided that the request was in violation of traffic ordinances. More important, there is no question that Women In Black earned the respect of much of the media. Whatever his or her opinion of the issues, any trained observer could not fail to be impressed by the deep commitment and phenomenal endurance of Women In Black.

Democracy of Demonstrators

Women In Black never established a formal organization. Each vigil was a totally autonomous grouping. Participation in the vigil was the only form of membership and there was no other form of attachment to the group. If any issues arose, these were discussed either at the vigil, immediately afterwards or at ad hoc meetings. Representatives from different vigils met to discuss proposed activities which required the assent of more than one vigil. Just as there was no formal local organization, there never was a national organization, in any sense of the word.

Women In Black in Jerusalem, which often drew more than a hundred participants to a vigil, did develop a system of meetings, consultations and committee work designed to meet the needs of the group. Meetings usually discussed issues connected directly to recent incidents and problems affecting the vigil. In periods of intense provocation from the right, discussion centered on reports of contact with the authorities and the tactics of the vigil. However, there were instances of intense political discussion concerning the vigil's main message. The Jerusalem group deliberated suggestions by members that the group authorize additional slogans in addition to the single call for an end to the occupation. Most of the proposals were designed to broaden or detail the anti-occupation program by adding slogans such as "Negotiations with the PLO" or "Two-States for Two-Peoples." These suggestions were invariably rejected by a majority which feared that any new slogan would serve as a precedent and the group would face the danger of a constant debate on the issue of new slogans, thus creating a danger of eventual divisiveness. In fact, many of the other vigils outside Jerusalem did raise additional slogans true to the anti-occupation spirit of the vigil, without any deleterious effect. This might have been a simpler affair outside of Jerusalem, where the vigils tended to be smaller and more politically homogeneous.

The Jerusalem group devoted several discussions to a proposal arguing that it would be wise to raise the national flag at the vigil. The thrust of this proposal, which met with bitter opposition from many radicals in the group, was that Women In Black should not allow the right a monopoly on the use of the national flag. In this case, as in others, the mechanics of the consensual approach meant that it was difficult, if not impossible, to make any serious changes in the presentation of the group's basic image and message and the suggestion was rejected.

An internal information sheet published by Women In Black in Jerusalem shows how the group managed to deal with complex issues and gives a comprehensive overview of the impressive scope and the innovative style of Women In Black activity. In simple, technical, matter-of-fact language, the information sheet reveals a rich, almost mosaic-like composition of political shrewdness, organizational savvy, collective determination and an attention to detail which is the hallmark of any serious group of people who have a good idea of what they want and how they intend reaching their goal.

Information Sheet – Women In Black, Jerusalem

After the incident on Friday, July 7, 1989 there was a meeting on July 12 with 40 women present. Here is the summary: Decision #1: We have three fundamental and irrevocable rules: (1) Only women can participate; (2) black clothing; (3) "End the Occupation" signs. Decision #2: Vigil rules: Come on time. The vigil should appear respectable and attractive; refuse to respond to provocations and do not be drawn into arguments. A duty usher will be there; listen to her instructions and try to help.

Announcements:

(1) The best way to improve security is to increase our numbers; come and bring your friends . . . ;

(2) A workshop and work-out devoted to non-violent response to violence will take place next Thursday.

(3) *Support meeting* After any incident a meeting (to talk, to be together and to strengthen each other) will take place immediately after the vigil. For details . . .

(4) *Tear Gas* Do not rinse with water – do not cover with a handkerchief – Do not rub. Do get out of the area into an area with clean air (it will stop after a short time). Do wash your clothes immediately afterwards. Asthmatics and sufferers of heart disease should go immediately to the duty hospital.

(5) *First Aid* There will be a nurse and a first-aid kit.

(6) *Dispersal* When the vigil is over or when we decide to end it – do it quickly and evacuate the area. DO NOT REMAIN for conversations, etc.

(7) An observer on behalf of the Association for Civil Rights will be present.

C. *Police*

1. Every week, and especially in tense periods we call the police to be present. 75 percent of the time, the police show up . . .

2. In the big cities and other places where there are Women In Black vigils, the police do not only refrain from help and protection, but often adopt a harsh and antagonistic policy. It was decided to collect affidavits from these places. These will be processed by the Association for Civil Rights in Haifa and will be brought to the attention of the policy makers in order to receive an unequivocal reply as to the right of Women In Black to demonstrate legally.

D. *Proposals tabled but not acted upon –*

1. Different women expressed a desire to add signs linking the occupation with violence.

2. It was suggested to put out a position paper expressing the essence of the vigil.

3. Some of the women discussed the necessity for political work designed to change opinions in society (in the street).

E. *Organizational Committee*
Women who are interested and want to participate in policy making, are
invited to participate in meetings that will take place the first Monday
of every month at 17:30 . . .
And finally – We are growing and getting stronger. Today Women
In Black vigils are scattered from the far north (Western and Upper
Galilee) to the South (the Aravah and soon, Elat); At inter-city
intersections, in the big cities, and even adopted by the kibbutzim
and this is only the beginning . . .

Women In Black Jerusalem, July 14, 1989

The Jerusalem Focus

The Jerusalem group was doubly important because it alone had
the capacity to launch appropriate national initiatives. Decisions on
holding a national meeting of Women In Black at Kibbutz Harel
(September 3, 1989) or calling for a national Women In Black vigil
and march in Jerusalem on (December 30, 1989) were reached after
extensive consultations with women from other vigils. Even so, only
the Jerusalem group could assume the responsibility for most of the
political and organizational efforts involved in getting a national
initiative off the ground.

Despite its pre-eminence, when the Jerusalem group finally
worked out a position paper to express in broader terms the
political meaning and message of the vigil, it never pretended
to speak for other vigils. The Jerusalem document, finally issued
in March 1990 bears witness to the intensive consultations and
compromises which accompanied its birth. A special committee
circulated one draft after another at the weekly vigil, calculating
support and opposition to various formulations. The document is
probably the most representative political statement ever issued
by Women In Black. Though it was issued by the Jerusalem vigil
and only in its name, the formulation was so careful as to ensure
it being acceptable to the broadest spectrum of views represented
at all Women In Black vigils. It expressed a unanimous rejection of
the occupation but presented alternative approaches to the solution
of the conflict: "Many of us believe that the PLO is the partner
for peace negotiations based on the principle of two states for two
peoples – while others are of the opinion that it is not for us to
decide who the Palestinian partner for negotiations is nor the exact
solution on which peace will be based."[6] This kind of flexibility built
unity between radical and liberal women and demonstrated, at the

same time, that the Women In Black vigil was drawing women from all sections of the peace movement, and not only from its radical wing.

Women In Black – Jerusalem

We, "Women In Black," citizens of Israel, have been holding a weekly protest vigil since the beginning of the Intifada. This protest vigil is an expression of Israeli society, and expresses our need to actively and strongly oppose the occupation. The black clothing symbolizes the tragedy of both peoples, the Israeli and Palestinian.

We are protesting against the occupation and against all its manifestations: destruction of homes, expulsions, administrative arrests, collective punishment, extended curfews, killings and bloodshed.

We have had enough of the legitimization of brutality, of violence, of insensitivity, the erosion of morality in our society and the heavy economic price paid by every family in Israel.

We are women of different political convictions, but the call "End the Occupation" unites us. We all demand that our government take immediate action to begin negotiation for a peace settlement. Many of us believe that the PLO is the partner for peace negotiations based on the principle of two states for two peoples – while others are of the opinion that it is not for us to decide who the Palestinian partner for negotiations is nor the exact solution on which peace will be based.

We are united in our belief that our message is powerful and just and will eventually bring peace.

More than twenty protests vigils, composed of hundreds of women in black take place simultaneously every week throughout the country. We call on all women to join us in our steadfast and unyielding non-violent protest.

Women In Black – Jerusalem, March 1990

To the Crossroads of a Nation, to the Capitals of the World

The growth of Women In Black found expression in the gradual spread of Women In Black vigils over the entire country. Naturally enough, the first additional vigils appeared in Tel Aviv and Haifa. Both these vigils were about half the size of their sisters' vigil in Jerusalem. While the Tel Aviv and Haifa groups tended to reflect, in their composition, a spiritual affinity to militant feminist circles or the radical left, in Jerusalem all shades of dove opinion and feeling were represented. Because of its strength and its representative character, the Jerusalem group played an effective role in disseminating the Women In Black idea throughout the country. The Jerusalem group was larger and comprised a broader spectrum of views and approaches. Women prominent in the local branch of the Civil Rights Movement, and others who had been affiliated with Peace Now were, along with more radical women, among the most dedicated and active participants. Moreover, there were many women who had no political affiliation aside from Women In Black – which for them became their "political home."

During 1988 and 1989, the Jerusalem vigil attracted on the average of 80–100 women every week. About half to two-thirds of these were a core group which came every week, many of whom tended to be more involved in additional facets of Women In Black activity. Other women "came and went," leaving the vigil for a wide range of individual considerations – some political, some highly personal. Many who left, returned afterwards.

Women In Black inspired the formation of new groups of women in the kibbutz movement who decided to organize vigils at principal highway intersections, usually in the vicinity of a number of kibbutzim. The first such vigils, sometimes towards the end of 1988, were organized by women in Kibbutz Artzi, at Megiddo, near the southern entrance to the Valley of Jezreal, Granoth, near Kibbutz Gan Shmuel and Nahshon, between Jerusalem and Tel Aviv. A call by kibbutz Women In Black from these areas was endorsed by the Political-Ideological Division of Kibbutz Artzi in a circular to the members of the different kibbutzim.[7]

The proliferation of Women In Black vigils throughout Israel during the second half of 1989 and the first half of 1990 was phenomenal, in every sense of the word. A Women In Black call to mark the twenty-third anniversary of the occupation at the vigils to be held on June 8, 1990, displayed a map marking the existence of thirty (!) different locations where regular Women In Black vigils were held. The list includes almost every significant intersection in the country as well as additional cities and towns such as Be'er Sheva, Naharia, Acre, Nazareth and Elat. The range of participation in most of these vigils was usually ten to twenty women. Every Friday afternoon, Women In Black blanketed the entire country with a vivid and insistent message against the occupation.

Though official support by the kibbutz movement was helpful, the proliferation of vigils could not be traced to efforts by any outside sponsor. Nor can one cite any specific organizational drive by Women In Black to expand the number of vigils. Women In Black certainly encouraged other women to emulate their example but this was done through purely informal channels. The movement grew and developed because the protest format created by Women In Black – the distinctive feminist form, the forthright, clear and direct political message and the simple, but stark ritual – inspired and induced other women to go to the street.

Sisters Over the Sea

Thus, Women In Black spread through inspiration and emulation. The power of the image and the message was such that it also attracted and inspired women abroad to hold regular vigils of Women In Black in different metropolitan centers. Women In Black vigils met with various degrees of regularity in New York, Boston, Washington, D.C., Los Angeles, the Bay area (Berkeley and Palo Alto), London. A bulletin disseminated by the Jewish Women's Committee to End Occupation from New York listed Jewish women's peace groups which were active in twenty different cities in the United States and Canada, many of whom organized around a regular Women In Black vigil.[8]

Vigils were established in Europe and in Australia. The life-span of the vigils varied as did the political composition or message. Each vigil represented the Women In Black idea in a form that it considered appropriate. In Ann Arbor, Michigan, at the University of Michigan the group called itself Zionist Women Against the Occupation. In Minneapolis, Minnesota, the group was called the Hannah Arendt Lesbian Peace Patrol. The vigils in London, Washington and Berkeley were composed of Jewish and Arab women. Women In Black and other sections of the women's peace movement in Israel had given the impetus for the formation of a growing cluster of Jewish women's peace groups outside Israel. These groups, many of which sought to maintain some semblance of Jewish identity found a spiritual anchor and inspiration in the growing Israeli women's peace movement.

This process of "internationalization" certainly received a boost from an initiative of Women In Black in Jerusalem which wrote (December 1989) to women's groups abroad suggesting that they hold solidarity vigils on International Women's Day in March, 1990 in solidarity with Women In Black and the Israeli peace movement.[9] The Women In Black committee was able to report back to the group on the success of the initiative. More than 24 organizations responded to the call and held solidarity vigils in various places in Europe, North America and South America. In addition, many organizations sent expressions of solidarity and support.[10]

Thus, Women In Black found its way onto the international protest map. One pleasant result of this prominence was the award of the Aachen Peace Prize to Women In Black for 1991. However, the main achievement was that Women In Black became a highly visible and well-known international symbol, and sent a powerful message from Israeli women to women abroad: first, women in Israel were speaking out against the occupation and the repression of the Palestinian people and secondly, women everywhere can, if they so wish, play an independent role and make a unique contribution to the fight against violence and for peace.

SHANI, Women for Palestinian Women Political Prisoners, the Network

With all its importance and its uniqueness, Women In Black did not exhaust all possible avenues of women's peace activity. Two additional groups active from the first stages of the Intifada were SHANI (Israeli Women Against Occupation) and Women for Women Political Prisoners (WOFPP). A third organization, The Israeli Women's Peace Network, was formed in June 1989 as a direct outcome of an international conference, which took place in Brussels in May that year. Each group had its distinct political complexion and tended to concentrate in a specific area of activity.

SHANI was organized on the principle that the women in the peace movement needed to go beyond basic slogans, as important as these were, in order to delve deeper into politics. This meant that the group should have a clear position on the basic political issues and make a conscious effort to disseminate its ideas. SHANI also stressed that as a political group, and not just a protest formation, it had to devote a significant part of its efforts to educational work in order to deepen its members understanding of current issues. SHANI negated the approach that a women's organization should shy away from specific, detailed political positions and emphasized the urgent need for a framework where women could discuss political issues, take clear, concrete positions and create appropriate forums for educational work. SHANI took it upon itself to fulfill that role.

The core group of SHANI activists had their political roots in various groups of the left and the militant peace movement. Several were members of SHASI (Israeli Socialist Left) and others had been active in the Committee for Solidarity with Bir Zeit University and the Committee Against the War in Lebanon (November 1981–83). The group's first statement, close to its formation, considered it sufficient to express a strong women's concern over the effects of repression in the occupied territories.[11] However, under the impact of the events and after a series of internal discussions, SHANI issued a more programmatic document at the beginning 1989. In addition to negation of the occupation, SHANI called for talks with the PLO and expressed clear support for the two-state solution.[12]

Regular Meetings, Constant Activity, Palestinian Contacts and Coalition Work

SHANI's greatest skill was its intensive, consistent combination of political and educational activities. During 1988 and 1989, SHANI held approximately thirty lecture meetings which centered on current aspects of the situation in the territories. SHANI regularly hosted Palestinian speakers from the occupied territories, organized visits to women's centers and organizations in the territories and met regularly with leading Palestinian women activists. This partial list of activities does not include innumerable planning meetings and the more conventional activities of the peace movement such as rallies and demonstrations. SHANI's weakness was that it was unable to inspire the organization of similar groups, outside of Jerusalem. Most of its activities in Jerusalem attracted between thirty and fifty participants. The SHANI women made up for their numerical shortcomings by their ability to work with and in other groups and to combine this coalition work with their own projects.

Empowering Jewish Women

Two important Jewish establishment organizations from abroad, the American Jewish Congress and the World Jewish Congress decided, in conjunction with the Israeli Women's Lobby, to hold the first International Jewish Feminist Conference in Jerusalem at the end of 1988. Since the conference intended to ignore events in the occupied territories, one of the main slogans of the conference – "Identifying Problems – Finding Solutions" – seemed particularly hypocritical to SHANI. In an open letter to women attending the conference, SHANI challenged the attempt to ignore the Intifada, pointing out that the "empowerment of women is connected to securing rights for all disempowered groups," and suggesting that the participants should "be aware of how the subject of the occupation and its abuses were prevented from being raised at the conference."[13]

The letter went on to describe SHANI's unsuccessful efforts to convince the organizers to place the subject on the conference agenda. SHANI came up with the idea of putting together a "post-conference" to get its message across. And it appears that the "post conference" did just that: "More than 300 women, Jewish and Arab, Israeli and American, some of whom had also attended the Feminist Conference, spent the morning listening to a panel discuss the occupation and the need for a clearly articulated feminist response . . . [and] There was a sense of relief among the women . . . that their concerns as feminists and peace-seekers were being seriously addressed. There was also a palpable sense of excitement that Jewish and Arab women seemed to be meeting on common ground."[14] When the "post conference" ended, most of the participants joined the Women In Black vigil which drew four hundred women that Friday afternoon.

Women for Women Political Prisoners – Solidarity

No women's group made a clearer statement of its identification and solidarity with Palestinian women than the Women's Organization for Women Political Prisoners (WOFWPP).[15] The first group of women concerned with the fate of Palestinian women prisoners was founded in Tel Aviv in May 1988 after hearing a report from women in Jerusalem. The group received lists of female prisoners from the United States.[16]

WOFWPP was creating a new model of protest activity, distinctive in that it centered on a very practical and concrete goal, namely, alleviating the suffering of a specific group of women. Yael Renan, a university lecturer, stressed that she became involved in the group because this was a kind of activity that had immediate effect and did not depend on long-range political developments. WOFWPP attracted activists who were tired of demonstrations and endless strategy sessions, people who wanted to concentrate efforts on achieving measurable and tangible results. This organizational prototype later served as the basis for additional formations during later stages of protest during the Intifada.

Yael Oren, one of the group's founders, summed up six months of activity which included handling the cases of about 100 women prisoners, the adoption of prisoners by Israeli women, appeals to the High Court of Justice when necessary, gathering information and data and media exposure.[17] By the end of the year, additional groups had been formed in Jerusalem and Haifa. A statement issued by the group defined its goal as "support for women held in Israeli prisons . . . who because of their resistance to the occupation . . . are being denied fundamental human rights."[18] The statement goes on to declare the group's objective to prevent abuses such as illegal and administrative arrests; censorship of information regarding torture and sexual harassment, use of women as hostages to apply pressure on male prisoners, denial of the right to an attorney, lack of medical treatment and inhuman conditions of detention.[19]

The group published regular monthly reports on the arrest, interrogation and prison conditions of women prisoners, documenting the aforementioned abuses. One of the reports contains the group's sober assessment of its achievements:

> WOFPP's achievements are not always measurable in concrete terms. Detainees have mentioned that [the] mere presence at the Russian Compound and the daily delivery of necessary items and newspapers – sometimes WOFPP arrive before the families or the lawyers – are an important source of moral support. Improvements in conditions of detention, minute as they are, should not be belittled. In cooperation with other organizations, the number of weekly visiting hours have been increased from two to four. Recently, a shelter for visitors has been built . . . On the other hand, visiting arrangements and conditions, collective punishments and the stubbornness of the authorities counter these achievements. In a few cases, public campaigns did influence the release of detainees who are ill, detainees against whom there was no evidence or of breast-feeding detainees denied access to their babies. This kind of struggle also facilitated the provision of medicine and the granting of adequate medical treatment . . . WOFPP's most important achievement, however lies in its existence as a "public eye" examining and reporting, and countering the prevailing indifference towards the negation of political prisoners' basic rights . . . The basic, critical struggle

– against detainee's complete lack of legal status and against the
prison authorities negligence towards what is happening inside the
security service branch – remains to be won.[20]

The motivation and emotions which brought the WOFPP activists
to the prison gates and to a deep sense of solidarity with Palestinian
women prisoners deserve deeper analysis. Most supporters of the
peace movement considered Palestinians who participated in armed
struggle as enemies and defined the Palestinian resistance organizations as basically terrorist in nature. The feminists and radical
women who organized and sustained the work of WOFPP were able
to cross this "national divide" because they saw the Palestinian
women first and foremost as women and sisters. And once Israeli
women saw them as such, it was easy for them to understand
that the Palestinian women's motivation was political and not
criminal. This different perspective showed Palestinian women as
victims of the occupation and made it perfectly reasonable, even
commendable, that they were active participants in the Intifada
and the resistance movements. Sisterhood can and did transcend
the conventional bounds of national discourse, which invariably
demonizes the "enemy" in order to better pursue goals that include,
inter alia, the mass repression of a civilian population.

Distinctive Features of the Women's Peace Movement

The women's peace movement was distinctive in three important
respects. The first was, of course, the strength and the uniqueness
of Women In Black and the tremendous respect that Women
In Black earned in the peace community. Second, the women's
peace movement achieved a level of cooperation and understanding
between its various groupings that enabled it to avoid tensions that
usually marred relations between radicals and liberals in the peace
movement. This is not to say that the political divergences which
existed in the entire peace movement were absent or irrelevant
in the women's peace movement. However, given the existence
of the different political approaches, it appears that women were
better at compromising and found ways of making political statements which were amenable to all concerned. Third, the women's
movement achieved an exceptionally high level of cooperation and
interaction between Israeli and Palestinian women. This is not to say
that the activity in all these fields of endeavor were "unadulterated

success stories." The point is that the women's movement was considerably more advanced than its heterosexual counterparts in finding ways to dramatize the inhumanity of the occupation and to work with other women, Israelis and Palestinians, to further common aims.

Our discussion of the peace movement up to this point has concentrated on the newer and more radical elements in the peace movement. However, the full strength of the peace movement came into play with the mobilization of Peace Now, the chief mass-based section of the peace movement and the only force that could hope to bring tens of thousands of people to the street. It was the combined efforts of moderates and militants, of radicals and liberals which crystallized opposition to the status quo. Peace Now had been and remained the single strongest force in the peace movement; it enjoyed the confidence and the support of many of the voters for Labor, and most of the voters of the left-Zionist parties: the Citizen's Rights Movement, MAPAM and Shinui. The leadership of Peace Now was on record against the settlement drive in the territories; the movement's leadership was convinced that the diplomatic deadlock could not continue for ever; but it had decided to wait for events to prove this to its mass constituency. The Intifada was such an event.

7

Back in Harness – Peace Now and the Intifada

Peace Now had been relatively inactive during the period preceding the outbreak of the Intifada. This did not perturb the Peace
Now leadership which attributed periods of relative inaction to the
normal ebb and flow of protest activity. Peace Now's leadership
developed its own organizational approach according to which it
saw the movement as a specially sensitized conduit for feelings
of anger and indignation as these appeared and crystallized in its
broad constituency. For this reason, the leadership attached only
secondary importance to the day-to-day functioning of the organization. Peace Now preferred to wait until part of its constituency
actually called on the organization to "do something," in response to
dramatic events. Tsali Reshef, Peace Now's spokesperson, explained
its strategy by describing Peace Now as a "mood and not a movement." The implications of this approach were that is was advisable
to wait until there was actually a certain amount of pressure from
the movement periphery before suggestions for action received
serious consideration. This approach is almost the opposite of the
"vanguard" conception of leadership which held that the organized
formation should move into action in order to arouse the public.
More than anything else, the Peace Now feared running ahead of
its constituency and criticized tendencies in the left to hold small,
unimpressive activities which served, in its opinion, mainly as a
catharsis for the frustrations of the more militant and politically-
conscious activists.

Critics of Peace Now had a different explanation for Peace Now's
relative inactivity in the years preceeding the Intifada. They argued
that the main reason for Peace Now's lack of viligance stemmed
from a desire to avoid confrontation with the government during the

period that Labour Party Prime Minister Shimon Peres was serving the first two years of the rotating premiership in the National Unity government (October 1984–October 1986).

The Palestinian Intifada Brings Peace Now Back into the Street

The reports coming out of the territories were just the catalyst that Peace Now needed to move back into action. In a matter of weeks, the movement quickly assumed a central role in the response by the peace movement to the Intifada. Peace Now called its first demonstration in Tel Aviv on December 19, 1987, less than two weeks into the Intifada. The turn out was mild, somewhere in the vicinity of 1,500 participants, many of whom reached the demonstration via a "feeder" demonstration called by Dai La'kibush.[1] But this was only the first of a long series of demonstrations called by Peace Now during the first year of the Intifada.

Peace Now appealed to the broad peace constituency by posing the question of "'Why the territories are really burning' and replied that the government of 'national paralysis' is unable to offer any hope to the Arab population, especially since Shamir, its Prime Minister, is gripped with fear by the thought of any compromise."[2] Peace Now's message remained basically the same as it was before the Intifada, despite the new circumstances. Peace Now reiterated its demand that Israel must be willing to give land for peace, but did not articulate a clear approach to the Palestinian question. Even so, innovations in the list of speakers at the first demonstration in Tel Aviv did reflect changes in the political climate. For the first time, there were two Palestinian speakers on the Peace Now podium. Israel's Arab population was represented by Ahmad Abu Asneh, deputy-chair of the Council of Arab Mayors and Local Council members, the main umbrella organization of Israeli Palestinians. The appearance and speech by Dr. Zakariyya al-Agha, Chairperson of the Association of Physicians in the Gaza Strip, who gave a detailed description of events in the territories, was even more indicative. Dr. al-Agha was placed in administrative arrest a few days after the Peace Now rally.

Peace Now broadened the scope of its message on the occasion of its first major demonstration during the Intifada in Tel Aviv on January 23, 1988. The organizers were right in assuming that the

flow of reports of more civilian casualties and mass arrests were convincing the dove community that it was indeed time to take to the
streets. The calculated risk in "returning" to the enormous "Kikar
Malkhei Yisrael" square, the site of the massive 400,000 participant
demonstration in September 1982 after the massacre at Sabra and
Shatilla, turned out to be justified. Press reports acknowledged
the strength of the turn out, and stressed that it was the biggest
demonstration held in Israel on events in the territories and the
largest demonstration by Peace Now since Sabra and Shatilla six
years earlier.[3] It is worth noting that the same evening, a Peace Now
representative, Eli Shimoni, spoke at a mass meeting in Nazareth
– organized by a wide coalition of the main forces in the Israeli
Palestinian Arab sector.

A flyer, "What Do We Say?" issued for the "Kikar Malchei
Yisrael" demonstration added new elements to Peace Now's traditional message. The flyer explained that "In the wake of events over
the last weeks, all countries in the world have united to condemn
us and we might find ourselves excommunicated like South Africa.
World Jewry finds it difficult to defend Israeli policy . . . We call on
the government to initiate immediately a dialogue with Palestinian
representatives."[4]

It is worth comparing Peace Now's message in this early stage of
the Intifada with the politics of the militant groups which sprang up
to its left. The more militant sections of the peace movement such as
Dai La'kibush, Yesh Gvul and The Twenty-first Year all stressed
that the Intifada created a new situation. The new reality demanded
that Israel understand that Palestinian self-determination was a
principle with the force of an idea whose time has come. The
militants were calling for recognition of the PLO and negotiations
on the establishment of a Palestinian state. Peace Now, on the
other hand, avoided concrete proposals regarding the key issues
of Palestinian representation and the fate of the territories and
centered its argument on the government's blame for creating an
intolerable impasse; it reiterated its previous, conventional positions
demanding Israeli readiness for territorial compromise. Though it
favored self-determination in principle, it was not willing to go out
on a limb and demand recognition of the PLO and the establishment
of a Palestinian state.

Peace Now prided itself on its practice of raising practical, concrete political demands and it was uncomfortable about not being
able to present any concrete demand during the first months of

the Intifada. However, by February 1988, less than a month after the successful mass action in Tel Aviv, Peace Now presented its own suggestion for meeting the challenge created by the Intifada: a five-point plan for "immediate elections for municipalities and local councils on the West Bank and Gaza." Peace Now considered "the cessation of violence on the West Bank and of terror from outside of Israel" as "preconditions for elections." The elections were to be held "within two months" and under proper supervision. The plan's main purpose appeared in the fifth and final point:

> A delegation should be selected from among the chosen candidates. With other representatives from the territories, those chosen should join the Palestinian–Jordanian delegation to negotiate a peace agreement with Israel, which should determine the future of the territories on the basis of mutual recognition.[5]

This attempt to be relevant by making "practical" suggestions proved to be vacuous. Peace Now was indulging in a tendency, for which it had often been criticized by the Israeli right, of "playing chess with itself." There was no reason to believe that the Palestinian leadership would agree to elections in such conditions – nor would it be impressed by Peace Now's stubborn adherence to a disappearing "Jordanian option." The five-point plan was helpful in proving that the government had no answer to the Intifada, but convinced few that Peace Now did have such an answer. Fortunately, Peace Now was able, in a few weeks, to throw its weight behind a more serious initiative.

The United States was growing increasingly concerned about the results of the Intifada. Though Israel had enjoyed a long and uninterrupted honeymoon with Ronald Reagan in the White House, US diplomatic policy had never officially approved the occupation as a new status quo. The working premise in Washington was that as long as the Israelis assured a modicum of stability, Washington would "leave it alone as long as it works." The Intifada was a stark reminder to the United States that it "was not working," that the Israeli-Arab conflict harbored too many unsolved problems and the potential for radical deterioration in the region was still there. In order to find an answer to the new reality created by the Intifada, US Secretary of State George Shultz came to the region. Shultz had the blessing of Peace Now, which hoped that the US Secretary of State would find a way to budge Shamir from Israel's stand pat approach. True enough, there was not much new in the Shultz initiative. The United States felt that it was sufficient to go back and work on the Camp David formula, albeit under the sponsorship of the five permanent members of the UN Security Council. The thrust of the initiative was a plan to resume the ill-fated negotiations on an interim agreement between Israel and an undefined Jordanian–Palestinian delegation which had taken place in 1978–79 in the framework of the Camp David Accords.

The Palestinians never accepted the Camp David formula and, inspired by a sense of empowerment achieved with tremendous sacrifices during the first months of the Intifada, refused to meet with Shultz. Peace Now, on its part, submitted a memorandum to the Secretary expressing full support for his mission and his proposals and accusing both the Palestinian leadership and the Shamir government for the impasse."[6]

Many readers familiar with various peace movements may be surprised at Peace Now's avid support for United States policy in general and for the Shultz initiative after three months of Intifada. There was nothing unusual in these circumstances. From its very inception, Peace Now's main enemy was the Israeli right, dominated and motivated by the Movement for a Greater Israel, which had been calling for the annexation of the occupied territories since the June 1967 war.

Though there were differences about the fate of the occupied territories, there was no basic difference in international orientation between the Labor–Zionist parties that ruled Israel up to 1977 and the Begin government which came to power with the "upheaval" of that year. Both main currents in modern Israeli politics considered a political and strategic alliance with the United States as the cornerstone of all other policy approaches. However, there was always some tension between the objectives of Israeli annexationists and US policy in the region, which had to express consideration, to one degree or another, for the Arab and Palestinian cause.

Peace Now sought, therefore, to advance the cause of peace by driving a wedge between the United States and Israel's right-wing government. In these circumstances, Peace Now considered it politically wise to accuse the right-wing of undermining Israeli security by endangering the special relationship between Israel and the United States. The main difficulty with this conception was that the United States did everything to avoid confrontation with Begin and Shamir and showed little readiness to exert itself to impose its own policies on Israel. To realize Peace Now's central strategy, it seemed only necessary that time and events in the region would convince the United States to be serious about its own positions. However, once again, this time regarding Shultz's initiative to check the Intifada, it was a case of "Shultz proposes, and Shamir disposes." Nothing came of Peace Now's demand that the Shamir government "Say Yes to Shultz" for the simple reason that Shultz was not willing, after all was said and done, to put any real pressure on Shamir.

Peace Now's clear and open orientation on United States policy and interests in the region was a source of surprise and dismay for many in the international peace movement who tended to equate the fight for peace with opposition to the United States. In Israel, Peace Now's orientation on the United States was yet further evidence among the more radical and militant sections of the peace movement that Peace Now lacked certain essential attributes of a genuine protest movement. If Peace Now was willing to put its trust in the United States' good intention, the opposite was true among the militants in the peace movement. Many of the militants grew up on a steady fare of anti-imperialist discourse, while still others had been influenced by radical movements in Europe and the United States. Small wonder that when Shultz visited Israel, Dai La'kibush demonstrated against his visit, the same week that Peace Now called on Israelis to give him their full support.

The militants identified with the Palestinian leadership which refused to meet with Shultz. Peace Now, to the degree that it felt necessary to rationalize its support for Shultz, could point out that the main forces in Israel which feared and opposed Shultz's intervention were the settlers and their supporters. Peace Now, for its part always considered the United States as its "strategic ally" and hoped that sooner or later the United States would exert all its influence to move the Israeli government from its catatonic immobility.

Shultz Gets Bogged Down

On March 12, 1988, on the eve of Shamir's visit to Washington, Peace Now succeeded once again in bringing tens of thousands of Israelis to Kikar Malchei Yisrael. The dove community fervently hoped that Washington would give Shamir a working-over, forcing him to relate seriously to Shultz's proposals. Tzali Reshef, who spoke at the rally for Peace Now, called on Shamir to stop ignoring the opinions of hundreds of thousands of Israelis who had recently demonstrated their abhorrence for his policies in the territories and against his complete negation of any initiative that hints of peace. Reshef added, "It is not enough to say that we are all for peace. We have to say what kind of peace is possible. There can be no peace between the occupier and those under occupation . . . "[7] Peace Now's call for the demonstration on the eve of Shamir's trip to the United States was issued during the days that Peace Now was marking a decade of activity. There was a surprising similarity in the circumstances attending this demonstration and the first massive Peace Now demonstration on the eve of Menahem Begin's trip to Washington in April, 1978. Peace Now's message was identical at both events: Do not miss an important opportunity to make peace.

Yossi Ben Artzi, one of the founders of Peace Now, commenting on the anniversary, explained the reasons for the creation of the movement: "the existing political frameworks did not facilitate or even permit expression of a common sense of protest." Ben Artzi listed a long series of crossroads in recent history where Peace Now had been successful in influencing democratic processes, in and outside of parliament; these included Camp David, the fight against settlements, the war in Lebanon, Sabra and Shatilla, and the current events.[8]

Shamir succeeded in effectively burying Shultz's initiative by making some vague declaration about the possibility of elections in the territories. The deeper reasons why Shamir could get away with this kind of evasiveness and the techniques for implementing this holding operation is outside the limits of our inquiry. What is important for our inquiry is the fact that United States' inaction convinced many in the peace movement to deepen their commitment to the "Palestinian orientation." Since elections built on the idea of creating a local leadership in the territories as an alternative to the PLO were not even on the agenda, the most hesitant supporter of Palestinian rights had to conclude that recognition of the PLO was the only serious possible step forward. Though it seemed, at the time, the most pragmatic of all options, nothing came of Peace Now's support for the Shultz initiative for the simple reason that the United States abandoned its own enterprise. On the background of the United States' inability to influence Shamir, the demand to include the PLO in the peace equation seemed, in the eyes of the militants all the more justified. The militant sections of the peace movement were more and more convinced that the demand for Palestinian statehood must be advanced even though both official Washington and official Jerusalem were not willing to countenance the very idea.

Peace Now, though it was still able to bring out the largest crowds and spoke for the widest constituency, was as we have seen only one part of the protest scene. "Between Peace Now demonstrations," as it were, the profusion of other more militant organizations which supported negotiations with the PLO, covered broad sections of the protest map. We will return to Dai La'kibush, The Twenty-first Year, Yesh Gvul, Women In Black and their sisters and other various protest formations. However, at this point it is vital to point out that in the summer of 1988, a set of processes commenced that were to bring Peace Now much closer to the Palestinian cause.

Basam Abu Sharif Writes an Article

In June 1988, PLO spokesperson and one of Arafat's close advisors, Basam Abu Sharif, published a position paper in the international press which went further than any previous mainstream PLO statement towards acceptance of a two-state solution. Though Abu Sharif's article lacked official status, his standing in the PLO indicated that it was one of those classic trial balloons with which politicians test response. Naturally enough, the document also made quite a stir in Israel.

Peace Now invited two prominent Palestinians, Faisal Husseini and Radwan Abu Ayyash, to a public discussion of the Abu Sharif document. Peace Now was understandingly favorably disposed to the quasi-official Palestinian document that included some kind words about Peace Now, itself. This was the beginning of a serious opening and the invitation to the meeting featured direct quotations from the Abu Sharif document, which showed that the Palestinians were ready to negotiate with the current government.[9]

One of the two Palestinians invited to speak at the discussion, Faisal Husseini, had been recognized by the Israeli media (basing themselves on informed security sources) as the leading Fatah activist in East Jerusalem – or even in all the territories. He had gained status and prestige over the previous years and had recently been released, after being held in administrative arrest for almost nine months. Faisal Husseini represented a radical departure in Palestinian politics. Though he had impeccable credentials as a mainstream Fatah spokesperson, he developed a clear and consistent line of support for Israeli-Palestinian understanding and opposition to violence and terror.

Faisal Husseini had established the first joint Israeli-Palestinian peace group back in 1986, before the Intifada. The Committee Against the Iron Fist was composed mainly of circles under Faisal Hussein's influence in East Jerusalem and several Israeli militant anti-Zionist activists. Though the Committee Against the Iron Fist received scant public attention, it was an important link in the chain of Israeli-Palestinian joint action. There was an interesting paradox in the combination of forces that established the group. Husseini and his people had quite obviously decided that they were going to make a serious and sustained effort to develop contact with mainstream Israeli organizations including both the Alignment and the Likud, but they began by joining forces with left-wing radicals on the margins of Israeli politics who were willing, one could say eager, to create a united Israeli-Palestinian peace formation. The left-wing radicals, many affiliated with Matzpen, were closer to the official PLO line supporting the creation of a "secular democratic state in all of Palestine" than Faisal Hussein and his people, who were laying the foundations for a two-state solution.

In fact, Faisal Husseini did widen his Israeli contacts. During the summer of 1987 he held several meetings with Moshe Amirav, Likud activist in Jerusalem who reported on the meetings to the party leadership. Revelations of these meetings were a momentary sensation in September 1987. But Amirav, unable to bring the party leadership around to accepting the importance and the wisdom of the contacts with Husseini, was renounced by the party and eventually read out of the Likud.[10]

Respectable Host and Dangerous Guest

Radwan Abu-Ayyash, head of the Journalist Association in the territories and Faisal Husseini who appeared at the meeting called by Peace Now, both came out clearly in support of the Abu Sharif document and expressed optimism about chances for the establishment of an independent Palestinian state alongside of Israel. The meeting, which brought central PLO activists from the territories to the Peace Now rostrum in West Jerusalem before a crowd of sympathetic Jerusalemites, was an important step forward in the contact and cooperation between the two groupings. However, as often happens, the significance of this meeting expressed itself in a gripping sequel, when Israeli security forces decided to arrest Faisal Husseini just a few days after the meeting.

Faisal Husseini had been in administrative arrest before, from April to June 1987 and from September 1987 to June 1988. The police announcement on his re-arrest and the closure of the Arab Studies Institute which he headed had a "classic" texture:

> Despite the steps taken against Husseini a number of times, immediately after his release from prison in June 1988, he renewed his subversive, hostile activity, in the framework of the Fatah organization. This activity encompassed many fields in Jerusalem and the Jerusalem area and included inter alia: coordination, incitement, the institutionalization of the uprising and the achievement of its goals . . . The Institute is run and financed by the Fatah organization and serves as an instrument in order to serve its objectives and the achievement of the goals of the uprising. Among its other activities the Institute helped distribute inciteful material calling for strikes, disturbance of public order and state security . . . [11]

All sections of the peace movement condemned the arrest and its obvious political motivation. Peace Now was incensed and tens of its activists hurried to the Russian Compound in Jerusalem where Husseini was being held to hold a vigil against the government action. The movement wired Rabin and demanded Husseini's release and also approached heads of government and friends of Israel abroad requesting their intervention. Faisal Husseini was being victimized by the Israeli security apparatus headed by Labor Defense Minister Yitzhak Rabin, and responsible to a government of national unity in which the Alignment held fifty percent of the stock. Peace Now had always made every effort to avoid any confrontation with the Israeli Defense Forces or the General Security Services (SHABAK) and usually limited its criticism to government policies. But this time Peace Now was directly involved and felt that it could not very well turn its back on Husseini after providing him a public platform just a few days before his arrest. Peace Now could have limited its intervention to the personal and the humanitarian level and tried to use its influence privately on Husseini's behalf but it decided to pick up the gauntlet by calling for a demonstration at Rabin's private residence in Tel Aviv. The call for the demonstration expressed a sense of anger and frustration. It emphasized that Husseini had come out for the two-state solution and demanded that the government start talking with Husseini and his colleagues instead of jailing them.[12] About three thousand demonstrators marched past Rabin's residence calling on him to resign for the sake of peace, after they heard speakers demand Faisal Hussein's immediate release. MK Dedi Zucker (CRM), who spoke at the demonstration, noted that there were, at the time, three thousand Palestinians in detention under administrative arrest.

Peace Now still hesitated to come out for recognition of the PLO. Instead it developed a middle-of-the-way position after Husseini's arrest by issuing a collection of his statements at the now famous July 27, 1988 meeting in Jerusalem and concluded:

> Peace Now considers the statements by Faisal Husseini and the Abu Sharif document a basis for direct talks between Palestinians and Israelis. Peace Now calls on the PLO to adopt the document officially and the government of Israel to agree to direct negotiations with the Palestinians on the basis of the principles in the document.[13]

Expeditions to the Land of the Intifada

During the first year of the Intifada, Peace Now organized two mass trips to the West Bank. At the end of May, 1988, Peace Now marked the twenty-first anniversary of the occupation by holding a Peace Convoy under the slogan "Free Israel of the West Bank." The main focus was criticism of Rabin's policies in the territories and the reiteration of Peace Now's standard call for negotiations and compromise. The May convoy was the first time a Peace Now action marked the anniversary of the June 1967 war. Though Peace Now fully supported the thesis that the occupation was a corrupting factor, marking the anniversary of the occupation was problematic for the movement. The problem stemmed from the fact that Peace Now considered itself as part of the national consensus which considered the June 1967 war a just war of defense. Since the anniversary of the occupation and the "Six Day War" overlapped, Peace Now found it difficult to mark the anniversary, officially celebrated in Israel as a day of national salvation, as the beginning of a catastrophe. This contradiction simply did not exist for the more radical elements in the peace movement who either negated the June 1967 war along with its consequences, i.e. the occupation, or felt no inhibitions whatsoever about marking the anniversary of the occupation without relating in one way or another to the June 1967 war. The fact that the anniversary of the occupation was a red-letter day for the radical sections of the peace movement nourished a current of opinion in Peace Now that the date was taboo as far as Peace Now was concerned.

Elections Leave the Parliamentary Deadlock Intact

Israel had been ruled since 1984 by a coalition built on parity between the two main parties and a complicated scheme by which the premiership was rotated between them. The results of Knesset elections at the beginning of November 1988, four years later and after almost a year of the Palestinian uprising, weakened Likud control slightly without creating a genuine parliamentary alternative. Both the two main parties, the Likud and Labor, lost support to parties to their right and left. The Likud and Labor (the Alignment between the Labor Party and MAPAM broke up before the elections, mainly because MAPAM became disenchanted with the national-unity government) remained by far the two largest parties and the possibility of forming any stable coalition depended on their reaching an agreement for joint rule.

MAPAM, an important component of the Zionist left, had been a member of the Alignment since 1969 and surprised most observers when it gained three seats in the 1988 Knesset elections, running as an independent party. An independent MAPAM and the increased representation for the CRM – up from three to five seats – made for a sizable block of doves, ideologically loyal to Zionism, but arraigned politically in opposition to the new government of national unity.

The Likud had a one seat edge on Labor and a theoretical possibility of forming a coalition while Labor did not. Labor had to choose between an extended period in opposition or agreeing to re-establish a government of "national unity" with the Likud. Labor opted for "national unity" but this time, because of the slight advantage of the Likud, Labor had to agree that the undivided premiership would go to Shamir. In exchange, Labor received two key cabinet posts – Defense for Rabin and the Treasury for Peres – and equal representation in a number of pivotal cabinet committees. The doves in the Labor party were manifestly unhappy about the decision of their party to join the government. However, the bulk of the party, especially the party apparatus, fearing the consequences of loss of power and patronage, supported the decision to form an even less attractive version of the national-unity coalition.

If the Intifada had any impact on voting patterns, it was to increase the strength of the doves to the left of Labor and the chauvinist forces to the right of the Likud. Since both Rabin and the Likud could only promise "more of the same" – more repression aimed at breaking the Intifada – many voters who sought a convincing answer to the challenges posed by the Intifada moved from the center and its two main parties to the right (which promised to smash the uprising) and to the left (which was pushing for negotiations with its real leadersip). One section of the electorate was convinced by the Intifada that the government should show genuine readiness to negotiate with the Palestinians, while another section demanded more severe and draconic measures, whatever the cost in Palestinian lives and the damage to Israel's image.[14]

Peace Now Very Much Back in Business

Negotiations between the Likud and Labor produced a new, if somewhat diluted, version of the previous national unity scenario. For those who felt a need to seek peace with the Palestinians, there was not a single ray of light in the emerging government. The election results and Labor's willingness to serve under Shamir strengthened Peace Now's resolve to battle the government in the extra-parliamentary opposition. Moreover, Peace Now became even more convinced that it was on the right political track by developments in the PLO. The PLO openly and publicly transformed its political strategy in November and December 1988 by a convincing series of dramatic moves which commanded world-wide attention. On November 15, 1988, the Palestinian National Council met in Algeria and proclaimed the establishment of an independent Palestinian state in terms that made it clear that the PLO was talking about a Palestinian state alongside Israel. The hopes which the Abu Sharif document had aroused in the Israeli peace movement were more than confirmed by the Palestinian National Council decisions. Furthermore, the PLO was conducting intensive talks with the United States about United States recognition of the PLO. These talks came to fruition in Arafat's speech to the UN Assembly in Geneva on December 13, 1988, when he proclaimed a clear PLO stand against terror. The United States agreed shortly afterwards to establish open relations with the PLO.

Peace Now had prepared itself and its supporters well for the message that came out of the Palestinian National Council session in Algeria. Peace Now now had an answer to the common Israeli complaint that there was really no partner with whom it could talk about peace. Over the summer, Peace Now had suggested that the PLO was preparing itself politically for participation in such a dialogue. Even so, when Peace Now actually came out and supported negotiations with the PLO, observers noted the magnitude of the shift in its position. "For the first time in its history, Peace Now came out with a call for direct negotiations with the PLO. Until now their were differences of opinion regarding direct talks with the PLO, and only in the wake of the Algerian conference, the declaration of a Palestinian state and the new circumstances, did the 'right-wing' activists in the movement accept the position . . . "[15]

The movement announced plans for a series of meetings and conferences to mobilize support for its new position. The call for negotiations, though clear and unequivocal, was formulated with caution: "In response to Arafat's call for flexibility, moderation and realism, the government of Israel has adopted the path of refusal . . . The government of Israel must call for direct negotiations with the PLO on the basis of mutual recognition and the cessation of violence. Only through negotiation will we know if the PLO has really adopted the path of peace as declared in Algiers. Speak with the PLO."[16]

In a matter of weeks, speakers at well-attended Peace Now meetings in Tel Aviv and Jerusalem were on the attack against the official government line that there was "nothing new" in the Algerian decisions. Dan Margalit, a prominent center-of-the-road columnist, had to admit – though he criticized Peace Now for allowing itself to be blinded by the PLO formulations – that "when Shamir and Rabin argued that the language of the [Palestinian National Council] resolution contained nothing new, there was a need for a contrasting perception which could expose their duplicity. This was achieved by Peace Now's far-reaching step."[17] Arafat's unequivocal denunciation of terror in his speech at Geneva December 13, 1988 created conditions enabling Peace Now to go on the political offensive. The PLO peace strategy and its warm reception in the international arena could not fail to impress broad sections of the Israeli public. Peace Now issued a special call to the Labor doves, bitter over the renewal

of the national unity government, to join it in a campaign for talks
with the PLO.

It Was Like Old Times

There was some excitement in the air when Peace Now's national
"forum of forums"[18] met in Tel Aviv on Sunday, December 18.
Expectations ran high because there were more people in the room
than usual: new faces of young enthusiasts who were "ready to go"
and veterans who had dropped out of activity for one reason or
another. Even more important, the entire movement felt it had a
an urgent, distinctive role to play: The government was trying to
sabotage a serious peace initiative coming from the Arab side and
it should be stopped. Only Peace Now could rally enough of the
public to make a difference. Everyone agreed that it was important
to activate as many Labor Party people as possible and to form a
broad front from all walks of Israeli life: Mizrakhim (or "Sephardic"
Jews) from the poor neighborhoods, Israeli Arabs, women and youth
as well as Palestinians from the territories. The meeting moved
quickly from a discussion of the main slogans to the second stage
– forming operational units of people who understood the technical
requirements for a successful demonstration.[19]

Blanket of Bright Umbrellas

And, despite the weather, there was a successful demonstration:

> . . . Tens of thousands braved the elements last night filling the Kikar
> Malchei Yisrael in a Peace Now rally billed as the most critical
> since the Lebanon War . . . The rally marked a new phase in Peace
> Now activity . . . A Peace Now spokeswoman said that most of the
> movement's supporters felt that Arafat's recent statements marked
> a turning point in PLO policy and created a new opportunity for
> peace.[20]

The list of speakers included Labor MK Lova Eliav, who referred
to a *Yediot Ahronot* poll published the same day which indicated
that 54 percent of the public were in favor of negotiations with
the PLO, and Labor activist, Yael Dayan, who called for bringing the peace message to the urban poor in Likud neighborhood
strongholds.

Peace Now rarely issued detailed political statements. On a day-to-day basis, Peace Now's politics were really the carefully chosen slogans it raised at its demonstrations. The movement related rarely to basic ideological issues and position papers designed to make a political statement, per se, were few and far between. However, important programmatic shifts when they did occur were usually published in pamphlet form in a format which helped to identify the publication as an authoritative political statement. Such a pamphlet came off the press during December 1988. As if to calm anxieties that might arise in the context of its new position, Peace Now began the statement by reasserting that "Peace Now is a Zionist movement . . . "[21] Indeed, the new position was couched in cautious terms:

> As a first step towards peace, the government of Israel should declare its willingness to conduct negotiations with the Palestinians, under the leadership of the PLO. The Palestinians will declare their acceptance of negotiations as the only path towards the resolution of the conflict. Simultaneously, acts of violence by all sides in the territories will cease; new settlements will not be established nor will existing settlements be expanded.[22]

In the ensuing text, Peace Now reiterates the principles on which the peace agreement should be based. The "Jordanian option" was dropped from the text. Israel will recognize the "national existence of the Palestinians in the West Bank and Gaza, to be realized in a manner agreed upon by both sides." "Undivided Jerusalem as the Capital of Israel . . . expression will be given to the place of Jerusalem in Islam and Christianity as well as to the national affinities of the Arab inhabitants."[23]

Thus, Peace Now limited the political shift it made to the more procedural level of negotiations, without changes regarding its substantive positions on the solution of the conflict. The document did admit that the "Jordanian option." was rapidly fading. Though Peace Now's open call for talks with the PLO was a positive development, critics on the left pointed out that Peace Now was still far from advocating a two-state solution based on the principle of equality between sovereign nations. Peace Now used the phrase [Palestinian] "national existence" instead of the clearer concept of "national self-determination and narrowed the Palestinian entity to the Palestinians in the territories. This complete negation of the Palestinian diaspora was especially disturbing coming from a Zionist group which sees the Law of Return as an inseparable aspect of Israeli sovereign existence. Peace Now's unqualified support for the unilateral annexation of Jerusalem by Israel was yet another reminder of the group's links to mainstream Israeli politics. Peace Now had made a bold step forward, but it was not prepared to undergo a political metamorphosis that would eliminate the distinctions between it and the militant section of the peace movement.

The Peace Now leadership believed that their support for talks with the PLO expressed the feelings of its membership and the entire dove community. Dr. Amiram Goldblum, Peace Now spokesperson, explained that activists who had previously opposed talks with the PLO had done so mainly for tactical reasons, believing that an international conference which included a Jordanian–Palestinian delegation was more acceptable to the Israeli public. This internal opposition to talks with the PLO actually disappeared and a new consensus emerged, in Peace Now's national "forum of forums," as a result of the PLO's Palestinian National Council meeting in Algeria.[24]

There was one notable exception. Yossi Ben Artzi, one of the founders of the movement from Haifa, accused the Peace Now leadership of alienating its broad base by "acting hysterically as if it feared that it would lose its dominant role in the protest movement to bodies such as Dai La'kibush, The Twenty-First Year or women in all sorts of colors. It was its responsibility to the broad public and its refusal to succumb to extremists which had kept Peace Now in the center of the struggle . . . "[25]

Peace Now's Internal Life and Lack of Organizational Structure

Ben Artzi's announcement that he was leaving Peace Now shed light on one aspect of the political mentality prevalent in that group. Since the movement existed primarily to do things, there was very little political life to speak of above and beyond the ad hoc discussions, which usually were of a pronounced tactical nature. Important decisions were reached through a complicated consultative process based on discussions in the various forums. Tremendous efforts were made to reach and maintain a consensus, and in many cases the majority on a certain issue would refrain from action until it had convinced almost everyone that the time was ripe for the movement to make a decision on the issue. However, since there was no formal organizational structure, and therefore no mechanisms that provide consistent expression to minority views, activists who found themselves at loggerheads with the movement's strategic line would tend to avoid a painful situation by leaving it. It appears that both those who agreed to a particular policy, and those who opposed it, considered the idea of an internal opposition as contrary to the spirit and the aims of the organization.

This particular distaste for the idea of any kind of internal opposition is just one aspect of the political philosophy that shaped Peace Now as an organization. When the Peace Now activists shaped their organizational environment, they sought to create a formation that was as unlike a political party as possible. It was their generation that grew up when the prestige of Israeli parties, and especially that of MAPAI, the historical forerunner of the Labor Party, crumbled, revealing an advanced state of decay. In school and in the youth movement they were taught about Zionist visionaries ready to sacrifice all for their ideals, but the day-to-day news was replete with exposures of party graft and corruption. The more idealist members of "old guard" appeared cut off from new realities and often served as a butt of jokes instead of an inspiration for emulation. Moreover, though the Peace Now activists were far from the radicalism of the "new left", they were impressed by its disdain for formal organizational structures and its emphasis on action as opposed to doctrine. Their own ideology (liberal Zionism) was not dead, but the generation that created and operated Peace Now tended to believe that many political movements had suffocated under excess ideological baggage.

These were the roots of Peace Now's rejection of any kind of formal organizational structure. It was not really a membership organization, there were no elected local or national bodies. Decisions evolved on the basis of constant attempts to create a consensus. Those who consciously created this state of affairs claim that the movement and its activists have been spared the tremendous waste of energy that more structured formal political forces devote to internal friction and the running battle over influential positions and offices. Internal party life is a demanding and enervating proposition and those who created Peace Now were convinced that any internal conflict or bickering would dissipate protest energy and probably drive away a lot of people who came to the organization to protest and not to endure the pressures of a highly politicized environment.

Critics of this organizational philosophy are quick to point out its major flaws. In the absence of formal decision-making bodies, an informal coterie of leaders determine de facto what the movement does and how it does it. The absence of annual conferences, periodic reporting back to the membership and the need to ratify basic strategy – all weaken the individual members' sense of belonging and responsibility. Moreover, members who wanted to challenge the leadership's general strategy were made to feel that they were directing criticism against fellow volunteers. It was much harder to argue against a fellow volunteer than to criticize an elected officer who holds his or her position on the basis of your vote. Whatever its defects, Peace Now's organizational structure, or more exactly, its lack of such a structure, was an organic expression of the political mentality of the people who created Peace Now and turned it into an effective vehicle for political protest.

Putting on Pressure – Shamir to the United States

The leaders of Peace Now (which continued to feel itself part of the Israeli mainstream) asked for a meeting with Yitzhak Rabin, the Defense Minister, towards the end of February 1989. The Peace Now leadership had met with Rabin six months earlier in order to express its anxiety over the rampant repression of the Intifada. That meeting had been extremely tense and did nothing to bring the sides closer, nor did this one. Peace Now had hoped to move Rabin on the PLO issue, and found him totally unconcerned at the current state of affairs. According to Rabin, US contacts with the PLO were at the lowest possible level and were really a stalling tactic on the part of the Americans. Moreover, according to him, the Palestinians in the territories were close to the breaking point. The Peace Now leadership was totally unconvinced.[26]

Shamir and his Foreign Minister, Moshe Arens, were invited to the United States at the beginning of April 1989, to meet the new President, George Bush and his Secretary of State, James Baker. The reason for the meeting went beyond protocol and tradition in

US–Israeli relations. The US had agreed to contacts with the PLO in order to find some solution to the Palestinian problem and wanted to know what Shamir and his government intended to do about the Intifada, which was in American eyes a crisis which demanded attention.

It was by now common practice for Peace Now to "throw a farewell party" for an Israeli prime minister on the way to Washington – in the form of a demonstration on the eve of his departure. Shamir "earned" special attention by having lodged a frontal attack on Peace Now just a few weeks earlier when he told a Likud audience in Tel Aviv that Peace Now was a "marginal element that can't influence anything" and charged it with sabotaging Israel's political and security struggle "which is a battle for our very existence."[27] On the eve of his departure, approximately 1,000 Peace Now demonstrators demanded that he agree to negotiatiate with the PLO.[28]

The call for the demonstration cited a recent poll to the effect that some two-thirds of the population support negotiations with the PLO if and when it should recognize Israel and cease terrorist activity. This is probably one of the few instances when Peace Now overstated its case. Almost all polls showed an increase in the willingness of Israelis to contemplate negotiations with the PLO, but there was a tremendous and not unexpected variance, depending on the formulation of the question and the date of the poll.[29]

Guests in Palestine

Peace Now entered an intensive period of activity with a clear-cut political agenda and many ideas about moving it forward. It also entered a period of organizational expansion whose main goals were to increase the number of active branches and to strike roots in the poorer neighborhoods. Cooperation with the Palestinian leadership in the territories created new opportunities for Peace Now to prove the efficacy of its main current slogan: Stop shooting and start talking. Peace Now called for a "Day of Peace Meetings" between Peace Now supporters and Palestinians in different cities and villages on the West Bank at the beginning of March 1989. The operation demanded unprecedented coordination with the Palestinians and careful planning to prevent offending the sensitivities of either Israelis or Palestinians. A special leaflet by the Palestinian National Leadership called on the populace to refrain from attacking the Peace Now convoy and to participate in the meetings.

The Israeli Defense Forces, acting on Rabin's orders, blocked the entry of five convoys, though activists in some locations managed to bypass army roadblocks and hold small meetings. Peace Now did everything to prevent any confrontation with the Israeli Defense Forces, but went on the attack against Rabin the next day. The settlers, argued Peace Now, were free to move in the territories and constituted a continuous provocation against the Palestinians 365 days in the year. But why, asked Peace Now, when hundreds of Israelis wanted to meet with Palestinians who wanted to host them, was this suddenly a security problem?

It took some time and some pressure before Rabin relented and permitted the meetings to take place. Peace Now had to agree to some modifications of the original plans before the Israeli Defense Forces would grant permission. Basically, it was the very same type of activity that the Israeli Defense Forces banned two months earlier when 2,500 Israelis and 1,000 Palestinians held "peace meetings" in six West Bank locations.[30]

Nahalin, one of the locations, was a remarkable site for such an event. Five local youths had been shot and killed by the Israeli Border Police six weeks before the scheduled meeting and charges that the police had gone berserk over some personal insult were still being investigated by the Israeli authorities. MK Dedi Zucker noted that though the bitter memory of the bloody raid still hung over the village, the residents, by greeting the peace convoy with warmth and open arms, were sending a signal to Israeli society, one clearly calling for reconciliation.[31]

There were a few hitches here and there but none that dulled the overall effect of masses of people involved in a "face to face" Israeli-Palestinian dialogue. Peace Now supporters were greeted by the local population in an effort sponsored and organized by their own leadership in cooperation with an Israeli, Zionist peace organization. Communication between Israelis and Palestinians had reached a new stage with the meeting of large groups of hundreds of Israelis with the residents of a whole village. The "state" of Palestine, which came into existence, largely as a spiritual entity, after the Palestinian National Council in Algeria, was ready and able to extend a semi-official welcome in the territories to Israelis who supported negotiations with their national leadership, the PLO.

Peace Now and the Law Against Contact with the PLO

Peace Now, along with all sectors of liberal opinion in the country, condemned the Amendment to the Prevention of Terrorism Ordinance, which made any contact between Israelis and the PLO – even open and clearly political in nature – a crime punishable by law, from the moment of its enactment in August 1986. Even so, true to its principle of working within the limits of the law, Peace Now announced that it would respect the restriction. Later, soon after it came out for negotiations with the PLO in December 1988, it argued that the law no longer should apply to the PLO because of the changes in the program and the nature of the organization.[32]

Peace Now had entered into a regular working relationship with many leading Palestinians in the territories such as Faisal Husseini, Ziyad Abu Ziyad, Seri Nusseiba and Rassan El-Hativ (paradoxically, since membership in the PLO was a crime, none of the leaders in the territories was actually an official member). When Hativ was arrested by the Israeli authorities in May 1989, Peace Now had no hesitations about condemning his imprisonment and expressing full confidence in his innocence, despite the fact that Hativ, who was released a few days later without being charged, was one of the leaders of the Palestinian Communist Party. Even so, the excellent working relationship with the leadership "on the inside" was no substitute for contact and discussions with the PLO leadership abroad.

A number of circumstances made such contacts possible without running afoul of the new law. The first trial of four Israeli leftists, Latif Dori (MAPAM), the writer Yael Lotan, Eliezer Feiler and Reuven Kaminer who participated in the first open meeting with the PLO in Romania in November 1986 held after the law was passed, in August 1986, showed that marshalling evidence from abroad and getting it to an Israeli court was a difficult and complex, though not impossible, affair. It became clear that the Minister of Justice, though he wanted the law on the books, was not over eager to seek out and prosecute offenders who claimed that their meetings were conducted in accordance with one of the exceptions permitted by the law. One of these exceptions, which allowed Israelis to participate in academic conferences, was particularly suited for Peace Now which counted a surfeit of academics in its ranks. Wisely enough, the important open meetings were held at academic institutions – Oxford in February and Columbia in April of 1989. It was highly doubtful whether, strictly speaking, these meetings were permissible – since political meetings were excluded from the exception – but the prosecutors and the political echelon were quite conscious of the difficulty of holding a trial against a perfectly innocent act sponsored by a major academic institution.

At a particular point it became clear that – if an Israeli really wanted to – he or she could meet with the PLO without being charged if the host of the meeting was sufficiently prestigious and the Israeli participant was circumspect about photographs and seating arrangements. It was under this kind of "arrangement" that tens of meetings between Israelis and leading PLO officials took place before the law was finally abolished in December 1992. Peace Now chose not to defy the law, but like many others, found ways to evade its restrictions and to maintain serious contacts with the PLO leadership.

Over the years, the PLO leadership had failed to mobilize genuine material and political support for its efforts to eliminate the Zionist entity in Israel. The success of the Intifada enhanced the Palestinian cause and created new political options for the PLO. These options were utilized and enabled the PLO to elaborate a new line based on a two-state solution. In consequence, the most moderate and influ-ential section of the Israeli peace movement, Peace Now, revised its initial rejection of Palestinian self-determination, and demanded that the Israeli government take the path to peace by negotiating with the only authentic representatives of the Palestinians, the PLO. When it adopted the slogan calling for negotiations with the PLO, Peace Now adopted the most central plank in the platform of the militant sections of the peace movement. This change, which "robbed" them of a major distinction between the militants and the moderates, demanded a creative response from the leading militant formations: Dai La'kibush and The Twenty-first Year. However, such a response was not forthcoming.

8

The Demise of the Militants

Dai La'kibush and The Twenty-first Year were, as we have seen, driving forces in the protest movement during the initial stages of the Intifada. They were by far the most active and influential components of a wide network of organizations and groups which came into existence in response to the Intifada. Both groups continued to make major contributions to the protest movement during the second year of the Intifada, 1989, but began to suffer more and more from the lack of any effective long-range strategy, so necessary after the initial enthusiasm and excitement wears thin.

Into the second year of the Intifada, it became progressively clearer that though the Intifada had succeeded in refocusing international public opinion on the Palestinian question, a solution to the Israeli-Palestinian conflict was not around the corner. It was only natural to start thinking in terms of priorities and planning and Dai La'kibush was a group which did not lack for members who had thoughts on this subject and who knew how to articulate their ideas. Practical considerations underscored the necessity for long-range strategic thinking. There was a slow but steady drop in the number of people attending the weekly forum. Many activists had "disappeared" and many others complained openly of "burn-out."

A sense that many discussions were a rehash of previous arguments added to a collective sense of weariness. And, perhaps more important than any of the internal difficulties that had arisen, Dai La'kibush had to evaluate the meaning, for it, of what was, by all accounts, an encouraging and positive development: Peace Now's decision to come out clearly for talks with the PLO. One of the major criticisms of the militants against Peace Now was no longer valid.

The arguments over strategy developed gradually. After all, Dai La'kibush was functioning intensely and still a very important force on the protest scene during all of 1988 and the first half of 1989. Dai La'kibush cemented a broad coalition of groups in order to commemorate the twenty-first anniversary of the occupation in June 1988. There were about 5,000 demonstrators; the size of the march and the impressive coalition which included large contingents of marchers from The Twenty-first Year and Women In Black, indicated that the militant wing of the protest movement was succeeding in overcoming its traditional isolation.

Other important activities by Dai La'kibush were devoted to "spoiling" the festive atmosphere at cultural events such as Jerusalem's film festival in July 1988 by reminding people of events in the occupied territories, including the Arab part of Jerusalem just several hundred meters from the festival center in the Jerusalem Cinematec. Dai La'kibush took particular exception to a film festival held during March 1989, which was devoted to the special theme "In the Spirit of Freedom," and which omitted any film material dealing with the Intifada. For their part, the sponsors of the event felt that they had gone out on a limb by suggesting in the festival program that "an egocentric Israeli society should clarify the crises it encounters by studying events in other places, even if the analogy is not always exact . . . " It was one of those classic confrontations: liberal film people thought that they had acted with daring – while Dai La'kibush indignantly demanded an answer to the hard question: "how long will people hide behind those three dots?"

Other relatively successful Dai La'kibush activities during the summer of 1988 included a stormy demonstration in the center of Jerusalem in support of the "Rumanian four" on trial for meeting with the PLO, a mass visit of 300 Israelis to Beit Sahur, a town near Bethlehem which had spearheaded resistance to the Israeli authorities, a well-attended public meeting against administrative arrests, and visits to the homes of Palestinians who had been expelled or were on the verge of expulsion. Feisel Husseini was warmly received at a packed Dai La'kibush meeting in February 1989, held in a Jerusalem Reform Temple and during the spring of 1989 Dai La'kibush was active in exposing sub-human conditions in the Dahariyah military prison. This is only a partial list of the more outstanding activities. Visits to the territories continued every other week and the group put out and disseminated a variety of publications.

Is This Pamphlet Necessary?

Indeed, one of the first debates about strategy was touched off by a bitter controversy around a proposal to compose and publish a 30-page educational pamphlet on the causes and the solution to the Israeli-Palestinian conflict. A number of activists felt the need for a publication designed to prove to a skeptical reader that the Palestinians had expressed readiness for a reasonable compromise – while Israel was turning its back on a serious opportunity to end the conflict.

Those that objected to the project argued that any detailed exposition would include an historical analysis and argumentation that had never been discussed or approved by the group. The thrust of this argument was that Dai La'kibush's goal was to express its members sense of shame and outrage by drawing media attention to the most repulsive manifestations of repression in the territories. It was further argued that the creation and dissemination of programmatic educational material was not the proper role of a protest organization, but more appropriate for a full-scale political organization.

The "pro-pamphlet advocates" in Dai La'kibush argued that there was a dearth of updated material for political education. The creation of good reading material and its dissemination was the way to overcome genuine doubts in the public and to effect real changes in people's opinions. Moreover, though it was becoming clear to many that the occupation was disgusting and even evil, people would still be willing to accept the status quo unless they were convinced that there was a real political alternative to government policy. And this had to be explained and proven – just saying that peace was possible was not enough.

As the discussion dragged on, the different approaches about a single aspect of Dai La'kibush's aims developed into a comprehensive debate about long-range strategy. In an attempt to work out a strategic program, a number of position papers were submitted to the forum. These papers provide both the background for understanding Dai La'kibush's unsuccessful attempt to develop a strategic consensus, and at the same time afford considerable insight into the complexities of protest strategy faced by the entire protest movement.

"Actionists" vs. "Politicizers"

This period of introspection in Dai La'kibush shed light on the political and tactical problems that were the daily fare of protest activity. The key question was rather simple. How could a small militant peace formation hope to make a major impact on Israeli society? Two opposing tendencies emerged as the group grappled with this question. For want of better terms, the first tendency can be described as "actionists" and the second tendency as "politicizers." The opposing tendencies in Dai La'kibush first clashed on the relative importance of the Dai La'kibush political program (in political shorthand, the "two-state solution)." As far as the "actionists" were concerned, the program's basic function was to ensure a modicum of political unity, while the real objective was activity – action that would mobilize more and more people against government repression in the occupied territories. Dai La'kibush's "political calling card" was to be considered as no more than some sort of an internal agreement so as to defuse dangers of a clash or a split between different groups or ideologies represented in the formation.

For the "politicizers," the real objective was to build a bigger and stronger organization to further Dai La'kibush's political goals. According to this opinion, activities were not a goal in themselves, but a means to mobilize new people and to conduct political education aimed at convincing people to support Dai La'kibush's solution to the Palestinian question. The differences of opinion can best be understood by contrasting the different scenarios of success for which people aimed.

Success for the "actionist" trend of thought meant a quantitative leap in the number of protesters, i.e. genuinely massive participation in protest activity. This meant that politics, in the programmatic sense, were of subsidiary interest and it was the job of Dai La'kibush to identify and raise issues that would move people into the streets. For this purpose it was necessary to concentrate on the evils of the occupation – since the negation of the occupation was the widest possible denominator of democratic public opinion. From this point of view, the entire liberal constituency in the country were prospective protestors. The potential for mobilizing people against, for example, administrative arrest, argued the "actionists," is immense. Bringing people into the circle of protest is the way to radicalize them and cause them to question the overall policies of the government; Dai La'kibush's political program was not, according to the "actionists," particularly useful, since it had a relatively narrow appeal. Dai La'kibush's actions were what counted and its militancy against repression could evoke sympathy among a wide section of Israelis who do not want to support any particular political program. Dai La'kibush should be blazing the following path: convince people to oppose a specific feature of the occupation, convince them to act on this basis and their opposition to the occupation will radicalize them to the point of being willing to retreat from the occupied territories unilaterally. The "actionist" strategy was naturally supported by several key activists who questioned Israel's right to exist because of its "colonialist essense," but "tolerated" the two-state program for the sake of united action. However, it must be stressed that many sincere supporters of the "two-state solution" agreed with the "actionists" and felt that politics – in the programmatic sense – was of secondary importance.

The second major trend of thought in Dai La'kibush, the "politicizers," held that a line oriented on action, action and more action carried the seeds of its own failure. If no attention was devoted to organizational basics, the movement would be unable to educate and organize new cadres and without seriously broadening the organization base, the devoted, but small band of activists would suffer from fatigue and burn-out. The "politicizers" favored the gradual transformation of Dai La'kibush into a political organization based on membership and elected bodies. Much of the burn-out and drop-out stemmed from a tedious and onerous way of reaching decisions in the forum. Several highly devoted but politically naive activists would load every agenda with suggestions and challenges which demanded greater militancy and sacrifices from a dwindling constituency. Most of these proposals never got off the ground, but they did burden the organization with a sense of frustration and impotence. The "politicizers" held that spontaneity and direct democracy (whoever was in the room voted and decided on action) were good and fine in the period of initial enthusiasm, but after a year of activity, anyone could see that Dai La'kibush would have to become more practical and more business-like. Dai La'kibush had to build an organization that would capitalize on the experience of the protest movement and combine action with political education and organizational work. Success was achievable only by launching steady grass-roots work designed to educate the public.

The two trends had profound differences in their evaluation of Dai La'kibush's "solidarity activity," which turned into a sore point of contention. The "politicizers" observed that, those involved in such efforts began to identify – politically and psychologically – with the victims of the occupation. This identification inspired the introduction and the use of an essentially Palestinian discourse – which grows out of such identification – into the organization. Disproportionate emphasis on solidarity work was, in the eyes of the "politicizers," a certain prescription for political isolation and alienation. The "politicizers" argued that when peace workers appear to be concerned mainly about the welfare and the suffering of the "other side" and contemptuous or indifferent to their own national interests, they lose contact with the Israeli public and appear as advocates of the Arab Palestinian cause.

The "actionists" did recognize the tension between solidarity work and the feelings that it evokes and the responsibility to disseminate reliable and convincing information about the occupation. However, since solidarity work tended to radicalize those involved, the "actionists" minimalized its dangers and rejected the concern of the "politicizers" that Dai La'kibush was spending a disproportionate amount of its efforts on solidarity work and developing an image of a group motivated only by its empathy for the victims of the occupation. The "politicizers" were convinced that such an image would weaken the ability of Dai La'kibush to influence the politics of the more moderate sections of the peace movement. The "actionists" felt that first-hand contact with Palestinian suffering was a radicalizing force that had unlimited potential. Internal tensions over strategy and tactics had their debilitating effect on the group and its ability to mount effective actions.

Dai La'kibush did not realize any of the different scenarios for success. Neither did it succeed in moving masses into protest action, nor was it able to muster the resources to indulge in steady political education and grass-roots organizing. More and more activists became discouraged by the group's inability to attract new activists or to mount militant actions.

By the end of 1989, the group had been reduced to a shadow of its previous strength. Conceivably, the group might have succeeded in working out a joint strategy if Peace Now had not "stolen its thunder" by transforming its position on the PLO. As it were, Dai La'kibush could be proud that it had played a pioneer role in exposing the realities of occupation and placing regular Israeli-

Palestinian contacts on the agenda of the entire peace movement.

"The Twenty-first Year" Faces Reality

The Twenty-first Year continued to be one of the most interesting new developments on the protest scene into the first months of 1989. During this period, its main efforts were devoted to translating the principles of the Covenant into a day-by-day agenda of political work. This was, as we shall see, no simple task.

The Twenty-first Year had greeted the decision of the PLO Palestinian National Conference in Algeria calling it a "decisive step towards a just peace in the Middle East and reconciliation between two peoples." But strangely enough, The Twenty-First Year added a number of reservations which echoed the caution of Peace Now. Identifying themselves as "those who carry on the path of the Zionist movement," the group announced that "we still await explicit recognition of Israel and total abandonment of terror.[1]

Interestingly, The Twenty-first Year had returned to classical Zionist discourse in responding to a major political development which had not been dealt with specifically by the movement's Covenant. The Covenant, it will be recalled, concentrated exclusively on the relations between Israeli society and the occupation. This kind of "Zionist" response confirmed the criticism of many skeptics regarding the Covenant who argued that for all its radical phraseology, the Covenant skirted major historical and ideological issues by ascribing all the negative features in Israeli society to the occupation which began in 1967. The group's adoption of the Zionist "argumentation" on such a critical issue seemed to suggest that the differences between The Twenty-first Year and Peace Now were not all that deep.

The activity by The Twenty-first Year at the Ansar prisoner camp in the Negev, though reasonably successful by most standards, had posed some difficult unresolved tactical dilemmas. The chief of these was how to reconcile its basic message of total resistance to the occupation with its strict observance of the law, including the demands of the military authorities in the Ansar camp area. This dilemma was especially painful as The Twenty-first Year had explicitly attacked Peace Now on more than one occasion for its scrupulous observance of the law both in Israel and especially in

the territories where Peace Now abhorred the idea of any confrontation with the IDF. Many people in The Twenty-first Year
and other organizations had expressed an interest in the tactics of
civil disobedience and non-violent, passive resistance, but no one
had found a way to put these ideas into practice.

Caught in the Occupation Machine

The ideas of civil disobedience or non-violent resistance have fared
poorly in the rocky soil of the Arab-Israeli conflict. It is not because
the concepts of pacifism or the great examples of Gandhi and others
were unknown or lacked devoted individual adherents locally.
Moreover, there were considerable efforts from abroad to import
the theory and practice of the non-violent approach to peace activists
in Israel. Indeed, there were many individual activists in the peace
movement during the Intifada who were motivated by these very
ideas. But, there was no important, organized group which adopted
these concepts as the starting point for their political program or
strategy. At this point, our account must dwell, unfortunately, on
a critical juncture where these ideas were rejected without giving
them a fair chance.

At the end of May 1989, just one day before Peace Now's first
mass visit to the territories in coordination with the Palestinian
leadership, activists from The Twenty-first Year tried to carry
out a plan which had been brewing for quite a while. The
destruction of homes of "terrorists" (and this included homes
of suspects before trial) was a common punitive action by the
military authorities. The idea of physically preventing such an
act of destruction by non-violent resistance had a particular
appeal for members of The Twenty-first Year movement, which
sent a group of 27 protesters to Kalkilya in the West Bank.

Dr. Ilana Hammerman, a prominent editor, critic and translator
and one of the founders of the movement, explained that the group
went to express solidarity with the thirteen occupants (including
ten children) of a house in the village designated for demolition.
Hammerman noted that the family had petitioned the High Court
of Justice, but all such petitions had been rejected in the past.[2]

Though the IDF declared the area "closed," the group managed to
enter the town on foot in a roundabout manner only to meet up with
an Israeli Defense Forces contingent which started to escort it out of

the "closed area." It seems that everything was going to end quietly when one of the protestors flashed a "V" sign to the local residents (later, the "V" sign became the basis for the charge that the 27 had incited the local population to rebellion . . .)[3] The officers were incensed and began arresting; first, several men in the group, and then all the women who refused to abandon them. In a matter of minutes, 27 demonstrators were being held in the local police station and a chain of events was set in motion which forced the 27 to remain in prison for five full days. The arresting officers, the duty judges and the court of first instance all seemed to be motivated by a desire to show these intellectuals and their friends that it was no small matter to trifle with the workings of the occupation.

One of the 27, Daphna Golan, an academician at the Hebrew University and a central activist in The Twenty-first Year wrote to her friend, Deena Hurwitz, an American pacifist with a special interest in the Middle East, a letter which analyzed the limits of Israeli protest in the light of the Kalkilya events.[4] For Golan it was clear that the "idea [of The Twenty-first Year's Covenant] was that we can no longer merely say that we oppose the occupation; we must do something against it, even if it entails paying a personal price."[5] Golan explains that the original intention was to employ non-violent tactics to prevent the demolition but the plan had to be altered: "People did not say that they were afraid, but if they had been ready to go to jail for months, missing that day of work could not have made such a big difference . . . So we had to rethink our strategies . . . We decided, then, to forget our training, and our plans for civil disobedience, and simply go there and pay a visit to the family . . . and found ourselves in jail for five days."[6]

Golan summarized a debate that broke out among the arrested protesters. Most sought the quickest path to an acquittal, while only a minority sought to challenge the legitimacy of the court by refusing to be judged according to unjust laws. Golan stresses with complete honesty and candor that she was simply unwilling to pay the price involved in such a challenge. Though there were ample opportunities for non-violent resistance in the future, nothing would ever come of it since, "No one was really ready to pay that high a price . . . I know we need radical measures to take us out of our paralyzed situation, our feelings of hopelessness and failure; yet the kind of steps that we, middle-class parents, people who still live too comfortably, will be able to adopt."[7]

There were a number of immediate causes for the Kalkilya failure of nerve and its dire consequences. First, though Adi Ophir and Hanan Hever had become the authoritative exponents of the movement in matters of theory, neither of them (nor anyone else for that matter) emerged willing and able to set an example of how to wage "total struggle" against the occupation. Secondly, in all fairness to the 27 "prisoners" and the bulk of The Twenty-first Year's membership, neither the leadership nor anyone else prepared the 27 for the often shocking and bewildering results of direct confrontations with the authorities. Thirdly, as a group and as individuals, The Twenty-first Year had very little experience in dealing with events like the Kalkilya jailing. For the uninitiated, the prosecution attempt to portray every infraction of the law a major violation and the court rigmarole seemed to constitute a major threat. Even Golan, an astute observer of the protest scene, revealed exaggerated fear when she thought that she faced the "prospect of six months'" imprisonment as a possible price for taking a militant line. She certainly was wrong when she wrote about no one caring about the 27 being in jail. When news of the detention reached Jerusalem, Peace Now (!) succeeded in organizing a rally of 400 protesters opposite National Police Headquarters the very next morning at 7 a.m. Moreover, the arrests evoked extensive, sympathetic media coverage, which highlighted the difference between the authorities' permissiveness toward settler violence and their over-reaction to a rather meek bit of protest activity.

It is worth considering why concerted activity on the basis of The Twenty-first Year's Covenant did not produce anything near the "readiness to pay a personal price," which was at the heart of the programmatic document. It is impossible to avoid the conclusion that a sizable section of the young intelligentsia did not take the trouble to read and understand the document that they signed. Though it was blessed with a highly literate cadre, there was a dearth of political experience in The Twenty-first Year. A textual analysis of the Covenant should have been sufficient to show that The Twenty-first Year would be doing illegal activity which had to involve personal danger. The plain fact is that no one, and its seems that this includes the leadership, had the faintest idea how the group's theory would be put into practice. In the absence of any clear idea of how the movement should act against the occupation machine, the ideas of civil disobedience and the techniques of non-violent struggle had much appeal for many members of The

Twenty-first Year. But a strategy for on-the-ground struggle was never worked out.

It is necessary to go back to the weaknesses of the Covenant in order to understand why The Twenty-first Year did not undergo a process of radicalization. In the final analysis, the Covenant's theoretical framework did not really provide an alternative ideology to the prevailing Zionist discourse. The members were disgusted by the occupation but had no clear idea of where their allegiance to Israel began and ended. They wanted to fight the occupation, but never seriously thought about the consequences of their thesis that the Israel polity had turned into a function of the occupation. The Covenant posed these questions but did not provide a clear answer to them. This lack of clarity kept pulling the movement back from the challenges of confrontation. The Twenty-first Year failed to explain to its advocates or to the public how their "total opposition" to the "total occupation" would change things. Thus, it happened that at Kalkilya, The Twenty-first Year squandered an opportunity to challenge the occupation on precisely the ground that it had sought.

The Twenty-first Year was never the same after Kalkilya. Devoted cadres continued to be active, but the malaise that was affecting many sections of the protest movement took an even greater toll on The Twenty-first Year. The psychological and intellectual damage that resulted from doubts about the movement's strategy in the post-Kalkilya period undermined the foundations of The Twenty-first Year existence. The pledge that members of The Twenty-first Year would be "fighting the occupation with a readiness to pay a personal price" was not fulfilled. Even so, the Covenant of The Twenty-first Year was the first serious attempt, outside traditional Marxist analyses, to examine the occupation and its impact on Israeli society on a theoretical level. There is reason to believe that, despite the failure of The Twenty-first Year, the seeds of critical thinking embodied in the Covenant will be felt in Israeli intellectual life for years to come.

The Intifada led, as we have seen, to the rejuvenation of Peace Now and the movement's decision at the end of 1988 to demand Israeli recognition of the PLO significantly narrowed the political gap between Peace Now and the rest of the protest movement. This development required the militants to articulate new strategies which could serve to justify the continued existence of smaller and less influential formations. They were unable to meet this challenge.

As a result, Dai La'kibush and The Twenty-first Year, the two main formations which had led the initial response to the Intifada – and created a challenge to the hegemony of Peace Now in the protest movement – began to disintegrate during 1989. Dai La'kibush was unable, because of internal divisions, to decide what it wanted to do or how to do it, while The Twenty-first Year was unable to do, because of a failure of nerve, what it had promised to do. The inability of the two main radical protest formations to come up with answers to decisive questions of strategy stifled their growth and hastened their demise.

The demise of Dai La'kibush and The Twenty-first Year did not result in Peace Now becoming the exclusive actor on the scene. A rich variety of important protest formations showed remarkable vitality and went on to establish their own separate identity and to find important roles in the overall struggle against government policy. These groups – Yesh Gvul, the women's movement, various formations on the basis of professions such as writers, artists and others, and human rights organizations – tended to shy away from the promotion of an overall political program. Many potential protesters questioned the value of standard forms of political activity, such as demonstrations and petitions, and saw little value in conducting interminable debates on political strategy. These groupings satisfied the need for a more personal, direct form of protest by organizing around special issues and attempting to activate specific social groups. Protest, for them, had to include a personal element, a personal sense of responsibility, a personal desire to act as an individual.

9

Taking Protest Personally

Yesh Gvul's Mission: the Specter of Refusal

Yesh Gvul, unlike other militant groups, had no cause for concern that the reason for its existence had been "co-opted" by Peace Now, simply because Peace Now's shift towards talks with the PLO did not moderate its negation of refusal to serve in the occupied territories. Yesh Gvul continued to pursue its basic goals: to promote the idea of "selective refusal" of military service in the occupied territories and to support those who refused. Yesh Gvul and its message were pertinent every time a call-up order was sent, "by courtesy of the IDF," to one of the many thousands of reservists who opposed the occupation and everything it stood for. If the reservist opposed the occupation, he was forced, seriously, to consider Yesh Gvul's recommendation.

After the first wave of refusals to serve in the occupied territories at the outbreak of the Intifada, the numbers of reservists actually jailed for refusing to serve in the territories levelled off at approximately five to ten per month. The number of reservists who decided to avoid service in the territories and succeeded in doing so was undoubtedly much larger than the number of those who refused and were actually sentenced to jail – though there are no reliable figures on this kind of refusal. Moreover, Yesh Gvul undoubtedly inspired the establishment of an additional, more moderate grouping. "Concerned Parents" was composed of uneasy parents, whose children were facing induction and who had deep reservations concerning their service in the occupied territories.

"Concerned Parents of IDF Soldiers" was a rather impressive collection of middle-class Israelis who banded together to warn the military and political authorities that they too had a limit, a limit to their endurance as parents. The group called on the authorities to "stop acting like the Intifada can go on forever and as if it were not doing damage – whose price we are paying and will pay for years to come" and "called on every parent to demand that the Knesset and the government stop passing the buck to our children by evading a political solution."[1]

Understandably, the number of "refuseniks" who actually went to jail was never great. By July 1990 – after thirty months of Intifada, 120 "refuseniks" had served jail sentences. At the same time, there was a growing sense in wide circles that service in the occupied territories was morally unjustifiable. The ideas of Yesh Gvul, and the moral dedication of the "refuseniks," met with respect, and even admiration, among the broadest circles of the peace constituency.

The moral challenge posed by Yesh Gvul made life a bit complicated for the political leaders of the two main dove-Zionist parties. Both MAPAM and the Citizen's Rights Movement were dismayed by the prestige of Yesh Gvul and growing interest in the option of "refusal". It was inevitable that many young supporters of the Citizen's Rights Movement and MAPAM would take the denunciation of the occupation by their political leaders seriously enough to consider refusal to serve in the occupied territories as a logical response.

MKs Yossi Sarid and Ran Cohen of the Citizen's Rights Movement, and the leaders of the two kibbutz movements, Kibbutz Artzi and the United Kibbutz Movement (Takam), were particularly active in trying to stamp out "refusenick" tendencies that continued to resurface in their ranks. Of the 120 refuseniks who went to jail, 28 were kibbutz members – less than a quarter (18 from Kibbutz Artzi, associated with Mapam and 10 from the United Kibbutz Movement, affiliated with the Labor Party). Though statistically a marginal affair, "refusal" was constantly discussed in the kibbutz movement. It should be recalled, in this respect, that the kibbutz movement took pride over the years in the fact that kibbutz youngsters made up a disproportionally high percentage of Israel's elite fighting units – and death casualties.

The kibbutz movements considered it their ideological and political duty to fight Yesh Gvul's influence. The leadership of Kibbutz Artzi took steps to encourage the youth movement connected with it, Hashomer Hatzair, to debate and adopt a resolution against "refusal". High-ranking officers, members of Kibbutz Artzi, were mobilized to dissuade any individual kibbutz member who considered refusal. One of the more convincing arguments used was that the presence of humane, decent soldiers in the ranks served to restrain unauthorized acts of cruelty by chauvinists and right-wing soldiers.[2]

The refusal issue appeared on the agenda of an important meeting of the United Kibbutz Movement's 300-member Political Council. The question was of importance because most of the few "refusenicks" who went to jail were leading members of the kibbutz community and more often than not occupied positions of administrative or educational authority. Moreover, the immediate resonance of such an act in a kibbutz was much greater than a similar act by citizens who enjoyed some degree of urban anonymity.[3] The kibbutz leadership succeeded in passing a resolution against "refusal" by 280 to 13, but only after the motion had been reworded and modified to exclude elements of condemnation and a threat of sanctions which had appeared in the original text. Moreover, the vote was taken only after a suggestion to leave the matter to each member's individual conscience was voted down by a slight majority, 120 to 80. It was clear that those willing to support the refusenicks were a small minority, but it was also clear that kibbutz members could still refuse to serve in the occupied territories without endangering their kibbutz membership.[4]

Flood Control

It had all the makings of a fierce inner-party row. Thirty-four members of the Citizen's Rights Movement, almost all of them elected officials in various municipal, local and labor movement councils, announced their solidarity with four Citizen's Rights Movement members who were "doing time" for having refused to serve in the territories. The message was short but pointed: "We, the undersigned respect their courageous step, their principled moral stand and their readiness to pay the price of their convictions."[5] When the announcement was published in the press, the Citizen's Rights Movement was thrown into a turmoil. The signatories rejected accusations that their announcement was either a call for or an endorsement of refusal. MKs Yossi Sarid and Ran Cohen accused the signatories of downright deception for citing their status as elected officers and implying by this that they were speaking for the Citizen's Rights Movement.[6] Public interest in the Citizen's Rights Movement row was intense. Ha'aretz columnist, Dan Margalit warned the Citizen's Rights Movement of the dire consequences of coddling refusenik tendencies: "Refusal might spread and create a split that would undermine democracy and result in military weakness that could encourage aggression. Sarid and Cohen understand this but they may not move quickly enough and the last dam against irresponsible refusal will burst."[7]

The 70-member Citizen's Rights Movement secretariat adopted an almost unanimous decision against refusal or encouraging refusal, adding a minor qualification to the effect that "a change in government policy is the only effective barrier against the spread of the phenomenon."[8]

MK Shulamit Aloni, the leader of the Citizen's Rights Movement, who had expressed respect and admiration for refusenicks on more than one occasion, made a rather acrobatic effort to distinguish between the position of the Citizen's Rights Movement as a political party bound by the "rules of the game" to respect the law, and the role of the Citizen's Rights Movement in defense of "freedom of conscience" as a movement based on citizens' rights. Sarid was less equivocal. He warned the secretariat that they had their "finger in the dike." "If we support refusal, it will flood the country. If this barrier is breached, the army will be destroyed and I have no assurances from Sadaam Hussein or Hafaz El-Asad that they will be impressed by our moral rectitude."[9]

One could say that the specter of refusal haunted large sections of the thinking public. Everybody who knew something about what was happening in the territories, and that included the well-informed Sarid, had to think about the limits of compliance – the proverbial "red line", a point at which he or she would refuse to follow orders. At the very same Citizen's Rights Movement meeting which Sarid had demanded in order to throw up the roadblocks against refusal, he himself declared: "There is a red line, however, which has not been crossed. If, for instance, there is an order to deport entire [Arab] villages and their residents, it will be a blatantly illegal order and it will be not only our right but also our duty to refuse to carry it out."[10]

Yesh Gvul had remarked on a number of occasions that all too many "red-lines" had already been crossed and those who hesitate to refuse orders until they actually receive undisguised and unequivocal instructions to commit obvious atrocities, would find themselves an integral part of the machine committing more and more serious crimes.

Protest By Profession

As we have noted, from the very beginning of the Intifada, a large and heterogeneous community of protesters emerged and proceeded to create novel forms of organization. Among other innovations, there was a pronounced tendency to protest "according to profession." The tendency found initial expression in a flurry of petitions by members of various professional groups which appeared in the form of newspaper advertisements during the first weeks of the Intifada. The most prominent groups represented were, inter alia, psychologists and mental health workers, writers and painters and other creative artists, university lecturers and teachers. For some professions, for example, architects and ceramicists, the petition was a one-time affair, the first and last time that the signers took a public stand during the Intifada. Other groups – such as Imut, Mental Health Workers for the Advancement of Peace and the Israeli-Palestinian Physicians Committee for Human Rights – went on to establish permanent frameworks which combined professional interests and protest activity.

The decision to organize on a professional basis was the single common denominator of many such groups, which tended to differ in almost every other respect. The Playwrights Association was by its very nature a select group; even so the entire profession made an important contribution to the protest community when it donated its offices to serve as the coordinating center between the different groups during the first months of the Intifada. In some professions – psychologists and mental health workers for example – the protesters comprised a significant segment of those in the field. Moreover, the group could often take pride in the activity of leading figures in the profession. On the other hand, the group of medical doctors which formed the Israeli-Palestinian Association of Physicians for Human Rights never exceeded a tiny percentage of the medical profession in Israel. Despite this, the Association commanded, because of the tremendous sensitivity of the problems and issues it dealt with, considerable public interest. Teachers and educators were active sporadically and their main project was a special campaign against the extended closures of schools. There was little success in the formation of a group within the legal profession which was willing to confront the degeneration of the legal system in the territories. This task fell mainly on individual lawyers such as Avigdor Feldman and Leah Zemel, and several staff persons and volunteers who worked with the various civil rights organizations. We shall deal here with those professional groups whose contribution was felt over a considerable period of time.

Creative Vanguard

Creative artists, Israelis and Palestinians from the occupied territories, must be considered the pioneers of protest by profession, having found the path to joint activity well before the beginning of the Intifada. In August 1988, a group of Israeli and Palestinian painters launched an exhibition of portraits of young Palestinians killed during the Intifada with the aim of bringing the victims out of their anonymity. It was the fourth time that Palestinian and Israeli painters held a joint exhbition and another link in long-standing cooperation between the artists.

> This is the fourth time that Palestinian and Israeli painters meet in a joint exhibition. The first attempt by the Palestinians to forge a link with the Israelis met with many difficulties. It was decided to abandon attempts to link up with the establishment and instead to establish links and contacts on an individual basis. The first contacts were with Gershon Knispel and David Reeb and they developed into exhibitions with wide participation of Israeli artists . . . A third exhibition was organized last year to mark 20 years of occupation . . . It wasn't just any group exhibition but a message against the entire occupation. Several works were censored.[11]

Cooperation between Israeli and Palestinian painters was facilitated by the fact that they had at their disposal a relatively simple form of joint expression – the art exhibition. Even so, putting together such an exhibition involved sensitive questions. Suliman Mansur, from East Jerusalem, was chairperson of the Palestinian Artists Association when the August 1988 exhibition was planned and held. Mansur, who was the only Palestinian from the territories who had studied at the Israeli Betzalel Art Academy in Jerusalem, was highly conscious of the tremendous differences between the two worlds of art. The Palestinian artists, who first organized in 1974, considered themselves, first and foremost, a part of Palestinian society and the Palestinian liberation movement. Their group was small in number and there were only two galleries where they could exhibit their work. Though the press followed their work closely, art criticism, as such, was practically non-existent. The occupation was so much the central theme of their work, that Mansur doubted whether there could be "normal" Palestinian art before it ended.[12]

The Israeli artists who worked with the Palestinians could not have been more different than their colleagues. By all the conventional standards, Israeli art was more sophisticated. Moreover, all the Israeli artists considered themselves completely "liberated" from any type of collective responsibility, aesthetic or otherwise. The Israeli artists who worked with the Palestinians acted as individuals and their individualism actually helped them overcome conventional Israeli inhibitions. Given the tremendous gap in the social conditions and the technical level of artistic development in the two societies, the number and quality of joint actions – and this includes joint exhibitions held in Israeli art centers and abroad – was certainly a success and an inspiration for additional kinds of joint Israeli-Palestinian cooperation.

Writers Work on Texts

It is, of course, easier to organize a joint art exhibition than to work out a joint, detailed political statement. But the Israeli writers, Jews and Arabs, who were organized in the Committee of Creative Artists, decided to draw up a full draft of an Israeli-Palestinian Peace Treaty, in conjunction with their Palestinian colleagues. It was a serious project designed to demonstrate that creative artists were both willing and able to work out the details, howsoever complex, of a practical and just compromise to the conflict. It was not easy.

> The contacts which culminated this week in a final draft of an Israeli-Palestinian Peace Treaty by the joint Committee of Jewish and Arab Creative Artists continued for more than four years, during which the joint efforts experienced many crises, including meetings which broke up in rancor and mini-boycotts.[13]

It appears that finding a compromise formula regarding the rights of the refugees was a particularly complicated problem, as many of the Israelis opposed any unqualified acknowledgement of the Right of Return. All in all it was a serious dialogue and a step forward in working out a compromise between opposing positions:

> The basic principles that guided the Israeli side were far to the left of Peace Now . . . On the Israeli side, an enlarged group of

writers, academicians and actors joined a nucleus, composed of
Yoram Kaniuk, Nathan Zakh, Gedalia Besser and Yael Lotan, who
had sustained the initiative from the beginning. Other writers,
prominent in the ranks of Israeli liberalism or the moderate left
such as A. B. Yehoshua, Amos Oz and Yehuda Amichai refused to
join this initiative in which, according to their opinion, the Israeli
side made excessive concessions.[14]

The Committee had attracted, in addition to the known leftists,
quite a number of colleagues with solid standing and political roots
in the liberal Zionist establishment. These newer members joined
out of a feeling that cooperation and dialogue with Palestinians was
the key to solving the conflict. While the Israelis spoke, at the best,
for an important minority of Israeli public opinion, the Palestinians
from the territories were, for their part, semi-official representatives
of the main political forces in the occupied territories. This caused
quite a bit of hesitation on the part of the Palestinians, since
any compromises they made with their Israeli counterparts could
be considered as potential concessions based on discussions and
deliberations within the PLO.

Most of the major literary figures affiliated with the Zionist left
usually acted in close coordination with Peace Now. However, on
at least one occasion they took an independent step considered
exceptional in the Israeli context. Amos Oz, A. B. Yehoshua, Yehuda
Amichai and Amos Eilon published a letter in the *New York Times*
in February 1988 in which they called on United States Jewry to
oppose Shamir's policies. It was yet another indication that most
Israeli writers sensed an urgent need to go on record against the
Shamir government.

No attempt is made in these pages to describe the impact of
the Intifada on Israeli art and literature. The reflection of the
Israeli-Arab conflict, the Intifada included, in Israeli art has received
more serious attention in recent years. There is a growing body of
criticism on this theme, published hitherto almost exclusively in
Hebrew. The subject is, at any rate, well beyond the limits of our
present inquiry.

Mental Health and the Occupation

It was, by any criterion, a tremendous success. In June 1988, over six
hundred mental health professionals came to a conference originally

planned for one hundred and fifty participants. In addition to the Israeli Jews, Israeli Palestinian Arabs were well represented and there was an impressive contingent of Palestinian professionals from the occupied territories. It was an auspicious beginning for one of the most successful of the "professional" protest organizations.

The idea for the conference and the possibility of establishing a permanent organization stemmed from the relative success of the mental health workers' original petition published at the beginning of February 1988. More than five hundred members of the profession signed a call which noted that:

> . . . the accumulative effect of the prolonged occupation will lead, inevitably, to social sickness, to the loss of sensitivity for the rights and the suffering of others and to a disregard for human life and honor. These influences seep into day-to-day life and corrupt the society in which we live.[15]

In the same period, Dr. Immanuel Berman, from Haifa University, published an article about the "Silence of the Psychologists," arguing that a series of defense mechanisms created a "conspiracy of silence by the psychotherapists in Israel about the effect of the cumulative trauma on the personality of many in the country and the role of the wars in shaping the psychotherapeutic profession."[16]

Should We Be Meeting Like This?

The very idea of a politically-based organization of psychologists met with severe criticism from many colleagues. There was the obvious reservation by those who disagreed with the basic political argument of the protesters. However, there was also a strong current of thought in the profession which believed that it was unwise, or even unethical, for psychologists to act as individuals or as a group in the political sphere. As if to reassure one another on this issue, much of the plenary discussion of the first conference was devoted to these hesitations – which do have strong roots in the profession. Freud, himself, it appears was against getting involved in "non-scientific" questions. Dr. Joachim Stein, arguing for the right and duty of psycholgoists to intervene as such in the political process, claimed that had Freud lived to the beginning of World War II, he would have changed his mind.

Several prominent academicians put forward a variety of arguments against the demand that psychologists should observe strict political neutrality. Prof. Y. Shuval (Chair of the Psychology Department at Tel Aviv University) argued that any separation between humanist values and psychological thinking is artificial. Prof. Aaron Antonovsky was of the opinion that the official professional organization of the psychologists, which included all psychologists in the country, should not take political positions, but psychologists who organize on a voluntary basis have every right to work for common values and political goals. Dr. Ruhama Marton observed that activity deemed perfectly legitimate for professors at the Weizmann Institute of Science is unquestionably permissible for psychologists. Dr. Charles Greenbaum, from the Department of Psychology at the Hebrew University, was the most impassioned defender of the organization. Greenbaum referred explicitly to the comparison between Israel and Germany. "I was born in Germany and personally experienced Kristalnacht . . . the problem in Germany was not that people remained silent in the forties. The problem was that in the thirties, when it was still possible to speak out, people preferred to remain silent."[17]

Almost a Full-Scale Professional Conference

Fifteen workshops and discussion groups dealt with a wide range of topics such as comparison of Palestinian and Jewish children's dreams on the conflict, conditions for joint field research between Palestinians and Israelis, interaction and special problems of Israeli Jewish and Palestinian families and women, educators, and adolescents. The feeling was that the general debate and the workshops were a significant beginning and the foundations for a permanent organization had been laid.

Imut then proceeded to create organizational tools for ongoing activity, including the preparation of its next national conference. The stated goals of Imut, Mental Workers for the Advancement of Peace, established in the wake of the first conference, were in no sense a program calling for an alternative, highly partisan "mobilized" psychology. It was the spectre of a partisan, mobilized psychology which had been raised by the opponents of any kind of organized action by the concerned psychologists. The goals were: (a) the acquisition and dissemination of knowledge of individual and group practices under Israeli rule in the West Bank and Gaza, harmful to both the Israeli and Palestinian populations; (b) the promotion of professional meetings between Palestinians and Israelis. Provision of services to those suffering mental stress as a result of the occupation: (c) the acquisition of information on psychological processes which create barriers to peace."[18]

Imut – Permanent Presence

Imut became a permanent force on the professional and protest scenes; it sponsored annual conferences and was particularly active in advancing cooperation with Palestinian health workers in the occupied territories. Its second annual conference, held in May 1989, was devoted to the theme: "Psychological Barriers to Peace." Three main opening addresses dealt with central questions for the mental health community: Dr. Immanuel Berman spoke on "Involved Psychology or Mobilized Psychology", Dr. Munir Fasha, from Bir Zeit University talked on "Empowerment as a Strategy of Hope and Change: The Case of the Palestinian Intifada"; and Prof. Stanley Cohen, of the Hebrew University, and a leading figure in Critical Criminology, spoke about the "Psychology and Politics of Denial." For two days, five hundred participants attended panels, workshops and open discussion groups. The cumulative effect demonstrated that a sizable part of the mental health worker community felt the very general principles and values expressed by Imut had created solid intellectual ground for professional debate and interaction.

Analyses and Issues

The examination of the psychological aspects of the Intifada and the prolonged Israeli occupation of the occupied territories proceeded on a number of levels. The broadest level of concern dealt with the effects of the occupation on the mental health of individuals and groups. The specific question of how participation by Israeli soldiers in the brutal repression of the uprising might affect them was particularly urgent since many Israeli psychologists, not few of whom were associated with Imut, performed their reserve duty as psychologists in the IDF. Another recurring theme was the positive, liberating psychological effects of the Intifada on the Palestinians under occupation and the need to explain this phenomenon to the Israeli public. Fears, demonization and the effects of the conflict on the mental make-up of the populations concerned were other objects for attention and research.

The use of psychological and psychoanalytical methods in the analysis of Israel, as an occupying power, was particularly noteworthy. The most prominent practitioner of this approach was Prof. Joachim Stein, who claimed that the Israeli occupation was exceptional by virtue of the "mental disposition" which enables the conqueror to consider himself as the "conquered". This results in an irrational streak that prevents the Israeli occupier from accurately analyzing political realities and the direction in which his own interests lie.[19]

Dr. Ruhama Marton based her analysis on experience in group therapy and spoke of infantile regression which appeared in the Israeli-Zionist-Jewish collective after 1967. This deterioration increased dependency and involved an inability to get past the childhood "splitting" stage when everything is completely good or bad. Marton felt that Israeli society was really quite ill and on the verge of a permanent and unalterable need for an enemy and that the Israeli-Jewish community would have to undergo a process similar to withdrawal symptoms which occur in drug abuse, and that only peace and the subsequent definition of Israeli borders could help repair a deficiency in maturity and give the Jewish population a clearer sense of identity.[20]

Prof. Stan Cohen made a serious attempt to understand the relative inaction of Israeli liberals, namely that "small (and dwindling) group of liberals: the educated, enlightened, Western-oriented sectors of the middle class; those supposedly receptive to messages of peace and co-existence; those who are the first to condemn racism and human rights violations in South Africa or Chile."[21] The familiar patterns of denial by which people block off or routinize information about atrocities perpetrated by sons, husbands, neighbors, friends and colleagues were certainly present. However, explained Cohen, the application of concepts from individual psychology to social conditions does not really examine the situational factors and explain what is happening in Israel. Using an analogy from the area of victimology, Cohen suggested the relevance of the "bystander effect" whereby intervention apparently dictated by an observer's values and convictions does not occur. In the Israeli context, Cohen, identifies three syndromes: (a) diffusion of responsibility or "why is it my job to blow the whistle?"; (b) lack of sympathy for the victim (the Palestinian) – and here everything from real historical experience to demonized racial stereotypes are combined together, i.e. "they started it and they are getting what they deserve"; and (c) simply not knowing what to do.

Most important, in Cohen's opinion is the historical-political level which "conditions" the other levels of response. Historical experience of being Jewish cultivates the image "of permanent victim." "However disingenuous it might look from the outside, the insecurity of the average Jewish Israeli – including our liberals – is too deep for the rational message of the peace movement to reach him or her." Moreover, the close identification of the group with the state during the period of nation building and wars created a "profound reluctance to take any public stand which may be interpreted as 'disloyal' . . . or worst of all 'anti-Zionist'."

Cohen did a brilliant job of delineating the complex sources of liberal paralysis, hoping, at least implicitly, that revealing the source of liberal paralysis would go a long way in removing obstacles to the creation of a deeply committed mass movement for peace in the country. This was highly improbable. Cohen's keen analyses of the weaknesses and the limitations of the Israeli peace movement actually created tools for a more balanced evaluation of the protest movement. Considering the real obstacles and historical conditioning, the achievements of the peace movement – which often fall short of having a decisive impact on events – are nonetheless highly important and noteworthy – and do create, through the arduous paths of practice, the possibility of overcoming the historical and sociological conditioning described so penetratingly by Cohen.

Protest Moves Off-Campus

The universities fulfilled a rather minor role in the protest movement during the Intifada. It wasn't that the mood on campus was any less dovish than it had been over the years. During the first weeks of the Intifada, a new group called "Lecturers Against Imposed Rule in the Territories – The Inter-University Movement for a Political Settlement" had gathered more than 700 signatures on a petition calling for a "reassessment of Israeli policy" and "immediate steps toward political negotiations."[22] Most leading professors had signed, and the massive support for the petition was an impressive reminder that the majority of the intelligentsia was dissatisfied with government inaction.

The message was about as "mild" in political terms as it could be and was couched in the language of concern and responsibility rather than condemnation. It was the voice of liberal Zionism, painfully aware that the Intifada was hammering at the status quo and efforts to maintain the occupation would mean more and more brutal suppression. At the same time, the message avoided any clear suggestion for transforming Israeli-Palestinian relations. A number of discussion forums were held by the new formation but the group never got off the ground. It appears that most of the young academicians who were slated to shoulder day-to-day responsibility for the movement's projected plans were "siphoned off" by other more militant and energetic frameworks growing and developing off campus. Moreover, the new group was covering the same ground as Peace Now and the fact that so many lecturers had renewed their activity in Peace Now, tended to render a new formation superfluous.

One reason so little happened on campus was that so much was happening off campus. Over the years, protest activity on campus – when it occurred – had been the sole or the main expression of the protest movement. This was, of course, a weakness recognized by teachers and students alike – who always hoped for the day that the students and faculty would be part of a wider social movement. The protest movement that developed in the wake of the Intifada was such a movement. It certainly drew many of its activists from the universities and if this meant that more was happening in the streets and cities and less on the campuses – it was a small price to pay.

Even so, there were a number of activities at Israeli universities which reflected new levels of political concern. Sectors not usually heard from appeared in the protest camp. Six hundred teachers and students at Bar Ilan University, known as a stronghold of the ultra-nationalist Gush Emunim (Bloc of the Faithful), sent a statement calling for "immediate negotiations with Palestinian representatives" to President Herzog.[23] More than 1,000 students and teachers in Israel's medical schools published a petition which, according to a student activist, jolted the ivory tower.[24] An ad hoc group of twenty law professors presented a petition to the Minister of Justice warning of the "certain havoc resulting from the existence of two legal systems, one for Israelis and another for Palestinians under occupation."[25] But these and other similar

actions were usually sporadic acts and did not lead to permanent
organizations.

This Far and No Further

One development signified an auspicious change in the protest
scene in Israeli academia – the establishment of the Ad Kan ("No
Further") group of professors and lecturers at Tel Aviv University.[26]
Ad Kan was established during the first days of the Intifada and
distanced itself, from its very inception, from the traditional liberal
Zionist approach previously dominant on Israeli campuses. For all
practical purposes, Ad Kan adopted the main points of the program
of the militant wing of the peace movement, including the demand
for Palestinian self-determination and recognition of the PLO as the
representative of the Palestinians. For a faculty organization, Ad
Kan was exceptionally active: it disseminated information on the
occupation, organized numerous demonstrations and seminars, and
participated in an organized fashion in the activities of other protest
organizations.

The appearance of Ad Kan was possible because the ideological
hegemony of Zionist liberalism had weakened considerably. This
weakness was linked to trends in the intellectual climate abroad
which had, naturally enough, a serious impact on Israeli academicians. Commitment to any establishment ideology was under fire
on a wide front and the independence of the academic, individually
and as a group, became the more acceptable norm. In the Israeli
context there were more and more lecturers who considered it
their intellectual duty to criticize the establishment discourse –
especially as the main base of liberal Zionism, the Socialist-Zionist
movement, had entered the throes of a prolonged ideological crisis.
Members of the new generation of academics tended to consider
democratic values and principles more important than any kind of
political affiliation and felt themselves psychologically distant, if not
alienated, from the Israeli establishment.

There is no way of knowing if Ad Kan was as representative of
the faculty opinion as the more traditional liberal Zionist trend.
It probably was not. However, Ad Kan did become the dominant
political force among the faculty at Tel Aviv University; it had
many highly prestigious members of the faculty in its ranks and
had broad support among "junior" faculty" – including many of

the non-tenured teaching staff. Thus, it also enhanced the prestige of the militant wing of the protest movement, which could show that it had serious support among the academic intelligentsia which hitherto had given almost exclusive support to Peace Now.

Doctors Lend a Helping Hand

The Association of Israeli and Palestinian Physicians for Human Rights did not claim that it mobilized a considerable segment of this traditionally apolitical profession. Despite this, the Association did become an important factor on the protest scene because it succeeded in finding ways to intervene in a critical area, where the repercussions of the occupation had clear and acute consequences.

The thousands of clashes between the IDF and the Palestinians in the territories intensified the need for urgent medical attention. The necessity of treating thousands of their people who had been wounded, often seriously, in these clashes, and the increased complexity of delivering medical care in almost "battlefield" conditions, threw a gigantic burden on the frail Palestinian medical infrastructure. The suffering of the civilian population and the desperate efforts of Palestinian medical personnel to deal with enormous challenges inspired a number of Israeli physicians to do something in an attempt to assist their Palestinian colleagues.

The Association of Israeli and Palestinian Physicians for Human Rights (AIPPHR) was established at a meeting of approximately one hundred physicians in Tel Aviv on March 19, 1988. The objectives of the group were (1) to maintain ongoing contacts between Israeli and Palestinian physicians; (2) to study the health-care system in the territories and to disseminate information aimed to improve it; (3) to monitor and report unethical practices such as delays in providing health care; (4) to investigate complaints of avoidable deaths and injuries; (5) to protect Palestinian physicians from arbitrary arrest, harassment, and physical harm; (6) to organize volunteer work by Israeli physicians in Palestinian clinics and hospitals; (7) to hold professional meetings with Palestinian colleagues; (8) and to maintain contact with human rights organizations abroad.[27]

The Israeli medical establishment – there are 12,000 physicians in the Israeli Medical Association – was non-political (in the narrow and formal sense of this concept) but it certainly had an image to protect. This was equally true of the medical officers who served the

IDF Civil Administration in the territories. A report issued by the Association of Israeli and Palestinian Physicians for Human Rights in August 1989 on health conditions in the Gaza Strip infuriated the Chief Medical officer of the Civilian Administration, Dr. Y. Peterberg and the Chair of the Israeli Medical Association, Dr. Ram Yishai. Peterberg refuted the accusations that Gaza hospitals and clinics lack basic equipment and are unable to provide important types of treatment by observing that the Egyptian health services were rooted in the Egyptian health system and this fact made comparisons based on Western standards unfair.[28] Peterberg, undeterred by the fact that the "Egyptian roots" of the system had been under Israeli control for the last 23 years, went on to list an "amazing amount of health projects that came to fruition during the Intifada."[29]

The Association was the first to admit that many of its important achievements resulted from quiet (and insistent) complaints which drew the attention of colleagues in the military and civilian medical establishments to the more flagrant violations of medical ethics. The Association intervened regarding impediments to the delivery of medical service because of curfews, the practice of chaining sick prisoners to their beds, denial of medical treatment to prisoners, and the arbitrary arrest of Palestinian physicians for unspecified "security" reasons. Perhaps one of the most significant activities of the Association was the systematic collection of clear evidence on the routine use of torture by the Israeli secret service, the "Shabak."

Rabbis on the Watch

The religious Zionist establishment – the Mizrachi bloc in world Zionism and the National Religious Party (NRP) – originally a moderate, if not dovish, organization was transformed over the years into the main political sponsor of the Gush Emunim settler movement. A messianic interpretation of the results of the Six Day War in 1967 converted the settlement of the occupied territories into the most urgent of all religious obligations. And if the Palestinian Intifada got in the way, it had to be destroyed and moral considerations were simply irrelevant.

The ultra-orthodox religious parties, more fundamentalist than the National Religious Party, were usually less nationalist and

indifferent to non-religious issues, and willing to render support
to the given government so long as religious issues and budgetary
questions were solved to their satisfaction. During the Intifada,
these parties, namely SHAS and Agudath Israel, could find no
reasons to object to the government and the army's handling of
the Intifada. There was a significant minority of the Mizrahi rabbis and intellectuals who did disassociate themselves from the
unbridled messiahism and religious fervor of the Gush Emunim
settler movement. The dovish dissidents, whose spiritual leader
was Rabbi Yehuda Amital, ran a list for the elections in 1988, named
Meimad, which barely missed gaining a parliamentary seat. Two
small groups, Oz Va'Shalom and Nitzanei Shalom, whose politics
were similar to those of Peace Now, challenged the monopoly of
Gush Emunim on religious Judaism. Main support for the groups,
which were unable to develop any sizable following, came from
the more intellectual section of religious Jewry. It was important to
establish a religious presence of Israel's orthodox community in the
peace camp, though for the most part the contribution of the orthodox religious peace groups was more symbolic than substantial.

The formation of the Rabbinic Human Rights Watch in March
1989 was a valuable addition to the protest movement. The goals of
the group were formulated in religious and ethical terms, stressing
that "protest[ing] the acts of personal humiliation and group intimidation inflicted on Palestinians, including women, children and the
elderly" was necessary in order to "[guard] the moral and ethical
heritage of our people."[30] From its inception, the Watch was able to
identify and publicize, usually through personal on-the-site visits,
including condolence visits to the homes of bereaved Palestinian
families, some of the more flagrant violations of human rights. The
Watch saw itself more as a human rights group than a political
protest movement and argued intensively against claims that its
human rights concerns meant disguised support for the Intifada.

The composition of the group was its greatest strength and its
greatest weakness. Most of the Rabbis were former Americans and
usually former members of the Reform or Conservative movements
in United States Jewry. The group emphasized the participation
of several Orthodox members (in Israel, almost all the Rabbinate
is Orthodox, while the Conservative and Reform denominations
compose only a slight minority of the religious community). In
fact, the Watch had little support in Israeli clerical circles. On the
other hand, the Watch was successful in receiving an endorsement

from over 1,000 North American Rabbis, and was not reticent about publicizing this fact. Its composition and its connections gave the Watch, and its chief spokesperson, Rabbi David Forman, a certain standing with the authorities and the media. There is also little doubt that the Watch was instrumental in helping liberal sections of the United States Jewish community to understand the realities of Israeli occupation despite the country's reputation as "the only democracy in the Middle East."

Talking About Former Americans

A small but intensely active group of "olim" (new immigrants) from the United States were prominent in protest circles – especially in Jerusalem from the very inception of protest activity. "Olim Against the Occupation" was one of the first groups to call for a constant vigil outside Shamir's residence during the first weeks of the Intifada. The group had strong links with many observant immigrants from the US. Its militancy and its willingness to cooperate with all sections of the protest movement earned its activists the respect of the entire movement. Veronica Cohen one of the leaders of the group, went on to establish with Hillel Bardin and others the first Israeli-Palestinian dialogue group with the leadership of the town of Beit Sahur. This dialogue group, which continued in existence all through the Intifada, later became a model for other similar ventures. Most of the activists in Olim Against Occupation and the Israeli side of the dialogue groups had a personal record of militant activity in the United states during the Vietnam war and the struggle for the rights of Soviet Jewry.

For the record, there was even an organization of "Joggers for Peace," which, believe it or not, managed to arouse the ire of the military authorities who found it necessary to curtail its activity. "Joggers for Peace" eventually had to go to the High Court of Justice, with the aid of the Israeli Association for Citizen's Rights, before the IDF was willing to offer them a reasonable compromise recognizing their "right to jog" but requiring prior notice of plans for Israeli-Palestinian running.[31]

Disproportionate Presence of Americans

You did not have to be a sophisticated observer of the protest movement in Israel to notice a disproportionate amount of former "Americans" in almost all the protest organizations. Before making too much of this fact, it must be observed that it is equally true that immigrants from the United States make up a sizable section among the settlers in the West Bank. One commentator suggested that it was only natural that ideologically motivated immigrants would end up highly committed to their principles. It appears that most of the immigrants who grew up and were active during the civil rights movement and the anti-war movement during the Vietnam war almost invariably ended up in the ranks of the doves. Most of those who came to Israel during the Reagan area, having grown up in an atmosphere of conservative nationalism and religious fundamentalism, found their way to the settler right. Naturally enough, there were many exceptions to this generalization though it does seem to offer a certain insight into the sociology of Jewish-American immigration to Israel.

Two years into the Intifada, the protest movement had broadened and diversified. Even so, the continued existence of a national-unity government effectively neutralized much of the mainstream opposition to Shamir's stand-pat policies. The protest movement had to do more and do it better; it also needed a political break that would convince people, including many of those in power, that there could not be a military answer to the problems posed by the Intifada.

10

Dismal Deadlock

Everything about the second anniversary of the Intifada in December 1989 was somber. The Israel Defense Forces employed a virtual arsenal of repressive measures, but was unable to end the uprising which succeeded in keeping the Palestinian question on the international agenda. Ariel Sharon was leading a "get tough" lobby in the cabinet, supported by the settlers and the fanatic right, which demanded that the government "put a stop to the Intifada." Sharon talked about using "whatever force necessary" but he was really proposing that the Israel Defense Forces should shoot to kill in order to prevent any form of civilian disturbance and prepare the ground, if necessary, for mass expulsions. International public opinion and internal pressures – among them the presence and activity of the protest movement – prevented the government from taking his advice.

The result was a dreadful stalemate in the occupied territories. The Palestinians kept "coming back for more" and the Israel Defense Forces continued to do everything to prove that it still had the situation under control. Shamir, an expert in "muddling through," denied that he had failed to quell the Intifada:

> We did not fail. It is a difficult task. There are certain successes, not a few in preventing and diminishing dangerous developments. I am certain that we will reach an end to this phenomenon. I cannot say when. I can only say that after two years that it has raged, those who initiated it and organized it have not achieved anything, and if they continue, they will not achieve anything.[1]

Defense Minister Yitzhak Rabin's response was more detailed, but carried the same message:

> *Rabin*: "Israel Defense Forces has failed to end Intifada . . . it might go on a year or two years." But the Defense Minister insists that

Israel can bear the burden of the Intifada, no matter how long it goes on. "I have no doubt about it," he says. "We will continue with all the measures we used for the first years, including the confrontations, the hitting, the arresting, the introduction of plastic bullets, the rubber bullet, and curfews on a large scale." "Soldiers don't like it," he continues, "but they understand why we have to do it . . . " As it stands today, Rabin says, some 85 percent of the violent activity is stone throwing, and 60 percent of that is carried out by children 13 years or younger. "The strike, the closures and the other passive means, we tried to control them and we failed. Now we don't try again. We have reached a war of attrition. But I think they feel more attrition than we do."[2]

The summaries, after two years of Intifada, increased anger and frustration in the protest movement. Almost a quarter of the approximately 300 fatalities during the second year of the Intifada were youths or children under 16. There were no reliable figures on the number of wounded, many of whom stayed away from the hospitals whenever possible, but United Nations Relief and Rehabilitation Agency sources gave the number of wounded as 37,439 for two years of the uprising. There were about 13,000 Palestinian prisoners, under various forms of detention, languishing in Israeli custody.[3] These were only the more shocking statistics of an entire system of repression that included extended curfews, house demolitions, imprisonment without trial, censorship, closure of educational institutions, and expulsions.

Shamir's government hid behind its April 1989 "peace initiative" – a plan to hold elections in the occupied territories. Based on refusal to negotiate with the PLO, complete negation of Palestinian self-determination and the demand to maintain the territorial status quo, Shamir's initiative was clearly a "non-starter." The overall result was to reinforce on the political level the same kind of deadlock that existed "on the ground" in the territories. The only ray of light was the steady increase of mainstream politicians and media figures who came out in criticism of Shamir's perpetual stall and for negotiations with the PLO. A typical example was the *Ha'aretz* editorial marking the second year of the Intifada:

all the senior security chiefs are of the same opinion that the West Bank and Gaza Arabs have not reached the breaking point . . . it is impossible to end the uprising by force. If the government was really interested in finding a political solution, it would not veto the PLO as a partner for negotiations . . . the government of Israel will not be able to repudiate, in the long run, the right of the Palestinians to self-determination.[4]

In many senses, the protest movement felt that it too, along with the Palestinians, was being pressed into a long war of attrition. And there was no way of being certain that the protest movement had the resources or the necessary reserves for a long protracted battle. Protesters were motivated by anger, insult, moral indignation and political opposition, but after all was said and done, they and their families did not live under occupation. Even so, during this, the second year of the Intifada, the protest movement was steadily building its strength.

More Women, More Unity

Women were among the most dynamic forces in the peace movement. As we have seen, during 1989 there was a sharp increase in the number of Women In Black vigils. In addition to the larger vigils in Israel's main cities, a growing network of vigils had appeared all over the country, many of which resulted from the ability of Women In Black to inspire women in the kibbutz movement to follow their example. The leadership of the kibbutz movement had decided, after some hesitation, to welcome this development. Once the kibbutz vigils started, they attracted women from towns in the region, and many vigils included Arab women. It was another example of the women's movement success in overcoming conventional barriers between moderates and militants.[5]

The stubborn perseverance of the women, their determination to stand vigil week after week in order to stress their commitment was a totally new phenomenon in Israeli politics. Even the media were impressed. One columnist waxed poetic: "If you really want to know the superiority of women in terms of perseverance and tenacity, endurance and elegance, go then, you typical Jerusalem (or Israeli) male to the weekly vigil of Women In Black in Jerusalem."[6] It is reasonable to believe that the astounding success of Women In Black in bridging the gap into the more moderate sections of the peace community inspired yet another development in the women's peace movement, the establishment of the Israel Women's Peace Net.

Networking into the Political Establishment

The Israeli Women's Peace Net, which will be referred to here by its much simpler Hebrew name, the Reshet, was probably the only Israeli peace organization which came into existence as a direct outcome of the proceedings of an international conference. The conference, whose motto was, "Give Peace a Chance, Women Speak Out," convened in Brussels during the last week in May, 1989. Ms. Simone Susskind, who had given significant financial backing to various Israeli peace projects in the past, was the main coordinator. The conference also received assistance from the European Community which was showing increased interest in Israeli-Palestinian contacts, since the adoption of a balanced resolution on the Palestinian question in Venice as far back as 1980. The Venice resolution was updated by a 1988 European parliament resolution which stated that any solution would involve the creation of a defined territory for a Palestinian state.[7]

The organizers made every effort to include women from the Labor Party and succeeded in convincing MK Navah Arad, Yael Dayan, and Navah Eisen to join the Israeli delegation. There were Palestinian women from the occupied territories and officials from the PLO Women's section based in Tunis. Susskind noted, at a press conference summarizing the meeting, "We were not able to reach unanimous agreement . . . but we committed ourselves to go on working together in Israel and the occupied territories to promote our mutual goals."[8] The Brussels Declaration was explicit about sharing Palestine according to resolutions 181 (the 1948 UN decision on the partition of Palestine) and Security Council Resolution 242, but at the same time evasive about explicitly mentioning Israeli national rights. The Reshet had a difficult time with the exact wording of the Brussels Declaration and decided to circumvent it by basing its activity on the "spirit of the Brussels Conference" (see below). This stratagem worked out by the Reshet during the first weeks of its existence protected it from what might have been a nearly fatal attack from hawkish circles in the Labor Party. Even so, the more acceptable, abridged version of the "spirit of Brussels" was enough to situate the Reshet, to the left of Peace

Now and closer to the more militant sections of the women's peace movement.

The Reshet, in one of its first activities, decided on a petition campaign in conjunction with SHANI, Israeli Women Against the Occupation. The petition contained the full text of the Brussels Declaration, but asked women to support three "mutually acceptable principles which are necessary for achieving a durable peace." These principles, later referred to as the "Spirit of the Brussels Declaration" were: (1) "Any agreement will be based on the recognition of the rights of the two peoples, Israeli and the Palestinian, to self-determination and sovereignty, which are the basis for peace and security. (2) Each party to the conflict has the legitimate right to determine its own representatives. (3) The agreement will be based on international guarantes and recognition." Women were asked to sign the petition in order to "urge the Israeli government to be guided by these principles in negotiating a comprehensive and just peace settlement." [9]

A number of factors made for the success of the Reshet. First, though its aim was to attract members closer to the established women's movements such as Na'amat, the huge women's division of the Histadrut, the General Federation of Labor, it adopted an open and unpretentious attitude to other women's peace movements. In the same spirit, the Reshet defined itself as a "non-partisan movement" of "Women from the broadest spectrum of political opinion, different political parties and peace organizations and protest movements [are represented] on an individual basis in the Reshet." [10] Secondly, though its leaders came from the heart of the Zionist establishment, it shaped its political program in close contact with the organized Palestinian women's movement. After all, it was the desire to meet with and work with Palestinian women which brought the organization into existence. Thirdly, the Reshet did attract and involve new circles of women in peace activity. Masha Lubelsky, then Secretary-General of Na'amat, spoke on behalf of the Reshet on more than one occasion. Many members were spouses of high government officials and one Tel Aviv activist was the wife of a cabinet minister. By making protest more "respectable", the Reshet helped to frustrate attempts to marginalize the protest movement and its main messages.

Perhaps the greatest weakness of the Reshet was its inability to build a mass base commensurate with its political standing and influence. Aside from bringing middle-class Israeli and Palestinian women together, it seems that the Reshet and its leaders never devoted much thinking to goals above and beyond organizing its "natural constituency," i.e. women already linked one way or another to the Labor Party and the CRM. There was certainly nothing "wrong" with holding home meetings with Palestinian women, and it was productive to have Israeli women visit the homes and offices of their Palestinian sisters in the territories. But there was something in the conformist style of the Reshet which prevented it from sparking any kind of grass-roots enthusiasm or dedication. Its few attempts to go to the streets, to march or stand vigil leaned heavily on the more radical constituency of the women's protest movement.

Two years of Intifada saw the women's peace movement in a period of growth and expansion. There were many women's groups and many different kinds of activities, but converting these gains into a presence in the streets remained the prerogative of the most organized and the least "organizational" of all the formations, Women In Black. Peace Now's claim to be the single mass-based force in the Israeli peace movement was being challenged. But this challenge was neither competitive nor confrontational. With the women's movement a new dimension of mass protest had arrived on the scene.

Protesting Israeli policy was never easy as most Israelis felt threatened by the Palestinians and the Arab world and felt that criticism of government policy was somehow disloyal. Support from abroad was no substitute for support among Israelis, but there was some consolation in the fact that a broad range of political forces abroad expressed admiration for the Israeli peace movement. International solidarity is important for any peace movement and it is worth reviewing, at this point, the Israeli peace movement's international connections.

Foreign Affairs

The peace movement could not be indifferent to the international implications of the Intifada for Israel and for the protest movement. It had to rebuff charges that its activities were giving Israel a bad name abroad and had to deal with proposals to limit Israeli control of the territories by some sort of international intervention. The peace movement had to conduct its own "foreign policy" in its contacts with various peace groups abroad which expressed a direct interest in events in the territories and considered extending support, in one form or another, to the work of the peace forces in Israel. Last and by far not the least, the Israeli peace movement had to develop a strategy towards Jews abroad. The Jewish communities in the diaspora had created over the years a powerful political and financial support system for Israeli governments. It was important, in the light of Shamir's policies and the challenge of the Intifada, to examine the possibility of piercing this armor by mobilizing some section of the Jewish community to support peace as the alternative to the status quo.

What Will the Goyim Say?

Israel's response to the Intifada and its stand-pat diplomatic attitude were affecting Israel's international standing and prestige. The entire peace movement rejected suggestions that protest was inimical to the interests of the state because it supposedly supplied grist to the mill of Israel's foes. Instead it endeavored to convince the Israeli public that increasingly brutal means used to repress the Intifada must of necessity cause serious damage to Israel's international standing. Countries and international organizations, usually inclined to be pro-Israeli, would start to disassociate themselves, in one or another form, from Israeli policy. The more moderate sections of the peace movement, such as Peace Now, would stress that though anti-Israeli responses were undesirable or even unwarranted, they were part of international reality that had to be taken into consideration. The moderates rejected proposals that the Israeli peace movement join calls for international intervention in the occupied territories – usually to prevent or monitor human rights violations – as unrealistic and politically counter-productive. Instead they called on the Israeli electorate to pressure the government to take heed of the deterioration in Israel's international standing and to draw the necessary conclusions requiring policy changes by Israel.

The more radical sections of the peace movement did not hesitate to welcome signs of growing criticism and disaffection for Israel. Thus, the radical sections of the peace movement would tend to support suggestions – which usually came from Palestinian quarters – for international intervention to monitor human rights violations or for the protection of the inhabitants. On more than one occasion, radical sections of the peace movement considered calling for a boycott of cultural activities in Israel or on Israeli products. Such projects usually failed to get off the ground for practical reasons, but were considered fair weapons in the arsenal of protest.

One Peace Movement to Another

The various international peace organizations viewed the political forces in the region through the prism of their own politics. Many of these organizations were anti-colonialist in nature, tended to support the Palestinian cause and to be indifferent to the nuances of internal Israeli politics. One exception to this trend was a smaller grouping of organizations – the Netherlands-based "Pax Christie" was a good example – which combined a sense of solidarity with the Jewish people and their state with firm rejection of the policies of the Shamir government. Such groups took a deep and abiding interest in the prospects of the Israeli peace movement as a moral and political force. The pro-Soviet current was yet another exception to the exclusively pro-Palestinian orientation in the international peace movement in that it considered it vital to extend moral support to the "progressive forces in Israel" who were doing battle with official policies.

Moreover, as the Palestinian leadership tended more and more in the direction of a two-state solution, the majority of the peace groups abroad began to understand the need to support the Israeli peace forces, even though these forces considered their program a patriotic alternative to government policy. Support from abroad for a two-state solution created the political opening which enabled cooperation and joint action between Peace Now and other moderate sections of the peace movement in Israel and the overwhelming majority of peace groups and organizations abroad.

In the course of its activity, the Israeli peace movement, in its various components, entered into a dialogue with various individuals and groups in the Jewish community abroad. This was not a simple matter since, historically, Israeli governments usually basked in the sun of unanimous Jewish support from abroad. Though this support had its source in a sense of ethnic solidarity built on deep historical sensitivity, Israeli governments did not hesitate to mobilize it as over-the-counter political currency to back its current political line.

We have mentioned that support groups in the form of Women In Black vigils appeared abroad, some directly linked with the Israeli movement and its demands, others expressing more local interests and interpretations of events in the region. Yesh Gvul succeeded in organizing several support groups abroad, usually to adopt prisoner "refuseniks," providing financial assistance to their families. The growth of Americans for Peace Now was a major development in this respect. Americans for Peace Now was established as a Jewish organization in support of a mainstream, Zionist peace movement in Israel. It succeeded in expressing a growing mood in broad sections of the North American Jewish community which sought to disassociate themselves from the practices and the rhetoric of the Shamir government and the Israel Defense Forces under the tutelage of Defense Minister Yitzhak Rabin – without disassociating themselves from their conventional obligations as Jews to support Israel. Peace Now, which was always careful to stress that it was a Zionist and patriotic movement, commanded sufficient respectability and intellectual cadre in Israel necessary to ensure some sort of hearing in many established Jewish organizations and congregations.

The development of Americans for Peace Now during 1989 and 1990 was one indication of changes in the political landscape of US Jewry. The American movement, which was run by a single staff person up to 1989 had 15 staff and board members by the middle of 1990. More important, Americans for Peace Now was beginning to present itself as a political alternative to the powerful AIPAC lobby (American Israel Public Affairs Committee) and claimed that is was speaking for half of Israel's citizens.[11]

During the first years of the Intifada there was a steady stream of announcements in the press by groups of concerned Jews and peace groups from abroad. Jews expressed pain and anguish that Israel was acting against its best interests, while various peace groups stressed condemnation of Israeli actions in the territories and called for some form of international intervention. Michael Lerner, editor of *Tikun* magazine, was instrumental in organizing and crystallizing Jewish criticism of the Shamir government at a conference of 1,500 young adults in New York in December 1988. Tikun's Committee for Judaism and Social Justice sponsored a full-page advertisement in the *New York Times*, in April 1989, signed by prominent American Jewish intellectuals. Critics of Lerner and the Jewish doves claimed that these activities were the antics of a stylish minority, but there were more and more polls that indicated growing erosion of support

for Shamir among US Jews. A poll conducted by Professor Steve
Cohen at New York University among 800 of the most prominent leaders of US Jewry, from all currents and organizations,
showed a tremendous gap between this group and official Israeli
policy – with more than two-thirds of those asked expressing
concern that "continued Israeli occupation of the territories would
undermine the democratic and humanitarian nature of Israel."[12]
The discomfort with hard-line Israeli policies slipped into public
view on more than one occasion. A majority at the convention
of the American National Jewish Community Relations Advisory
Council voted against settling immigrants from the Soviet Union
in Judea, Samaria and Gaza and also declined to call on the US
Administration to discontinue its dialogue with the PLO.[13] It was,
of course, impossible to know exactly how Jewish public opinion
stood. One thing was clear. It was harder and harder for Shamir
and Israel to depend on the traditionally automatic support of the
entire US Jewish community.

It fell to the European peace movement and its parliamentary
section in the European Parliament to have a direct and immediate
impact on the protest scene in Israel. European public opinion
was generally more sensitive to the Palestinian question and the
European peace movement could go to the region in the name of
wide sections of the growing European community. Representatives
of the European peace movement had a bold, concrete suggestion: to
export to Israel the idea of a human chain for peace – which would
be composed of Israelis, Palestinians and European guests. The
success of the entire project depended on finding an organizational
format that would ensure the participation of all the main peace
forces. It was not easy, but the European peace movement had
succeeded in organizing protest action in the USSR during the
Brezhnev era and in Poland, in support of Solidarity when the
Polish trade union was still banned. Its activists knew something
about operating on unfriendly terrain.

Protest – When it Works!

Peace Now's readiness to organize a major activity together with
the Palestinians and overseas peace organizations marked a new
stage in the group's militancy. This militancy was also a decisive
factor in its decision to hold a demonstration to mark the second

anniversary of the Intifada at the beginning of December 1989. Though commemoration of the second anniversary of the Intifada was mainly a Palestinian affair – the date threatened to be the occasion for violent clashes between the Israel Defense Forces and the population in the territories – Peace Now decided that it could not bypass the significance of the date for the Israeli public. Taking into account the problematic nature of the anniversary, Peace Now exercised caution and tact in choosing to make the deaths of Jewish and Arab children the main theme of the demonstration called in Jerusalem on December 9, 1989. More than 3,500 participated in one of the largest Peace Now rallies held in Jerusalem.[14]

In a flyer issued in preparation for the demonstration, Peace Now spoke with unprecedented candor about its support for the establishment of a Palestinian state and called for: "Dialogue with the PLO on the basis of the principle of peace in exchange for territory in which a Palestinian state will be established alongside of Israel."[15] At the end of the rally, Peace Now announced that it was sponsoring an "arms for peace – human chain around the Old City" at the end of the month.

After initial contacts with Peace Now leader Tsali Reshef in Rome in June 1989, representatives of the Italian and other European peace movements visited Israel a number of times during the fall of 1989 and conducted a long series of meetings and negotiations with the Palestinians and the different Israeli peace groups. Cooperation between the Europeans and the Palestinians – given the similarity in their positions – did not involve any political difficulties. It was Peace Now that had the more serious misgivings about the whole idea. Janet Aviad, a key Peace Now representative, expressed anxiety that the coalition would be perceived as "anti-Israeli" by most Israelis. In the end, Peace Now decided to co-sponsor the event after it was satisfied that organizationally Peace Now would be representing the Israeli "side" and that the political platform would include explicit support for Israel's security.[16] Peace Now did not hesitate to agree to the inclusion of a cluster of women's activities, including a Women In Black march, in the schedule of events. Moreover, all agreed that visitors from abroad could – and actually did – use their five-day sojourn to divide into groups which participated in various programs organized by Palestinians and Israeli protest groups. The Europeans were able to meet with most of the Israeli protest groups, and even managed to take part in demonstrations by Yesh

Gvul at the Atlit military prison and by Hal'ah Ha'kibush in the Golan.

The European representatives, specifically Ciarra Ingrao and Tom Bentolli, impressed all sides with their patience and tact and above all – with their political savvy. The Europeans were involved in a risky and complicated project. They were not merely coordinating and lending their "good offices." The centerpiece of the project was the plan to bring over more than 1,000 activists from Europe. Their presence would ensure European interest and media attention and serve as a symbol of the international unity of the peace movement. On the other hand, tensions between the organizers or between them and the Israeli authorities could disrupt the proceedings and lead to the cancellation of the entire project without advance notice. Bringing more than a thousand supporters from one continent to another and into the charged atmosphere of Jerusalem demanded political daring and logistical resourcefulness. The Europeans, it turned out, were up to it.

Though the Palestinians were represented by Faisal Husseini (Fatah) and Rassan El Hativ (the Palestinian Communist Party), there was no guarantee that they would be able to bring out their supporters to a licensed and legal demonstration organized in conjunction with Israelis. Doubts on this score were particularly acute since other secular and Islamic Palestinian groups expressed open opposition to the project.

Red Brigades on the Walls of Jerusalem?

The government was unhappy about the scheduled event. The Prime Minister's Office and the Ministry of Foreign Affairs let the press know of their opposition and their efforts to curtail or to ban the activities, including plans to prevent Palestinians in the territories from reaching Jerusalem.[17] But, the government could not ban the event without confirming – for the benefit of the international media – many of the worst allegations about the anti-democratic nature of the occupation. Moreover, the government wanted to manipulate the event to prove that Jerusalem was sovereign, Israeli territory, where the right to assembly was fully protected (unlike the situation in the occupied territories). Insistent reports suggested that the Israel Defense Forces would restrict entrance to Jerusalem the day of the major activity. The authorities were not invoking the law, but they wanted everyone to know their low opinion of the planned proceedings. They were really "part of a PLO campaign to embarrass Israel," and "interference in Israeli internal affairs" by MPs from Europe, something like Israeli MKs "going to Italy to demonstrate with the Red Brigades."[18]

Protest Puts Peace on the Agenda

The following account of the main activities which took place under the rubric – 1990 Time For Peace – is based on a number of reports.[19] The events of Women's Day, December 29, 1989 were organized by "Women and Peace," a broad-based coalition of women's peace groups. The day's proceeding opened with a mass conference of 1,500 women convened on the basis of calls to end the occupation and negotiate with the PLO, and for "two-states for two peoples." The speakers included Masha Lubelski, General-Secretary of the Histadrut women's organization, Na'amat. Zahira Kamal, Chair-women of the Palestinian Women's Committee, Caterina Ronko of the Women's House in Turino, Rebecca Johnson, a leader of the Greenham Common women, Naomi Hazan, one of the founders of the "Reshet," the Women's Peace Net, Prof. Alice Shalvi, Chair of the Israeli Women's Lobby and many other leading activists.

In the afternoon, the participants of the morning conference joined an additional 1,500 women (all 3,000 dressed in black) to join the weekly Women In Black vigil in central Jerusalem. At the end of the vigil, thousands of Women In Black marched to East Jerusalem to be met by hundreds of Palestinian women. Police estimated that the procession of women, chanting and singing, swelled to 5,000 as the women poured into the area around the El Ha-Kawati theater. At this point, police moved in with clubs and tear gas against a small group of teenagers who were shouting slogans and waving the Palestinian flag. In the ensuing melee, many women were wounded and seventeen were detained (and later released) by the police.

The next day, approximately 30,000 Israelis, Palestinians and guests from abroad joined hands and created a 5.5 kilometer human chain around the Old City of Jerusalem. Expert observers put the number of Palestinian participants at over 5,000 and noticed that many Palestinians joined the activity spontaneously. The festive holiday atmosphere was dispelled when, towards the end of the activity, 2,000 police and border guards, equipped with clubs, rifles, tear gas canisters and water cannon smashed into a section of the human chain under the pretext that young Palestinians were shouting anti-Israeli slogans. The police action, which became the subject of widespread comment and criticism in the following weeks, led to the wounding of 50 demonstrators and 50 arrests.

The Aftermath

The echo of clashes between peace demonstrators and the police or the army usually die down a day or two after the events. Accusations of police misconduct are treated as part of the effort to command further media attention. This was not the case regarding the behavior of the police at the human chain demonstration.[20] Too many people were brutally attacked, arrested and wounded, and no less important, too many representatives of the media – including scores of photographers – were present for the police behavior to remain unchallenged. Criticism of police behavior and requests for an inquiry came from sources distant from the dove community. One editorial cited the shocking similarity between police brutality in Jerusalem and "normal" police behavior towards the Intifada in the occupied territories. "Collective punishment such as this, reminds us of the territories, and indeed, yesterday at the gates of the walls of Jerusalem, we received a shocking example of how the occupation norms are seeping over the Green Line. Only the uninformed will ignore the connection between the forms of repression to which we have become accustomed in the territories and the unprecedented spectacle of policeman shooting rubber bullets and showering blows on citizens exercising their right to demonstrate . . . and as the right to protest is indivisible, those who deny it to the Palestinians will end up denying it to the Jews."[21]

Peace Now prepared a detailed brief on police misconduct. Moreover, there was pressure on the government: "In a briefing for foreign reporters . . . Olmert, who is the minister in charge of Arab Affairs, faced a torrent of criticism from journalists who were at the demonstration yesterday . . . [who] charged that police 'randomly beat' the protesters . . . "[22] A day later, Police Commissioner David Krause ordered all films of the Peace Now demonstration on Saturday to be checked for scenes showing excessive police violence. Two weeks after the demonstration Peace Now submitted a copy of its report to Police Minister, Bar Lev. The report was based on evidence from 56 participants in the demonstration many of whom were injured during the police attack. Peace Now leaders also submitted documentation based on video clips filmed during the event by foreign news networks, as well as evidence gathered from many camera and news people who were covering the event. Peace Now threatened that if an independent inquiry, headed by a judge, was not instituted, it would petition the High Court of Justice.[23] Just a few days later, Commissioner Krause ordered a Jerusalem policeman, filmed needlessly beating two demonstrators, removed from his post and announced that the police were trying to ascertain the identity of yet another policeman, filmed while firing rubber bullets at fleeing demonstrators.[24] In the wake of continuing local and international pressure, an investigation team formed of representatives of the police and the Attorney-General's office was appointed. Its report, submitted to the Chief-Inspector on April 8, 1990, blamed the chain of events on the poor judgment of officers on the spot and determined, inter alia, that (1) "there was no escalation that justified the forceful dispersal of the crowd by force just a few minutes before the natural end of the event," and (2) "the escalation and the general confusion . . . resulted from the police action," and (3) "there is no doubt that there was no basis for the use of force against people who were following instructions to disperse . . . such use is against the law."[25] A series of criminal proceedings and disciplinary actions were initiated. Peace Now had the satisfaction, so rare in circumstances such as these, of having the last word in the affair: "The norm of false reports by police personnel such as those given during the internal investigations of the violent turn of events during Peace Now's demonstration in Jerusalem must be abolished . . . demands Peace Now . . . In response to the publication of the report issued by the State-Attorney, Dorit Beinish, Peace Now welcomed the fact that the truth has been revealed and criticized police spokesmen and the former Minister of Police, Bar Lev, for their hasty responses blaming Peace Now and concocting descriptions of non-existent violence, Palestinian flags and rioting."[26]

The violent turn of events near the walls of the Old City commanded tremendous media attention. Moreover, the successful effort by Peace Now and the dove public to expose the responsibility of the police for the way the events developed were an important success for the peace camp. However, with all their importance, the main significance of the protest action during the last days of 1989 lay elsewhere. The activity that hoped to define 1990 as the Year of Peace marked an unprecedented level of cooperation between the Palestinian leadership in the territories and the Israeli peace movement. The experience, mutual respect and understanding that had accumulated over the years created the basis for joint action on the ground – despite a myriad of political and technical obstacles to such action. The Palestinian leadership had the breadth of vision and the flexibility to engage in an ongoing dialogue with mainstream, patriotic (Zionist) political groups such as Peace Now. Peace Now had the courage to discard its previous tendency to view the Palestinian national liberation movement as "the enemy" and to link up with those representing the patriotic, but realistic trends in the Palestinian community under occupation.

This meeting of the minds, and some reported a meeting of the hearts as well, would have been inconceivable without a long "human chain" of meetings and dialogue that began early in the seventies – first between Israeli radicals and the Palestinian left and later between militant sections of the Israeli peace movement and forward looking elements in the PLO. This project, which involved mass participation of rank and file Israelis (women and men) and Palestinians (women and men) living in the grim world of Israeli domination and repression, could never have gotten off the ground without the preceding intensive interaction between Israeli peace groups and Palestinians from the first weeks of the Intifada.

It was clear that protest, alone, no matter how effective, could not move the "national unity" government on to the path to peace. The hope was that the protest movement, along with diplomatic pressures on Israel, would make life unbearable for those sections of the Labor Party which refused to remain in the Shamir government and become accessories to the execution of the Greater Israel settlement and annexation program. Life was indeed becoming unbearable in the Shamir–Rabin government of national unity.

11

Crisis at the Top

The growing tensions between the two main parties, Likud and Labor, in the Israeli national unity government, along with the successes of the protest movement, led to a long, bitter government crisis in the spring of 1990. Tensions in the cabinet led to the expulsion, on December 31, 1989, of Transportation Minister Ezer Weizman from the Shamir government for holding secret, "private" talks with the PLO. Formally speaking, Weizman's personal decision to meet with PLO representatives may have been "improper" and even against the law. In political terms, Weizman had joined a constantly growing list of establishment figures who came to the conclusion that there was no real alternative to talks with the PLO – if there was a real desire to break out of the deadlock. And this was exactly the central demand of all sections of the peace movement, militants and moderates alike, since the PLO moved towards recognition of Israel at the meeting of the Palestinian National Council (Algiers, November 1988). The demand to recognize the PLO – the central demand of the entire peace movement – was gaining advocates in the heart of the political establishment. Weizman had launched his own private initiative to examine the prospects for an agreement with the PLO.

Labor protested Shamir's sanctions against Weizman and threatened to leave the coalition. However, despite its ostensible indignation, Labor accepted a face-saving compromise in order to avoid leaving the coalition on an issue linked to the recognition of the PLO. Weizman was returned to his cabinet post after a degrading compromise stipulated his expulsion from the prestigious ten-minister "inner cabinet on security affairs." Weizman, one of Israel's most venerated war heroes, was treated as some kind of a security risk and publicly disciplined for talking with the PLO. Labor decided to swallow the bitter pill, enabling Shamir to come out of the mini-crisis with enhanced prestige. The partnership between the two major parties was, for all practical purposes, an effective excuse for avoiding serious discussion of any possible compromise with the Palestinians and the Arab countries. The result was that the Likud program which promised to attain peace on the basis of the territorial status quo – and not the Labor program of 'land for peace' – prevailed and determined the course of events.

The United States was pressing Israel at the time to agree to elections in the territories as an alternative to continuation of the Intifada. Formally, Shamir's answer to Baker's demand for concrete steps towards elections in the territories was affirmative, but it included enough reservations to guarantee continued diplomatic paralysis. When the Labor Party refused to go along yet another time with Shamir's delaying tactics, the national unity government fell by a non-confidence vote of 60 to 55, on March 15, 1990. Meanwhile, Shimon Peres, then the undisputed leader of the party, had obtained assurances from the ultra-orthodox religious parties, who were uncomfortable about straining relations with the US, that they would join a new Labor-led coalition. The difficulty was that the ultra-orthodox parliamentary factions were themselves fairly loose coalitions of different sectarian groupings and different MKs owed their ultimate allegiance to an assortment of rabbinical authorities. As their leaders moved towards the establishment of a slim Labor-led majority, several of the more hawkish ultra-orthodox MKs, bolted from their factions, leaving Labor short of the majority required to form a coalition.

As the weeks turned into months, the leaders of the two main parties found themselves competing for the favors of this or that venerated Rabbi, making deals to wean political non-entities away from the rival party, and staving off threats from disgruntled rank and file MKs to change camps in exchange for political (and even financial) perks. It was a disgusting scene and one of the low points in Israeli parliamentary history. Labor had taken responsibility for breaking up the coalition and was committed to winning the battle to form an alternative coalition at all costs. Peres had promised many party leaders, including Yitzhak Rabin, that the stratagem would work. However, the Likud was able to discover and undermine weak spots in the shaky edifice that Labor was trying desperately to erect. Most of the deflections were to the right and eventually Shamir was able to reconstitute a coalition, without Labor. The entire performance was so disgusting that many Israelis actually forgot what the real issues were.

Though the peace movement continued to be active during the first half of 1990, center stage was occupied by the long, drawn-out battle between the two main parties. Both were bogged down in the mire and equally open to public criticism, but for most doves there was still a genuine political distinction between Labor's flexibility and the Likud's intransigence on the question of peace. The peace forces in the country had, naturally enough, hoped for a Labor success which would have, at the least, broken the deadlock on the diplomatic front.

Ersatz Protest

During the long weeks of fierce and unprincipled competition between the two large parties for the favors of this or that individual member of the Knesset, a new and different kind of protest movement emerged and gathered strength. It was a movement aimed at protesting the degradation of parliamentary life since the fall of the national unity government on March 15, 1990 and it believed that it had a panacea for all the imperfections of the Israeli political system – electoral reform.

Critics of the Israeli political system have always berated the country's proportional representation election system and argued for regional elections which would ensure the formation of a stable government by one of two alternative ruling parties. As the "buying and selling" of MKs took on alarming proportions, and there was a sense that no stable government could emerge, a movement for electoral reform grew from day to day. In a number of weeks, a core group demonstrating outside the Knesseth attracted wide spread public support and funding. At the height of its activity, tens of thousand of Israelis came out to support the demands of the Movement for Changing the System.

Most intellectuals in the dove community were highly critical of the reform movement's aims and style. Prof. Leon Shelef, an expert in sociological and legal issues, pointed out that the real crisis in Israeli society did not stem from the system of government and could not be solved by changes in the system.[1] According to Shelef, there was a real danger to Israeli democracy but it stemmed from the "prolonged military occupation and domination of another people."[2] When the parliamentary crisis ended with the establishment of a Likud-led government, with Labor in the opposition, interest in electoral reform and the impact of "The Movement to Change the System" faded as quickly as it emerged.

The movement to institute a constitution in the country or the initiative for electoral reform, in and of themselves are, of course, legitimate and many of the fiercest critics of the Movement to Change the System have endorsed one form or another of modification of Israel's electoral system. Moreover, both major parties are on the record as favoring changes in the electoral system and as of now (1995), the next national elections will provide for the direct election of the prime minister. Even so, protest which deals with the symptoms of a problem and often distracts public attention from the essential problem is a poor substitute for the real thing. In the Israeli context, attacks on parliamentary democracy which exploit the complications involved in multi-party rule are doubly dangerous considering the fragile nature of Israel's democratic institutions and the lack of constitutional limits on the executive.

Business as Usual (Almost)

During the prolonged government crisis and the first months of Shamir's "new" government, roughly the first half of 1990, the peace movement went on to broaden and deepen its public influence. The Reshet (Israeli Women's Network for Peace) established itself as a new and fresh element on the protest scene. In cooperation with other women's groups, the Reshet held a daring Israeli-Palestinian rally on the boundary between West and East Jerusalem, marking International Women's Day on March 10, 1990. Masha Lubelsky, Na'amat Secretary-General, Yael Dayan, and MK Shulamit Aloni led the Israeli women; Zahira Kamal headed the Palestinian delegation. The two delegations concluded the rally by endorsing a clear "two-state" resolution. In the spirit of the event, after the rally, Lubelsky visited Faisal Husseini, then under house arrest, and invited him to address the Na'amat secretariat.[3]

Peace Now devoted much of its energy during this same period to expanding its organizational reach, geographically and sociologically. Regional conferences were held in places like the Negev with participants from Be'er Sheva, the development towns

of Arad, Ofakim, and kibbutzim in the area (February, 1990). Peace
Now attracted four hundred people to an open discussion in Be'er
Sheva and movement activists held meetings and distributed information during a "Woodstock-style" festival in Elat (April 1990).
There were several smaller demonstrations: (a) in response to settler
provocations – namely the establishment of a Jewish settlement in
the Christian Quarter of Jerusalem (April 15, 1990); (b) against the
establishment of a new settlement at Dugit in the West Bank (April
24, 1990); (c) against a official state celebration marking 13 years of
settlement at Elkana (May 13, 1990).

In truth there was almost an atmosphere of "business as usual"
in the country until, early in the morning of May 20, 1990, a
young Israeli, named Ami Popper, opened fire on a group of
workers near Rishon La'tsion, killing eight and wounding tens.
At a Peace Now rally at the end of the week, the author Amos
Oz told fifty thousand demonstrators that it was a disgrace that
such a crime could have been committed so leisurely and with so
little interference.[4] Hatred and racism were spreading and taking
root in Israeli society, especially among those who grew up during
the occupation and were unable to conceive of any alternative to
violence and repression in the territories. Educators and public
opinion samplers agreed that young people, especially among the
urban poor and working-class families, were increasingly suscep-
tible to flagrant anti-Arab racism. The peace movement may have
become stronger and more organized, but its members shared a
dreadful feeling that, in a process of polarization, they were losing
the battle to those who stood to gain from the politics of hatred and
violence.

Permanent Assets

A number of important groups formed by peace activists came
to the fore in the second stage of the Intifada during 1989 and
1990. Three of these – the human rights organization, B'tselem,
Kav L'oved, which dealt with the specific problems of Palestinian
workers from the territories who worked in Israel and the Israeli
Committee Against Torture – operated on the principle that there
were many immediate issues affecting the life and the welfare
of the Palestinians under occupation, which demanded continuous, specialized treatment. The founders of these organizations

expressed unease and dissatisfaction with what they considered stifling limitations in the peace movement which stemmed, in their opinion, from an over emphasis on the conventional and routine forms of protest. These invariably dealt with central political issues and events in the news. While no one doubted the importance of the pressing day-to-day political battles, the founders of these new groups became convinced that there was a place for action designed to ameliorate conditions under occupation or to expose, on the basis of methodical research and long term investigation, its worse aspects. These organizations could not base themselves on sporadic 'mobilizations' and spontaneous bursts of energy. Their success depended on creating and training a core of permanent staff people and volunteers who would acquire expertise on the basis of prolonged experience in the field. By far the most prominent of these groups was B'tselem, the Israeli Information Center for Human Rights in the Occupied Territories.

The idea for the establishment of a center to document the abuse of human rights during the Intifada circulated in more than one group during the second half of 1988. MK Dedi Zucker, of the Citizen's Rights Movement, who was, together with MK Yossi Sarid, exceptionally active in exposing the more sordid aspects of IDF behavior, was prominent among those working on the idea. In addition, Dr. Eddy Kaufman, a political scientist at the Hebrew University, previously associated with Amnesty International, was also working on a similar conception.

The fact that the United States stressed the "human rights" issue in order to criticize Israeli policy regarding the Intifada certainly encouraged concerned Israelis to undertake a documentation project. B'tselem,[5] created in March 1989 in direct response to the situation in the territories, defined its goals in the following way:

> Its primary task is the systematic collection of data on human rights issues in the occupied territories and dissemination of reliable information. Its second task is to educate the Israeli public about international human rights standards and norms, and to foster public debate within Israel on the nature and scope of human rights violations and their impact, both short-term and long, on Israeli society and its democratic character.[6]

A certain vacuum regarding the defense of human rights in the occupied territories reinforced the need to establish B'tselem. The

Israeli Association for Civil Rights, established in 1971, had a distinguished record in the civil rights field. However, the Association which patterned its work on lines similar to those of the American Civil Liberties Union (ACLU), decided not to take on the new and highly controversial responsibility for documenting violations of human rights in the occupied territories. There were different reasons for the hesitations. Technically and legalistically speaking, the occupied territories were not "in Israel" and did not fit into the Association's formal terms of reference. Moreover, the Association was involved mainly in issue-related litigation. Educational work regarding the territories was problematic because there were different approaches in the Association regarding the rationale for government activity in the territories. In all fairness, it must be said, the Association did eventually undertake a vast amount of important litigation in defense of Palestinian rights in the territories and in Israeli jails. For this purpose it employed a number of attorneys whose main task was representing Palestinians in the IDF military courts. In one noteworthy project, Attorney Tamar Peleg represented the Israeli Association for Civil Rights in a running battle during 1988 and 1989 against infringements of the rights of Palestinian prisoners in the Ansar Prison in the Negev. Peleg wrested a number of concessions from the prison authorities by a combination of techniques which included floods of formal complaints, press releases and threats to turn to the High Court of Justice. The close monitoring and protesting of conditions in Ansar was critical in defending the rights and the dignity of thousands of Palestinians.

B'tselem – "In His Image"

Conditions created by repression during the Intifada had sparked the establishment of several Palestinian organizations in the human rights area. Some of them, such as "al-Haq, Law in the Service of Man," in Ramallah, the Palestinian Human Rights Information Center and the Jerusalem Media and Communication Center, turned out credible, professional reports. However, in the given circumstances, no Arab or Palestinian source of information, however reliable or accurate, could hope to influence the Israeli media and Israeli public opinion. B'tselem explained, in this context, that "there is hardly any public debate on human rights in Israel" and that this is due "in part to psychological rejection of information from international and Arab sources."[7]

B'tselem's political orientation and the composition of its first Board of Directors placed it in the more moderate sector of the Israeli peace movement. Zucker, whose dedication and fund-raising talents were decisive in establishing B'tselem, was clearly interested in attracting support from Labor Party circles and two Labor MKs, Haim Ramon and Amir Peretz, agreed to serve on the 23-person board of Directors. B'tselem's original statement offered the view that Israel had attempted to maintain a delicate balance between . . . security and . . . human rights up to the outbreak of the Intifada.[8] This somewhat rather one-sided description of the pre-Intifada period suggests that the human rights violations were somehow a result of the Intifada and not the occupation itself. B'tselem took pains to stress that:

> B'tselem was created out of a deep commitment to and concern for the humanistic character and security of the State of Israel. These principles underlie all of the center's activities . . . Unlike other human rights organizations . . . B'tselem is directed and staffed by Israelis, issues publications in Hebrew, and addresses Israelis as its primary constituency.[9]

This approach contains a slightly veiled criticism of other, mainly Palestinian human rights groups which considered international public opinion as their "primary constituency." Fortunately, these concessions to establishment rhetoric – which may have been only lip service in the cause of respectability – did not impair the efficiency of the organization or the ethics of its staff. From its first publications, it became clear that B'tselem was not going to pull any punches.

From the spring of 1989, B'tselem issued a stream of monthly publications, and information bulletins. The bulletins covered current statistics and occasionally issued a special summary of the situation in particular areas such as Freedom of Expression or Closure of Educational Institutions. The first Annual Report (1989) of the Center is an amazing and agonizing catalog of repressive measures. The Center took meticulous care to explain all its sources, its verification techniques, and discrepancies in findings where these occurred. The material was accompanied by tables and graphs and included breakdowns by district, age of the victims and other relevant materials. The Center's report deals with fatalities, injuries, demolition and sealing-off houses, deportations, detention and imprisonment, administrative detention, curfew, limitations on the freedom of expression, the closure of educational institutions, deportation of illegal residents, discrimination in the enforcement of the law, trials of IDF personnel for manslaughter, beatings, and property offenses.

B'tselem made judicious use of contacts and cooperation with the Palestinian human rights groups, especially al-Haq/Law in the Service of Man and the Palestinian Human Rights Information Center. It submitted all its data to the IDF and took upon itself to print any official responses. Since denials by Israel Defense Forces spokespersons were few and far between, this practice by the Center served to enhance its credibility.

The Center overcame its initial hesitations about printing its findings in English. The arguments against printing and disseminating material in English were both ideological and pragmatic. It must be explained that there were human rights advocates who were willing, ideologically, to criticize their own government on such matters, but held that dissemination of the materials abroad was unacceptable as it would provide propaganda ammunition to Israel's enemies. The "pragmatic" argument was that if you appear to "wash your dirty linen" abroad, Israeli public opinion will assume that you have an anti-patriotic axe to grind and conclude that your motives are suspect. Despite these arguments, the attempt to limit the Center's service exclusively to the Hebrew-reading public collapsed early in the life of the Center. The plain fact of the matter was that Israeli media relate to human rights information directly in proportion to its international reverberations. Moreover, people in the human rights field quickly understood that any serious effort to restrain repression depended on international interest and concern.

No doubt that much of the credit for the success of B'tselem goes to it first director, Zahava Gal'on, and her determination to make the Israeli public aware of the abuses in the human rights area. Before the year ended, B'tselem received, along with al-Haq, the Carter–Menil Human Rights Award issued by the Carter Center at Emory University in Atlanta. The $100,000 prize, awarded at a ceremony with Jimmy and Rosalind Carter in attendance, helped the Center, which had received start-up funds from the Ford Foundation, the New Israel Fund and others to intensify its fund-raising activity.[10]

B'tselem and the steady stream of information which it issued made a difference in Israeli political discourse. The verification and documentation of human rights violations in the territories reinforced the urgency and enhanced the credibility of the message that the protest movement was trying to get across to the Israeli public. Protest often followed an effective pattern: journalists who had come to see the Palestinians as the underdog, succeeded in exposing various "excesses" by the occupation army.[11] Naturally enough, protest groups centered much of their efforts on such exposures and when successful, served to remind the public of its moral and political responsibility for these same acts being perpetrated in its name. Then, once again, at a later stage, B'tselem reports dealt with the same set of events and usually proved that (1) the media reports had been accurate or even understated, (2) protest action had been completely justified and in fact, repression was far worse in reality than most observers had assumed.

"A Moderate Amount of Physical Pressure"

Documented charges about the systematic use of torture during interrogations by the General Security Services (SHABAK) predate the Intifada and have been, on more than one occasion, the subject of international scrutiny.[12] It was the familiar scenario of a frame-up – based on a forced confession – which unravelled and led to the establishment of an official government commission headed by Supreme Court President, Justice Moshe Landau in June, 1987. The report issued on the eve of the Intifada found that the General Security Services (SHABAK) had systematically lied to the courts for decades (!) denying that it was using force to extract confessions. The report then recommended that officials involved in past perjury and torture be exempt from prosecution and went on to permit "non-violent psychological pressure" and concluded that "when these do not attain their purpose, the exertion of a moderate amount of physical pressure is not to be avoided." Operational instructions for exerting such pressure are included in a secret, unpublished section of the report.[13]

The psychiatrist, Yoachim Stein, who had been prominent in Imut and Stan Cohen, Professor of Criminology at the Hebrew University, who was one of the key figures in Dai La'kibush during the first years of the Intifada, were the moving spirits in the establishment of The Public Committee Against Torture in Israel towards the end of

1989. The constitutive declaration of the Public Committee Against Torture in Israel discusses the inherent difficulties in achieving its goal.

> For obvious reasons, it is very difficult to provide detailed proof of the existence of torture. Our main work will be to locate cases – particularly where there is evidence beyond the victim's testimonies – and carry out research on the circumstances of each case.[14]

The declaration goes on to enumerate other forms of activity such as "analyzing past decisions to determine possible influence of torture . . . publicity in the Israeli media, lobbying and influencing public opinion abroad."[15]

The torture issue always aroused intense emotions in Israel. Most liberals were sincerely convinced that there were mitigating circumstances in Israel's severe security problems. They tended to believe the government's "ticking time bomb" justification that torture was a legitimate method to force prisoners to divulge information in order to save lives. Maybe it was just too difficult for many Israelis to conceive of members of their own families as torturers. The extreme sensitivity regarding the torture issue goes a long way in explaining why the composition of the Committee was certainly more radical than that of B'tselem. Avigdor Feldman, the committee's legal advisor, Leah Zemel, and Dr. Ruhama Marton were among the founding members and were known publicly for their readiness to defend the rights of Palestinians, radicals and other unpopular causes. They and others who established the Committee were convinced that Israel was using torture systematically, and this meant that Israeli democracy was far from secure.

Sickening Regularity

The Public Committee Against Torture in Israel convened a press conference in April 1990 in Jerusalem, where it presented results of its research and first-hand testimony on cases under the jurisdiction of the police, the General Security Services (SHABAK) and the investigative arm of the Military Police. Stan Cohen dwelt on the special circumstances that led to the formation of the Committee: "Now in the context of the Intifada, every human rights organization and every lawyer working with Palestinian clients hears these stories with sickening regularity . . . As if this was not bad enough . . . the authorities actually ended up providing a formal justification for torture."[16]

The work of the Public Committee Against Torture in Israel certainly helped to convince B'tselem that the subject deserved special treatment and to launch an intensive research project that followed up individual cases over 1989–90. The 150-page report, "The Interrogation of Palestinians During the Intifada: Ill Treatment, 'Moderate Physical Pressure' or Torture?" authored by Stanley Cohen and B'tselem Research Director, Daphna Golan, was published in March 1991 and had an enormous impact. The Report was based on interviews with adult male Palestinians who were selected from among a list of 60 names (provided by lawyers and human rights organizations). Twenty-six of the 41 had been recently released and fifteen others testified via affidavits given to lawyers.[17]

The pattern that emerged was shockingly clear. During an interrogation period that ranged from 10 to 18 days, virtually every prisoner was subjected to most of the ten following abuses: (i) verbal insults and abuse; (ii) threats to the defendant or his family; (iii) sleep and food deprivation; (iv) "hooding", covering the head with a sack – usually wet – for hours; (v) prolonged painful confinement crouched in small cells (the "closet" or the "refrigerator"); (vi) being tied up for long periods in deliberately painful positions; (vii) use of collaborators to exact evidence through violence or threats of violence; (viii) forced physical exercise; (ix) cold showers and sitting on a wet floor for prolonged periods; (x) severe beatings on all parts of the body.

Not one of the 41 interviewees, all of whom except for one had been beaten, was found guilty or even suspected of the type of "hostile terrorist activity" for which the Landau Commission justified the use of "moderate physical pressure." Of the 26 released detainees, only 12 were ever charged and three were put in administrative arrest. No correlation was found between the severity of the interrogation and the seriousness of the offence. On the other hand, there was no evidence of the use of special equipment or electric shock. B'tselem cites three factors which served to undermine protection and prohibitions available in the legal system: (1) the long period of incommunicado detention – usually for a period up to 30 days; (2) the prestige and power of the General Security Services and the absence of public surveillance;

and (3) the difficulty of challenging confessions in court. B'tselem did not hesitate to note the additional responsibility of the Landau Commission for weakening the absolute moral taboo against torture.

B'tselem understood full well that the credibility of the victims could and would be challenged and that such testimonies were subject, by their very nature, to willful or unintentional exaggerations and inaccuracy. Even so, B'tselem was convinced that the detailed internal consistency in the interviews, often backed by medical evidence, together with information from the human rights groups and lawyers revealed beyond any reasonable doubt an accurate picture of the experience of this group of detainees. At first, B'tselem estimated that approximately 1,500 or 2,000 Palestinians experienced these interrogation methods in one combination or another. During research for a Follow-up Report, B'tselem realized that the number was probably closer to 5,000.

The Awful Truth

There is something about accusations of torture which grates the raw nerves of any political system. Israel was no exception, and the publication of convincing evidence of systematic violation of prisoners' basic human rights catapulted the B'tselem Report into the center of an intense public controversy. The coverage of the Report and the press conference which presented it was unprecedented. Sketches from the Report of contorted, trussed-up human figures were spread over the pages of the entire press. Much of the public response split along familiar ideological lines. Even so, the wrath of the right seemed particularly frenzied. Limor Livnat, a prominent Likud spokesperson, refused to read the Report in order to avoid being contaminated by the "moral obscenity" of its source and determined that "if a group like B'tselem had existed when Israel was being established, a Jewish state would not have come into being." Shlomo Goren, former Chief Rabbi of Israel and the IDF identified the writers of the Report as "traitors to the people of Israel . . . They serve our enemies. Because they are traitors they were not created in the image (b'tselem) of God."[18] One criticism of the Report is worthy of special comment. Justice Landau himself published an open letter in the mass circulation daily, *Yediot Ahronot*, denying any causal connection whatsoever between the allegations in the Report and recommendations of his Commission.[19]

The Deconstruction of the B'tselem Report

Interestingly, the B'tselem Report on torture was also the object of some specific criticism from the left. Dr. Adi Ophir, one of the founders of The Twenty-first Year (which no longer existed for all practical purposes when the B'tselem Report was published) had become one of the leading exponents of post-modernist ideas and concepts in Israeli academia. Ophir turned his attention to the B'tselem Report in a series of three lengthy articles in the literary supplement of *Davar*.[20]

His critique of the Report was radical and comprehensive. Ophir attacked the Report and its authors for accepting the rules and the self-limitations of standard human rights discourse since "the authors of the B'tselem Report are unwilling to link the nature of the abuse to the nature of the regime – the occupation regime – which institutionalizes and legitimizes it." Ophir understood that exposing this link was beyond the authors' mandate, but sees acceptance of such limitations as part of a fatal surrender: "Their [the authors] rhetorical strategy assumes . . . that it is possible to extricate a description of social reality from the forces which are striving to mold it. In a post-modern world . . . this approach appears naive if not ridiculous." By accepting the rules of the "alternative information" game, "this Report merges with the hegemonic political discourse, created by the occupation regime as the natural order of things, a discourse whose task is to 'normalize' the relations between the conqueror and the conquered." Ophir considers it a fatal fault that "there is no alternative world view, no real challenge to the forms of representation used by the occupation . . . to reproduce the occupation."

Ophir stressed the value of other, different forms of documentation, citing with praise a recent collection of interviews with soldiers, printed in the form of monologues and other fragments.[21] Ophir sees room for both the liberal approach, operating within the dominant discourse and radical strategy, which tries to undermine that discourse, but bemoans the sad fact that the B'tselem Report is a product of radicals who have forsaken their natural role of launching a frontal attack on the regime's forms of representation.

Ophir was answered, among others, by the poet Yitzhak Laor and by Stan Cohen. Laor argued that it was precisely Ophir, who by arguing that all distortions of Israeli democracy stemmed from the occupation, was narrowing the scope of the discussion and blocking a broader analysis about the nature of the entire Israeli state-system. In Laor's opinion, the B'tselem Report exposed collusion between the General Security Services (GSS) and the court system within Israel, proper. Laor chastised Ophir's ridicule of factuality and his attempt to put all presentations of fact on an equal footing, as if only context and political approach have any importance. This approach ignores a major task of the radical left, i.e. the exposure of many hidden and secret facts about the Israeli state apparatus and its duplicity. The exposure of facts about the state sponsored and state protected illegal operations of the GSS, the police and the army was an important, positive step in the right direction.

Stan Cohen, who was personally admonished by Ophir for deserting the radical barricades, pointed out that over the years, the nature of Zionist politics had undermined militant liberalism to the point that the civil and human rights cause became, by forfeit, a domain of the radicals. Cohen accused Ophir of trying to create a philosophical monopoly whereby the task of intellectuals would be limited to the articulation of meta-theories on the evil of occupation. This would be patently irresponsible as it ignores, in the name of an abstract system, the real suffering of real people, and the need to do everything possible to alleviate that suffering, "when we are involved in a world where death is not a metaphor." According to Cohen, the demand that the radicals restrict themselves to one type of discourse was inconsistent with the thrust of much post-modernist thinking, which stresses the importance and the value of a pluralism of genres.[22]

By the Sweat of Their Brows

The story of the Palestinian workers from the occupied territories who crossed the Green Line to find a livelihood for their families is a saga in itself. This saga encompasses the lives of hundreds of thousands of workers over a period of decades. The lot of the Palestinians working in Israel was hard and uneasy before the Intifada. The need to cross the Green Line daily as the uprising of your own people is being smashed by the people of your employer is fraught with pitfalls and dangers above and beyond the "normal" vicissitudes of exploitation of an unorganized work force in a foreign environment.

It was always hard to keep track of the number of Palestinians working in Israel. Only a small majority, who worked at permanent jobs in factories, could be considered as semi-organized. While these workers enjoyed many of the benefits of an organized workplace, their status was always clearly inferior to their fellow Israeli workers. The majority of workers were legal but unorganized; construction workers were typical of this group. Their presence at work was registered and their income and deductions from it reported to the authorities. Then there was a significant sector of "illegal" workers. These included restaurant kitchen help and day laborers in agriculture. One estimate put the number of "illegal" and unregistered workers at 30,000, roughly a quarter of about 120,000 Palestinians employed in Israel.[23]

"Kav La'oved" – Workers Hotline, established in January 1990, addressed itself to the defense of the minimal rights of these workers. Almost all of them suffered, in one form or another, from the greed of employers who did not hesitate to exploit their workers' vulnerable status in order to pay less or to pay later or not to pay, at all.

"Kav La'oved" cited a number of prevalent examples of violations of workers' rights: (a) "Illegal" employment where employers deliberately refrained from registering workers in order to avoid paying the minimum wages and other benefits required by law. After regulations made registration mandatory, employers reported fewer work days in order to pay lower wages; (b) many employers – usually small independent contractors took on workers for short periods of time only to disappear when payment was due; (c) non-compliance with the law requiring payment of severance pay due to workers when they were laid off or when their absence was due to conditions over which they had no control; (d) refusal to grant vacation pay, sick-leave."[24]

"Kav La'oved" operated as a legal aid service, contacting and pressing the employer for a settlement or initiating a suit in the Labor Court. The group handled hundreds of cases during its first years of activity. "Kav La'oved" collected information on new ways that workers' rights were being infringed, and channeled such information to the media and the Histadrut, demanding that the latter provide equal services to all workers.

The rankest form of discrimination against workers from the territories was institutionalized and sanctioned by law. Although Palestinian workers had the same sums for the National Insurance Fund deducted from their wages, they received only 20 percent of the benefits. The chief benefit denied the Palestinian workers was unemployment insurance. "Kav La'oved" was part of a coalition of groups which challenged this discrimination. The government's justification was that a certain portion of the funds was transferred to the territories to provide health, social and welfare services to the population. "Kav La'oved" estimated in a memorandum it submitted to a commission of the Ministry of Labor, appointed to deal with the issue, that more than 800 million Israeli shekels in deductions, ostensibly for the National Insurance Fund (or almost $300 million at the current rate of exchange) were transferred to the Israeli treasury during the ten years before 1990.[25]

Perhaps, the ugliest chapter of all in this pattern of discrimination was the open, official government policy to displace Palestinian workers and encourage the employment of Israelis, especially new immigrants from the former Soviet Union in their place. There was, of course, a "security rationale" behind this; it was based on preventing in the future the kind of instances where Palestinians who entered Israel as workers, perpetrated violent stabbings of Israelis, including women and children. Such incidents served to justify and fuel government schemes for sealing off the territories and the absolute separation between the two populations. Of course, the main victims of such a separation would be tens of thousands of totally innocent workers thrown out of work and their families. Moreover, whenever the Defense Minister and the IDF decided, in the wake of "popular pressure" to seal off the territories for extended periods, the Ministry of Labor and other government bodies launched intensive campaigns to encourage employers to take on and permanently employ Israelis in place of the Palestinians who were confined to their towns and villages by the curfews and the closures.[26]

Though human rights organizations are not always an integral part of a protest movement, in the Israeli case the establishment of these organizations was a direct outgrowth of the experience and the challenges of a broader protest movement. Most of the sponsors and the staff of these organizations had been schooled in the protest movement and participated in it as individuals. Human rights organizations which try and prevent or reduce the number of violations of human rights can be seen as an alternative solution, standing in opposition to the political fight to eradicate the root causes of such violations – and the very existence of the occupation, in our case. Fortunately, in real life, and this was true regarding human rights organizations active during the Intifada, these organizations were actually an important facet of a wider political effort. Their efforts "fed" into the overall political battle, they usually considered themselves part of the entire protest movement and were seen as such by its participants. B'tselem, the Public Committee Against Torture in Israel and the Workers' Hotline became "permanent assets" of the entire protest movement. Their day-to-day work, their professionalism and expertise added yet another dimension to a healthy and diversified peace movement.

Shadow from Kuwait

Peace Now remained the strongest and most faithful expression of the mainstream dove constituency. The women's groups, and especially Women In Black had grown into a national movement. Connections between Israeli and Palestinian women were yet another important link between the peace movement and the Palestinians. Yesh Gvul continued to tunnel under the props of the consensus. The professional groups such as Imut and the Israeli-Palestinian Committee of Physicians for Human Rights persisted in discovering and exposing different facets of the ongoing repression. Protest was a bit tired, but very stubborn. The government was suffering from internal quarrels in the Likud and becoming progressively isolated internationally. The parliamentary opposition was trying to recover from the fiasco that resulted from its attempt to unseat Shamir. Then, the contours of the political and strategic dynamics in the region were radically altered at the beginning of August 1990 when the Iraqi army moved into Kuwait.

12

The Gulf Crisis and the Peace Movement

Meeting of Minds at Notre Dame

The August 5, 1990 meeting at the Notre Dame Hotel on the boundary between West and East Jerusalem was a serious step forward in overcoming disagreement between the more moderate Zionist doves and the Palestinian leadership in the territories. A broad delegation of Knesset members included, in addition to MKs from the CRM, Mapam and Shinui, an important contingent from the Labor party comprised of MKs Yossi Beilin, Na'waf Masalha, Avrum Burg, Navah Arad, Amir Peretz and Lova Eliav. MKs David Libai and Shevah Weiss had planned to attend and were absent, it was reported, for technical, and not political reasons. Faisal Husseini headed the Palestinian delegation. The two sides agreed on a declaration which determined that the Palestinian issue was the heart of the Israeli-Arab conflict, that the Palestinians have the right to self-determination and the prerogative of choosing their own representatives.[1] The forum honored a request by the Labor MKs to desist from using formulations which would clash directly with those in the Labor program. As a result, neither the term "PLO" or a "Palestinian state" appeared explicitly in the statement.

MK Amnon Rubenstein (Shinui) utilized the occasion, just a few days after the crisis in the Gulf began, to express concern over the Palestinian position towards the events. According to this report, the Palestinians for their part, replied that, in their present circumstances, they were neither able or particularly interested in trying to solve all the world's problems.[2] The Gulf issue still appeared to be of no immediate or critical concern to the gathering. The Israeli MKs and the Palestinians felt a sense of satisfaction at reaching a new level of understanding. The peace movement had brought a distinguished entourage of mainstream Israeli political figures into a constructive and fruitful dialogue with the local national leadership of the Palestinians, a political force directly linked and clearly subordinate to the PLO in Tunis.

No less a figure than MK Yossi Sarid summed up the proceedings on an extremely positive note: "It was an exceptional meeting. If it were the participants who had the job of working out a peace treaty, we would be very close to its conclusion. It was an important step in a period in which it appeared that Palestinians and Israelis have stopped talking with one another. We are preserving the links to prevent the thread from being broken."[3]

Hawks in the Labor parliamentary faction were furious over the results of the Notre Dame meeting and demanded that the party institute urgent disciplinary action against Labor MKs for disregarding their party's program. Spokespersons for the Israeli right pronounced, as they were wont to do on such occasions, that the meeting and its results were dangerous to the security of the country. These responses simply underlined the fact that progress had been made in the Israeli-Palestinian dialogue.

The Gulf Crisis and the Peace Movement

Arafat flew to Baghdad a few days after the invasion of Kuwait and publicly embraced Sadaam Hussein, precisely at the moment when the US, its allies and the world media certified Iraq a major threat to world peace and regional stability. For reasons which predated and were unrelated to the Gulf crisis, the PLO had increased its contacts and dependency on Sadaam Hussein's Iraq. This pro-Iraqi shift was in line with the practice of Arafat and the PLO leadership to constantly mend and rebuild alliances in the shifting sands of Middle East politics. Over the years this kind of maneuvering between the different Arab countries had become one of the keys for PLO survival.

Even if many Palestinians were reluctant to approve any kind of unilateral military action between Arab countries, Kuwait included, few accepted the Western version that an independent, sovereign Kuwait was the innocent victim of naked aggression. Moreover, Sadaam Hussein's readiness to defy the United States and demand linkage between the Palestinian and Kuwait issues could not but arouse the sympathy of Palestinian public opinion, which rejected the right of the United States and its allies to "punish" Iraq militarily, even under the guise of the UN flag.

As the crisis in the Gulf developed, a political abyss was rapidly widening between the Zionist left, representing most of the Israeli peace movement, and the Palestinian leadership, in Tunis and in the occupied territories. The Zionist left, almost without exception, accepted the United States version of the crisis and readily accepted the official Israeli view that Sadaam Hussein was also a dangerous threat to the security of Israel. The PLO, for its part, expressed understanding for the Iraqi position and refused to cooperate with the United States led international effort to isolate Iraq. The first leader of the Zionist left to draw drastic conclusions from this new set of circumstances was MK Yossi Sarid.[4]

"Do Not Come Looking For Me"

Sarid left the Labor Party in 1984 after it agreed to establish the first National Unity Government with the Likud and joined the CRM, linking up with Shulamit Aloni, who had herself left the Labor Party eleven years before when she was unable to stomach the authoritarian and militaristic policies of the then Prime Minister, Golda Meir. During the Intifada, Sarid, an able parliamentarian and an effective publicist, had built an impressive record of exposing intolerable behavior by the Israeli Defense Forces. His energetic exposure of such "excesses," as they were termed in the Israeli media, made him one of the most hated enemies of fanatics on the right. On the other hand, Sarid, who prided himself on his sensitivity to genuine security needs, led the fight in the peace camp against the influence of Yesh Gvul, always stressing the importance of maintaining the Zionist left's links to the national consensus.

Sarid, several days after the Iraqi army moved into Kuwait, quickly determined that the "Iraqi invasion of Kuwait is the most vulgar violation of world peace in the last ten years . . . and the Iraqi ruler is an enemy of mankind."[5] Sarid's pronouncements went far beyond personal disappointment over the Palestinian position in the crisis.[6] The essence of the article was Sarid's conclusion that the whole-hearted participation of the Israeli peace camp, along with all other Israelis in the anti-Sadaam Hussein coalition, took precedent over every other consideration. The content and style of the attack were such as to precipitate a serious and irreversible crisis in the relations between the broad base of the Israeli Zionist peace camp and the Palestinians. Sarid assaulted the Palestinian leadership just a few days later with acid sarcasm:

> You need a gas mask to overcome the poisonous and sickening stench of the PLO position towards Sadaam Hussein. The cuddling between Yasser and Sadaam is nauseating and threatening. Every generation of Palestinian leaders made every possible mistake . . . For years, I explained to the Palestinians that they should not build their future on the USSR . . . and now Sadaam Hussein will redeem them from the occupation . . . the Palestinian leaders who have hopped from bed to bed have learned nothing . . . how many times will the Palestinians have to be betrayed until they learn that only they and we have a real interest in solving the Palestinian problem.[7]

Sarid went on to argue that Sadaam Hussein had done a colossal disservice to the Palestinian cause and predicted that irrespective of how the crisis would end, the Palestinians would come out as losers. He went on to attack the Palestinian public within Israel for supporting Sadaam Hussein and by so doing, placing a question mark on their loyalty as citizens. Sarid pronounced the policies of Shamir, Sharon and Rabin's "as white as snow" in comparison to Sadaam Hussein's crimes. Sarid concluded his attack by bidding the Palestinians farewell:

> If I supported a Palestinian state only because the Palestinians are worthy of a state – I would today rescind my support. However, I continue to support their right to self-determination and their own state, because I have a right to be rid of the occupation and its ugly effects. Maybe they deserve the occupation, but we do not. I am still trying to maintain my human image, but Arafat, Husseini, and Darousha have no role in this tremendous, almost super-human effort, which I have to make. Until further notice, they can, as far as I am concerned, look for me.[8]

Palestinians and militants in the peace movement discerned signs of a latent racism in Sarid's outburst. Even many of Sarid's colleagues in the Zionist section of the peace movement considered Sarid's response patronizing and over-emotional. However, even if many of his own colleagues were repelled by Sarid's style and considered his response unbalanced, these critics only rarely challenged the basis of his political logic. And, with all due respect to questions of style and form, it was the political basis of Sarid's approach that was the decisive element.

For Sarid, and many other liberal Zionists, peace was, first and foremost, an Israeli need, based on Israeli strategic and moral considerations. The primary and ultimate concern of Sarid and other like-minded leaders in the Zionist left was Israeli security and political power. There was no serious effort to deal with major issues from an internationalist or universal humanist perspective. Moreover, the Israeli-Arab conflict and the Palestinian question were almost always analyzed and evaluated within a traditional Zionist conception according to which relations with the Arabs were considered a function of Israel's relations with the main powers and especially the United States. According to this approach, the goal of peace with the Palestinians is openly and clearly subordinated to the larger strategic considerations of Israel and her "natural allies" in the region.[9]

Challenging Sarid

Yossi Sarid expressed the classic political tendency of many a loyal opposition to close ranks and opt for a policy of national unity in periods of military crisis. Sarid, naturally enough, received support from the right and the media. His position was decisive in moving large sections of the dove constituency into the national consensus. Even so, Sarid's approach was far from being the unchallenged or exclusive position in the Zionist peace camp. Among the first to take issue with Sarid were Yael Dayan and Professor Zev Sternhal, a political scientist at the Hebrew University. Yael Dayan wrote of Sarid and others:

> With the emotional rashness of a disappointed lover, they want to throw out the baby – genuine chances for Israeli-Palestinian peace – with the dirty water – the absurd and senseless folly and despair of Palestinian support for Sadaam Hussein . . . so far, no Palestinian leader has abandoned our mutual platform for peace in order to call for the destruction of Israel, and this is all the more reason to stick to our position.[10]

Sternhal analyzed the historical precedents for Sarid's retreat into the warm embrace of national unity in an hour of emergency, linking it to the behavior of the European Socialists in 1914 and that of the liberal camp in the United States during the 1960s.[11]

Sternhal stopped short of actually attacking Sarid's basic position regarding Sadaam Hussein, though he did propose an alternative strategy: "One must treat the Palestinian subject as though the crisis had never broken out, and one must treat Sadaam Hussein as if there were no Palestinians.[12]

MK Dedi Zucker (CRM) rejected what he termed Sarid's immaturity in turning his back on the Palestinians and expressed understanding for the fact that the Palestinian position stemmed from distress and desperation. He feared, nevertheless, that the Palestinian position *vis-à-vis* Sadaam Hussein meant a retreat from willingness to recognize Israel and make peace on the basis of the PLO policy shift in 1988.[13]

MK Shulamit Aloni felt that self-criticism on the part of the Israeli peace movement was more appropriate than Sarid's scorn. When asked if the Palestinians would have to "look for her," Aloni answered:

> Why should I be disappointed with the Palestinians? Did I do some-thing for them? Did the Israeli left do anything for them? . . . the Israeli left is a loyal part of the government and the establish-ment . . . we tried to raise a moral voice . . . de facto we did nothing. The government continued to control the territories, to deny human rights, to destroy and to kill, and we are part of this because we did not declare a rebellion . . . we were the fig leaf of Israeli democracy . . . the Palestinians do not owe us anything.[14]

Aloni felt that the "phone should be ready and in use" because any retreat by the peace movement would be a victory for the annexationists. Aloni's position regarding contact with the Palestinians was indeed diametrically opposed to Sarid's, though she did not question Sarid's evaluation of the Gulf crisis. It must be said of Aloni that on this and other occasions she displayed an ability to speak for both the militant and the moderate sections of the peace movement. Aloni never went so far as to question the articles of her Zionist faith, but she did reveal, on more than one occasion, a level of understanding and sensitivity for the "other" that transcended the traditional limits of nationalist discourse and establishment politics.

Peace Now in a Quandary

Peace Now could not have been less enthusiastic about Sarid's pretense to speak for the entire peace movement. It was clear to them that Sarid was acting irresponsibly, but at the same time they wanted to avoid confrontation with him. The Gulf crisis had created tremendous political obstacles in the path of the Israeli peace movement. But it was clear to Peace Now that nothing could be gained by an arrogant attitude towards their Palestinian counterparts, especially as Peace Now understood that the Palestinians and their leaders were caught in horrendously difficult conditions.[15] Peace Now understood that the wisest of options was to do everything possible to control the damage being inflicted on the peace movement. Peace Now spoke of its "disappointment" over the Palestinian position in the context of Palestinian "disappointment caused by the paralysis of the peace process, the establishment of a right-wing government in Israel and the cessation of the American-PLO dialogue," adding that it welcomed that part of the PLO statement that "called for Iraqi withdrawal from Kuwait."[16]

Most Peace Now activists accepted, like Sarid, the prevailing interpretation of the Gulf crisis to the effect that the United States represented "justice" in a battle against the forces of "evil." There were, of course, nuances in the way Peace Now activists expressed themselves. Tsali Reshef, by far the most influential leader in Peace Now, was quite open about supporting active US intervention, while other leading members hoped for a peaceful resolution of the conflict through UN mediation. But Peace Now's main concern was trying to preserve the Israeli-Palestinian dialogue and to prevent what appeared to them as politically irresponsible attacks on the Palestinians.[17]

Saying No to Bush

The main debate in the Zionist left was for or against Sarid's demand for a revision of the position supporting recognition and negotiations with the PLO, and not about the merits of the Gulf War. There were relatively few voices in the peace movement and the Israeli left which openly challenged the support for the United States position on the Gulf crisis. Criticism of the US position and Israeli willingness to cooperate – actively or passively – in the war against Iraq was restricted to a small section of the peace movement. This minority could not actually impair the national consensus supporting Bush. But it was able to raise its voice against the approaching war, thus proving that there was a trend in the

Israeli peace movement which did link the battle for Israeli-Arab peace to the battle for peace in the entire region. This minority was composed of the various Marxist groups, individuals linked to the more militant section of the peace movement and an ad hoc concentration of intellectuals which took the name, "A Minute Before War."

The Communist Party of Israel was highly critical of the US preparations for war against Iraq, but also criticized the invasion of Kuwait and took pains to disassociate itself from Sadaam Hussein's regime. An identical position was adopted at a meeting of Communist parties in the Middle East held in Athens, during the first week of September, 1990. Three smaller Marxist groupings also condemned war threats that emanated from Washington. SHASI, the Israeli Socialist left, condemned the US position but refused to see any saving virtue in Sadaam Hussein's role, while the Revolutionary Communist League (LE'KAM) and Nitzotz groups stressed that, whatever the nature of Hussein's internal regime, the struggle against US pressures did have anti-imperialist elements.

A number of individuals managed to convey to the public their scorn for the United States "peace keeping" role. Prof. Zev Sternhal reminded the public that the crisis "was connected with keeping warm during the winter, gasoline for automobiles, cheap electricity, comfort and not survival. If it was only a question of principle, namely the principle that invasion is illegitimate – it is doubtful that anything would have been done about the invasion."[18] The poet, Yitzhak Laor, denounced the enormous propaganda machine mobilized to convince the world that anyone who opposes this specific Pax America is opposed to peace in principle.[19] Res. General, Matti Peled, commented that the Israeli military establishment was even more eager to see a full-scale war in the Gulf than its US counterpart.[20]

"A Minute Before the War"

A group of professors, many of them members of Ad Kan at Tel Aviv University, formed a group in December 1990 based on the idea that the international community should take up Sadaam Hussein's offer of "linkage" between the Kuwait and the Palestinian issues. Hussein had declared that he would be ready to discuss evacuation of Kuwait in the same international forum that would also discuss Israel's withdrawal from the occupied territories. "A Minute Before the War" took the form of a petition campaign demanding that Israel participate in a diplomatic effort to defuse the Gulf crisis by expressing readiness to negotiate on the basis of Palestinian self-determination. Tania Reinhart, professor of Linguistics and Literature at Tel Aviv University, one of the initiators of the group explained: "Israel has the trump card in the form of the territories. If we decide on a tangible peace initiative, this will enable the world to increase its pressure on Iraq and to solve the crisis without war."[21] "A Minute Before the War" could boast an impressive list of sponsors and supporters and it had some success in engaging leaders of the dove community in a serious debate. "A Minute Before the War" was significant in that it posed the question of Israeli-Arab peace in a regional context and formulated a regional peace program as an alternative to the Gulf War.

On the Eve

"A Minute Before the War" hosted three MKs – Shulamit Aloni, Yair Tsahan and Mordechai Virshuvski – at an all-night vigil and discussion called by "A Minute Before the War" on January 14, 1991, the eve of the Gulf War. An acute observer summarized the situation as follows: Three schools of thought developed on the left . . . On the right wing of the left, stands Yossi Sarid who argues that the war is necessary for the peace process . . . since there will be no peace process if Sadaam Hussein is not roundly beaten. The second group is represented by the group of Tel Aviv University professors, headed by Tania Reinhart, which demanded that Israel show a readiness for an overall settlement in the region. The third group was represented by those MKs who attended the "A Minute Before the War" meeting but opposed its message. According to their position, Israel was not responsible for Sadaam Hussein's invasion of Kuwait, and the Iraqi aggression was not designed to help the Palestinians. Thus, Iraq's demand for "linkage" is artificial and fraudulent.[22]

Peace Now considered it the duty of the peace movement to make every effort to carry on 'business as usual' after the invasion of Kuwait and during the military build-up in the Gulf. This was the practical way to refute Sarid's line that everything had changed and nothing could be done for peace until Sadaam Hussein was defeated. Peace Now's organizational efforts during the pre-war period culminated in a mass human-chain activity sponsored by Peace Now in conjunction with the Council of Arab Mayors and Municipal Councilors held on Saturday, January 11, 1991, just a few days before the war. Approximately five thousand Jews and Arabs lined a ten-kilometer stretch along the Wadi Ara road in a call for Israeli-Palestinian peace, "despite everything," and in condemnation of anti-Arab racism. Under more normal conditions, Peace Now would have had the time to explain the significance of this new level of cooperation between the Israeli peace camp and the largest and most representative body of Israeli Palestinian Arabs. But war was just a few days off.

While activists from "A Minute Before the War" were making a valiant effort to use the "linkage" issue to organize against war in the region, the moderate section of the peace movement did everything possible to separate between the two issues in order to prevent the Gulf crisis from totally derailing peace activity in the country. The moderates were against any kind of "linkage" between the two issues because they were certain that such "linkage" would lead to the isolation of the peace movement in Israel from the general public and most of the liberal wing of the peace constituency. Clearly, the different approaches to the "linkage" question was yet one more expression of the deep division in the Israeli peace movement.

The chain of events set off by the Gulf crisis had, as can be expected, dire consequences for the peace movement in Israel. If, after years, the different trends of the Israeli peace movement had developed some sort of unity around the common demand to recognize the PLO and to negotiate peace with the genuine representative of the Palestinian people, the Gulf crisis presented a whole new set of challenges. The peace movement had to try and meet those challenges under the clouds of impending war, and at a time when the resolution of the Israeli-Palestinian struggle had been effectively pushed off the regional and international agenda. Perhaps, if the period had been conducive to calm, undisturbed discussions, it would have been possible to minimize the damage involved in this serious clash of opinion. But the period, the second half of 1990, was anything but calm. Blood was shed on the Temple Mount in Jerusalem and daggers flashed in quiet neighborhoods. It was a "good" time for religious fanaticism and racism and a bad time for peace and its supporters.

Blood on the Mount

The Wailing Wall plaza was packed with Jews at a ceremony marking the last day of Succoth (October 13, 1990) when a hale of stones rained down from the Temple Mount and scattered the worshippers. Initially, it seemed that the Moslems above, on the Mount, had used their vantage point above the worshippers at the Wall to prepare and launch an attack against unarmed Jews. However, in a number of hours, amidst conflicting accounts of how the clash started, it became dreadfully clear that 18 Palestinians had been shot to death on the Temple Mount by Israeli Police and Border Guards and scores of other Palestinians had been wounded. Israeli media reports were pushing the version that the violence originated in a premeditated attack by the Palestinians.

Even so, the killing of tens of unarmed Palestinian civilians in the heart of the holy places, the absence of any Israeli casualties and mounting international concern, including the despatch of a special UN emissary to Jerusalem, forced Prime Minister Shamir to hold an inquiry. Minister of Police, Ronny Milo, was confident that the findings would vindicate the police. Faisal Husseini had been picked up at the site and the police were busy building a case which had Husseini leading an uprising on the Holy Mount. The Minister of Police, Ronny Milo, told the radio: "I have no doubt that the findings of the commission will prove that there was a dangerous, frenzied attack on a holy place by Arab rioters. and that the police response was appropriate."[23]

A provisional B'tselem report issued on October 14, as well as a report by the Palestinian human rights group, al-Haq (Law in the Service of Man), concluded that there was no evidence whatsoever of any planned attack by the Palestinians. It appeared that the stones were thrown in the wake of a skirmish between police and Palestinian worshippers on the Temple Mount. Tensions were high because the Moslems had reliable information to the effect that a fanatical Israeli group was planning to violate the law and the customs of the holy site by praying on the Mount. Both reports accused the police of excessive violence and actually firing into the crowd of Palestinian worshippers on the Mount so as to regain control of the area which they had lost after an initial clash.[24] Shamir chose to appoint an administrative commission (thus avoiding a more powerful and independent judicial inquiry) to be headed by Reserve General Zvi Zamir. The official Zamir commission report – issued at the end of the month – did not find any basis for the "premeditated attack" version and criticized a lack of police professionalism.[25] Tsali Reshef, spokesperson for Peace Now and a lawyer by profession, characterized the Zamir report as a bit of "tight-rope walking between an unsuccessful attempt to sound credible and the attempt to avoid placing the responsibility for the death of tens and the injury of hundreds of Palestinians on Israel and its security forces."[26]

The authorities and the media had done a skillful job in convincing Israeli public opinion that Moslem fanatics had launched a premeditated attack on innocent, pious, Jews praying at the Wailing Wall. Devoted Moslems, for their part, were convinced that the massacre on the Temple Mount was the beginning of a master plan to evict them from Al-Aksa and the Dome of the Rock. The seeds of seething religious hatred and strife were maturing in the fertile soil of bitter, endless national struggle between Israel and the Palestinians. New poisons were spewing into the already polluted air.

Logic of the Long Knives

Less than a month later, by the time a screaming Palestinian youth, knife in hand, had finished his crazed spree, he had stabbed and killed three Israelis in the quiet Baka quarter in Jerusalem. For most Israelis it was one more expression of Islamic fanaticism. Few were willing to note the obvious connection between the Temple Mount events three weeks earlier and the new and latest outbreak of violence. The youth had come from Gaza to Baka that morning as a part of the massive, daily influx of Palestinian laborers into Israel. Thus, the means to prevent the deadly recurrence of such events seemed both simple and clear: seal off the territories and don't let the Palestinians into Israel.

The Baka killings, along with other similar events, made the decision by the government to close the territories for a limited period of time in order to cool tensions perfectly reasonable and actually popular in the Israeli public. The authorities appeared to be responding to genuine fear when they took steps to erect barriers separating the two populations. In the given circumstances it was hard to negate measures designed to "reduce friction" between the two populations and responding to the steps for separation between the two populations was no simple matter for the peace camp. When the government closed off the territories for a number of days immediately after the murder in Baka, the media were quick to observe that separation had supporters in the peace camp.

A Jerusalem Post commentator, Dan Izenberg, devoted an article analyzing support for the government move, from both the left and the right. Dr. Yael Tamir, one of the founders of Peace Now and a political philosophy lecturer declared that, "there was a need for separation between Palestinians and Israelis to stop the killing. The hatred was too deep, she said . . . "[27] Avrum Burg, a leading dove MK, drafted a bill to rescind the 1972 general entry permit which allowed Palestinians free access to Israel.

> According to Burg, there is a dialectic between right and left. They often arrive at the same conclusions but the contents are diametrically opposed . . . both sides urge separation. "The question is whether the separation will be humanitarian or transferist [forced expulsion]," said Burg. Nevertheless, Burg acknowledged that he had come a long way from his former belief in Israeli-Palestinian co-existence through understanding and good will to his current belief in immediate separation. "Things have happened in the meantime," he said – and began counting: "the killing of seven Palestinians in Rishon Le'tsion, the slaying of two teenage Israelis in Jerusalem and lynching of a Palestinian on Hebron St. [a main thoroughfare in southeast Jerusalem], Palestinian support for Sadaam Hussein, the Temple Mount riot, the stabbings in Baka. The possibility for coexistence is dead," said Burg. "That will come only after the two nations live separately. In the meantime, peace will come out of hatred. It will be based on self-interest, not good will."[28]

The attempt by many in the peace camp to present separation in a positive light, almost as if it were a step towards peace, aroused the ire of the radical sections of the peace movement. Dr. Azmi Bishara spearheaded the formation of an ad hoc group which circulated and published a petition against those in the "peace camp who allowed themselves to be dragged along to support nationalist and anti-Arab slogans which legitimized positions of the right."[29] For Bishara and the fifty-odd Israelis who signed the petition, it was vital to stress that there was nothing positive about the idea of separation between the two peoples, or in the words of the petition, "separation is not a value."

The petition denounced the racist atmosphere in which the Arab workers were pushed back across the "Green-Line" and attacked illusions among the doves that the restrictions on entry to Israel somehow reinforced the concept of a border between two sovereign entities. The signatories condemned all nationalistically motivated murder and killing, but pinpointed the occupation, itself, as the source of extremist acts and reminded the public that most of the victims of the occupation had been Palestinian Arabs who suffered daily oppression. The petition concluded with a call to the peace camp to fight racism and certainly to refrain from abetting it. The only solution lay in a political initiative to end the occupation.[30]

The separation issue was the subject of debate in Peace Now during the first weeks of November 1990. Intellectually, the racist motivations for some of the separation proposals were clear to Peace Now activists. However, in terms of pragmatic politics, many in Peace Now felt that it had to support concrete steps to alleviate public fears, "here and now" even before the peace camp could achieve significant changes in government policy. Separation did not seem all that bad as there were important Palestinian voices, such as that of Faisal Husseini, which claimed that the closure was tantamount to a "first step towards Palestinian independence."[31]

After no small amount of agonizing over the issue, Peace Now adopted a compromise formulation in its call for a demonstration marking the third anniversary of the Intifada in December 1990. Attacking Shamir for not having "any new ideas" on the eve of his trip to the United States, Peace Now observed that the "polls proved 70 percent of the people want a political separation from the territories." The Peace Now message was that "It is impossible to continue like this,"[32] as the illusions "that time would solve the problem" and that it would be possible to erase the "Green Line," have been shattered. "It is clear to all of us, the time has come for separation from the territories. Neither closure nor delusions about transfer will put an end to the violence and the hostility. We and the Palestinians need political and economic separation."[33]

A number of factors eventually reduced the intensity of the "separation" debate. The clouds of horror and the fear which are so pervasive after such incidents tend to disperse in periods of relative calm. Moreover, economic realities asserted themselves, as the specter of freshly-spilled blood receded. Hawk ministers such as Sharon at Housing and Construction and Raphael Eytan at Agriculture had to back measures to return the bulk of the Palestinian work force to their jobs, as their continued absence, in the absence of any viable alternative, meant the collapse of entire economic sectors. In addition, security advisors were issuing dire warnings to the effect that tens of thousands of unemployed workers would create ideal recruiting conditions for the outlawed "terrorist organizations."

The argument about "separation" as an ideal or a practical necessity would return to plague the peace movement in other circumstances. It would always be possible to see different and opposing implications in steps that create barriers between the territories and pre-1967 Israeli borders. Nationalist-minded Israelis believed that friction was inevitable and argued that Israel should learn to overcome its reliance on labor from the territories. For them separation was a value in and of itself, and had nothing to do with a search for a just solution to the conflict.

Opponents of the status quo on the left could point out that more than twenty years of occupation and unlimited Israeli rule were unable to obliterate the distinction between two defined communities and their territorial base. "Creeping annexation" could not change the basic demographic and social reality – it was and would remain a reality of two nations which would have to part in order to meet again in the future as equals. Some opponents of the status-quo approved of emergency steps by the government to lessen contact and friction between the two populations. Still others, mostly in the militant wing of the peace movement, insisted that separation – under unequal conditions of occupation – meant still further discrimination and repression.

Indeed, for those tens of thousands of workers who were denied their right to work and provide for their families, the meaning of "separation" was immediately clear and unequivocal – collective punishment at its worst. It was hard to see how such a clearly immoral act could be presented as a step in the right direction, merely because it made the "Green Line," the border between Israel and the territories more tangible.

As we have seen, the massacre on the Temple Mount, and the stabbings and the debate over the separation issue, were additional causes of frustration – above and beyond the mounting tension in the region. The worse was still to come as the crisis deteriorated and war came to the region – and to the heart of Israel.

13

The War and its Aftermath

When war came to the Gulf, it also came to Israel in the form of 40 Scud missile attacks which wreaked considerable havoc, chiefly in the Tel Aviv area, between January 18, 1991 and the end of the war, February 28, 1991. During this period, most Israelis were in no mood to criticize their government. They felt that the Palestinians had lined up with their worst and most dangerous enemy. There was something to this since, in their despair, many Palestinians hoped that the Scuds flying over their heads were an omen heralding the beginning of their deliverance from Israeli rule. The Palestinian feelings were exploited to the hilt by the mainstream media which cultivated, for the benefit of all Israelis, an image of Palestinians dancing joyously on the rooftops of their homes as the Scuds passed over on their way to Israeli cities.

Those who did feel a need to criticize the government had to operate in circumstances which seriously diminished their effectiveness. But, despite the circumstances, the peace movement was able to make its voice heard on two major issues. Strangely, on the first issue, the peace movement backed Shamir. Shamir was under attack from politicians on the right (and not only on the right) for complying with the US demand that Israel stay out of the fray. One leading dove, Dedi Zucker, announced that he wanted to hug Shamir for his policy of restraint.

The second issue related to the danger that the government might exploit the tense situation in order to expel masses of Palestinians from the territories. The war tension and the havoc wrought by the missile attacks created just the atmosphere which might be exploited for such a purpose. It was a government dominated by annexationists who had been praying for years for some kind of "miracle" which would open the way for annexation of the territories without their residents. But international circumstances made such a move by Israel highly problematic. At the time, the United States was doing everything to ensure maximum Arab participation in the anti-Hussein coalition, and Shamir could not permit himself to embark on a highly risky operation of this sort. However, he did make an attempt to legitimize the infamous "transfer" scheme by inviting its chief exponent, Rehav'am Ze'evi and his "Moledeth" party, into his government during the first week of February 1991. Peace Now responded by calling a demonstration at the Knesset on February 5, 1991, its first since the war began. No one was surprised that only hundreds participated; it was clear that the peace constituency, to the degree that it was still intact, was still reeling under the impact of the events.

The crisis in the Gulf revealed a deep division between the liberal majority of the Israeli peace movement's mass base, which accepted the proposition that Sadaam Hussein must be defeated, and the international peace movement which, at the least, questioned the motivation of United States policy and demanded a negotiated settlement of the crisis. At a special press conference for the foreign press, Amos Oz, A. B. Yehoshua and other leading writers affiliated with the Israeli peace movement, bitterly confronted the position adopted by their colleagues abroad, and accused them of appeasing Sadaam Hussein. Amos Oz talked about the danger of a "second Auschwitz."[1] Peace Now, for its part, made efforts to explain to activists in the peace movement abroad that this war was "different." In a letter to peace groups abroad, Peace Now wrote, "We do not believe that this war should be denounced, since according to all indications, it will prevent another war and possibly a whole series of wars, much worse than it."[2]

Opposition to the Gulf War

Opposition to the war was restricted to a small segment of the peace forces. The Marxist left, which had analyzed the pre-war crisis basically in terms of imperialist interests in the region, reasserted its position after the United States and its allies began military operations against Iraq. Considering the political atmosphere in the country after the first missiles hit Tel Aviv, opposition against the UN-sponsored operation was an act of political courage. The Marxist groups did indeed denounce the Iraqi missile attacks on Israel's civilian population. However, instead of joining the chorus calling for the annihilation of Sadaam Hussein, they called for an immediate cessation of hostilities in order to create the possibilities for a negotiated solution to the conflict.

It is easily understood that even the most militant sections of the peace movement found it difficult to organize activities against the war in the Gulf during a period of daily missile attacks on Israel's main urban centers. Even the activists who had launched the petition drive, "A Minute Before the War," despaired of formulating an alternative approach which could gain a modicum of public support. Simply stated, most of the peace constituency had joined the consensus supporting the US operation. In Peace Now and almost all the different peace groups, the feeling was that any activity regarding the Israeli-Arab conflict would have to wait until the "successful" conclusion of the Gulf War.

Despite the adverse conditions, there was one, single serious effort to convince the Israeli public that it did not necessarily have to choose between supporting either George Bush or Sadaam Hussein. An ad hoc group of individuals associated with the more militant sections of the peace movement initiated a petition under the heading "Dai" (Enough) which called for ending the war without supporting any side. (The campaign was similar to another petition drive launched under the same title during the first weeks of the war in Lebanon.) The text of the petition which appeared a number of times in the Israeli press over hundreds of signatures reflected the complex circumstances and tried to address anxieties prevalent in the public:

> As citizens of Israel, we are exposed to Iraqi missiles and condemn those who send these missiles. We also condemn the occupation of Kuwait and demand its independence. At the same time, we oppose the Gulf War.
>
> Bush's war is not motivated by the high-sounding principles of his speeches – just as Sadaam's aggression is not aimed at defending Palestinian rights. Both of them are motivated by desire for power and greed for oil.
>
> The horrible price of their war is paid by ordinary people: Iraqis, Americans, Kuwaitis, British, Palestinians and – of course – Israelis . . . [3]

The text also calls for a cease-fire and the convocation of an international conference. "Dai" showed that there was a solid core in the peace movement which could find the way to express its principles even as missiles were falling on Israeli cities, even when broad sections of the dove community had joined a national consensus dominated by the axiom that Sadaam Hussein was a modern-day Hitler. It was indeed the act of a small minority, and it did have symbolic value – though its practical impact was negligible.

Asides from a few modest activities carried out by the initiators of the "Dai" campaign – a press conference and several vigils and the Peace Now demonstration against the entrance of Ze'evi's "transferist" Moledeth party to the cabinet, peace activity ground to an abrupt halt when the war in the Gulf broke out and as long as Israel was actively threatened by Iraqi missiles. The entire Israeli population had spent many nights holed up in sealed rooms under instructions of the Civil Defense Authorities which warned that there might be poison gas warheads on the incoming missiles. Members of the peace movement, just like everybody else, sat out much of the war in the sealed rooms of their homes – it was the "sealed room" experience that was to be the hallmark of the war for most Israelis.

The Peace Movement Emerges from the Sealed Room

In many senses, the war was a "pushover" for the United States and its allies. The Palestinians along with the left and the international peace movement had seriously overestimated Sadaam's ability to challenge the regional status quo. US fire power had successfully enhanced, at least in the short term, the political prestige of the United States. Warnings from the peace movement to the effect that the United States and its allies were going to be bogged down in a long and critically dangerous confrontation, proved groundless. Many advocates of peace and dialogue had to admit, as it seemed, that military force and superiority were able to solve real threats and real problems. Detractors of the peace movement in Israel were quick to draw the inevitable conclusion. *Ha'aretz* columnist, Dan Margalit expressed a widespread tendency to pronounce the peace movement dead.

> The peace movement, of blessed memory, was killed during a salvo of missiles, not by a direct hit, but by the recoil which reverberated from the rooftops on which the Palestinians were celebrating the destruction being wrought on Tel Aviv and Haifa.[4]

After noting that only Sarid and his supporters had salvaged some honor, Margalit made short shrift of Peace Now, Yesh Gvul and

the professors who proved that protracted education was no prescription for short-sightedness. The leaders of the peace movement
were "naive", suffered from "political blindness" and "servility." In
short, they exploited democratic processes to influence policy while
ignoring the real nature of the enemy.

The fear and tension that descended on the country took its
toll on the most enduring and determined section of the peace
movement, Women In Black. Lily Galilee, who covered protest
activity for *Ha'aretz* over the years, started her analysis of the peace
movement with the sad sight of the empty square and went on to
describe the dire effect of the Gulf War on the peace movement in
Israel:

> The square was empty. For the first time since the Intifada, the
> women have stopped coming to the permanent vigil for three
> weeks . . . This expresses the confusion and the shock effecting the
> left since the crisis . . .
>
> It is in the nature of wars that they are not kind to peace
> movements. What seemed to be, a half year back, the unification
> of the peace movement on the basis of a single approach supporting
> the "two-state solution" has been transformed into division and
> confusion, emotionally charged with feelings of dread, disappoint-
> ment and a lost sense of direction. The break can be situated at
> two central points: the attitude to the war, itself, which separates
> between its advocates and the minority which opposes it, and the
> deep crisis in the relations of the left with the Palestinians. For
> the majority, there just isn't anything to do when the missiles
> start flying. There are also mutual recriminations. These people
> do not represent the peace camp. They have become part of the
> aggressive national consensus, opponents of the war will say of
> those on the left who support it. The camp which supports the
> war will answer: "they are hysterical marginal groups which lack
> any political understanding."[5]

Retreat, Repositioning, Comeback

The war in the Gulf and Israel's involvement in the war, chiefly
as an object of Scud attacks, brought about a serious retreat in the
prestige and influence of the peace movement in Israel. The reasons
are almost obvious but it is worth enumerating them in order to
describe the problems which the peace movement faced at the end
of the war.

The peace movement's crowning success during the Intifada had been to convince large sections of the public, if not, at certain points in time, even a majority of the people, that negotiations with the PLO offered a concrete and real opportunity for peace. With the advent of war, the public, as a whole, returned to its traditional suspicion regarding Palestinian motives. The general mood in the country was bitter and cynical: the public was convinced that Palestinian sympathy for Sadaam Hussein meant that Palestinian willingness to recognize Israel and negotiate with it was more of a maneuver than anything else. Here was proof that the PLO and the Palestinian public, given the first opportunity to do so, reverted to their original position – the hope to establish Palestinian sovereignty in all of Palestine. It seemed that the peace movement had been guilty of some degree of gullibility and its program appeared to have been built on sand. The Israeli hawks appeared to have had a deeper understanding of the inherent hostility of the Arabs and the Palestinians towards Israel. Here was another case of Israel's suffering an attack, without any provocation on its part. In short, Shamir's strategy – a prolonged, unending diplomatic stall – seemed reasonable, while the peace movement's alternative policies seemed flippant.

The peace movement had to fight an uphill battle in order to convince the public that the official interpretation of events was inadequate and distorted. Its feeling was that though the public might be stunned by the pressure of events and disappointed at Palestinian responses, the basic problems were going to reassert themselves and it was only a question of time until the peace movement could regain a place for its message in the ongoing debate concerning the national agenda. Shamir and his government were "helpful" in this respect when they began to use the temporary diplomatic respite to renew frenzied settler activity.

It was natural that a short period of re-evaluation preceded the return to post-war "normalcy." Nor was it surprising that the period immediately after the war witnessed a round of mutual recrimination between the two sections of the peace movement. The militants were convinced that the Zionist-left had shown its true colors by joining the national consensus. The leaders of the mainstream protest movement were hardly irked by these attacks from the left as their main problem was to convince their mass constituency that the movement's message was still relevant and that the period for a politics of national unity was over.

The Mainstream Found Wanting

One of the less sophisticated criticisms of the Zionist left held simply that, since the dialogue between the Palestinians and the Zionist left was predicated on Palestinian renunciation of "its Arab identity and its commitment to Arab unification and the uprising of the Arab peoples," the dialogue was doomed by the beginning of a new stage in the anti-imperialist struggle. This rediscovery of an unbridgeable chasm between the Palestinians and most of the Israeli peace camp assumed that the Gulf War was the beginning of a new epoch of anti-imperialist struggle in the region – a hope that was shot down in flames in a number of weeks.[6]

Dr. Azmi Bishara, an Israeli Palestinian intellectual with an intimate knowledge of the Zionist left, outlined its limitations in the following words:

> The Israeli Zionist left reveals neither serious understanding nor a real desire to understand the processes in the Arab world ... Instead the Zionist left becomes a warmonger and joins the Israeli nationalist camp which is interested in war in the Gulf ... The Israeli left is uninterested in struggles in the region and how can a left interested in peace and in integration in the region support total American hegemony ...[7]

This kind of criticism – though basically justified – was like barging into an open door, inasmuch as the Zionist left, and this includes Peace Now, were not in the least self-conscious about being open supporters of US policy in the region. This "pro-Americanism," so different from the approach of most peace formations, was built on two articles of faith. The first article of faith held that the United States was Israel's traditional ally (against Soviet influence and Arab radicalism) and a major financial and military backer of the country. Given the enmity of the Arab world and Soviet sympathy for the Arab cause, US support was a basic component of Israeli security. The second article of faith held that the United States, by virtue of its ramified interests in the region, had a basic interest in stability and this stability could be ensured only by curbing Israeli expansionism. The strategy of the peace movement envisaged an activist role for the United States as the surest remedy against Israeli intransigence. Thus, according to this approach, the more the United States intervened, the more it would be forced to disassociate itself from Israeli policies which sought to block any real chances for a compromise. The argument, in a nutshell, was that Israel should and could depend on the United States for its security and that, at some point, US interests would dictate the need for a compromise in the area, in opposition to the hopes and dreams of the Israeli right for a Greater Israel.

However, even if there were strong local considerations which shaped the pro-United States orientation of the Zionist section of the peace movement, Bishara was right in pointing out that the Zionist left showed a remarkable lack of genuine interest in the political and social dynamics of the region. After all was said and done it was the task of the Israeli peace movement to think in terms of processes and possibilities for the integration of Israel into the Arab world. This task was no less important, historically, than choosing the winning side in a particular crisis. Israel, without the benefit of the peace movement, already had enough advisors telling it how to come out on top by exploiting conflicts between Arab society and the world powers which saw the region through the familiar prism of oil and armaments. The Israeli peace movement could realize its basic goals only when and if it understood the Arab environment and took its needs and aspirations into account when developing a joint Arab-Israeli perspective.

An acute observer and participant on the protest scene, Prof. Stanley Cohen, was dismayed at the way the Zionist left and Peace Now responded to the Gulf crisis. However, Cohen stressed that there was no real basis for illusions about the mainstream sections of the peace movement who "have always taken care to operate within the national consensus and state security. They have never seen themselves as a protest movement on the edges of society."[8] In Cohen's opinion, the standard criticism from the left "is self-indulgent, unless we accept our dependence on these forces – and therefore, the need to understand their social base." Cohen's analysis creates room for debate with the Zionist left and warns against attempts to solve the problem by denouncing the treachery of the liberals in the peace camp.

Observers who had no illusions about the Zionist left had no reason to be disillusioned with its position during the war. Even so, there was something highly patronizing in the posture of many leading doves towards the international peace movement. Much of their criticism of the international peace movement was based on reactionary argumentation – attacking the peace movement abroad for being "soft" on aggression and assuming that Israelis had special, unique talents for analyzing trends in the region. This may have been partially true regarding concrete and immediate dangers to Israel. However, when it came to analyzing the real motives of the United States in the region, the international peace movement was certainly more knowledgeable and sophisticated than the leadership and the intellectuals on the Zionist left.

Peace Now felt little pressure to answer the criticism leveled against it from the left. The quick and decisive victory of the anti-Sadaam Hussein coalition was a political and ideological blow to the left, which had prophesied that the United States would get bogged down in Iraq. Instead of a new wave of anti-imperialist struggle, the region was readying itself for the local version of the "new world order." Peace Now's main interest was in finding ways, in the new political circumstances, of renewing the battle against the Shamir government. The moderates could find some comfort in the results of the war and the hope that the United States would use its enhanced influence "to do something" about the Israeli-Arab conflict.

Keeping Internationalist Hope Alive

For the militants and the radicals, the results of the Gulf War were another indication that a wave of conservatism and reaction had come to dominate international and regional affairs. The militants and the radicals feared that both the United States and Israel would seek to exploit the weakness of the Palestinians and the PLO. There was in Israel a solid core of peace activists who shared the values and the goals of the international peace movement and the mistrust (or opposition) for United States policy.

The capacity of the militant section of the peace movement to disassociate itself from the pro-war coalition in the region, though it took the form of an isolated "cry in the wilderness," had distinct moral and symbolic value. It kept a tradition of internationalism on the Israeli left alive in admittedly difficult circumstances. It sustained the obligation for independent thinking at a time when mass hysteria was prevalent. Even so, in practical terms, both the militant left and the mainstream of the Israeli peace movement suffered tangible losses. Much of the constituency of the more militant sections of the peace movement decided spontaneously to wait out the war. Much of the constituency of the mainstream felt uncomfortable, almost guilty over having been too optimistic about the path to peace. The Gulf War and the Scud attacks on Israel had moved the country to the right and moving it back to some kind of normalcy was not going to prove easy.

Comeback Trail

The interviewer, Gideon Levi, was known for his sympathies to the peace movement, but his job was to ask Tsali Reshef, Peace Now leader, the hard questions. He tried, unsuccessfully, to get Reshef to admit that Peace Now had made some wrong decisions. Reshef replied that the war actually confirmed Peace Now's basic approach by showing that Israel would be unacceptable as part of the Western coalition as long as the Palestinian question remained unsettled. But Reshef, who insisted that the left had not made any major mistakes, had to admit that "most of my associates think that we should keep quiet for the meanwhile, as if we have some reason to apologize."[9]

There was quite a bit of soul-searching in Peace Now after the war. Discussion in movement forums related to Peace Now's previous strategy and asked whether basic changes in Peace Now's policy were in order in light of the altered circumstances. A common criticism was that Peace Now had isolated itself from its mass base by drawing too close to the Palestinian leadership, or letting matters appear that way in the public. Zev Zachor, a political scientist at Ben-Gurion University in Be'er Sheva, affiliated with Peace Now from its inception, articulated severe criticism of Peace Now's basic strategy. "What a pity, wrote Zachor, "that precisely now Peace Now no longer represents the consensus of all those who are ready for peace in exchange for territories, as it has been pushed into that distant corner of the extreme left." Peace Now's big mistake, according to Zachor, was to become involved in issues like human rights, the condition of the population in the territories, negotiations with Palestinian leaders and support for the international recognition of the PLO.[10] These were, according to Zachor, side issues that isolated Peace Now from its mass base.

The Peace Now leadership denied that it had weakened the movement's links with its constituency. But the question "where do we go from here?" still hung in the air. The path that Peace Now chose was an attempt to build a new coalition of all the moderate forces in Israeli politics which supported the principle of territory for peace. The tactical move was a concession of sorts to those who felt that the movement had been too sectarian – without actually accepting the criticism. At the same time it was clear that this new coalition, which was to include a strong contingent of Labor MKs and hoped to activate leading moderates from the different kibbutz federations, was intended to rebuild Peace Now's mainstream connections and image. The coalition adopted a new name – "Time for Peace" – and a new logo featuring patriotic colors. The political logic for the move was based on two assumptions. First, the political scene had "returned to square one," and once more the basic division in Israel was between annexationists and those willing to give up territory for peace. Secondly, there were many dove circles in the country which were uncomfortable about accepting the open hegemony of Peace Now. These could contribute to building a broad coalition by agreeing to a new organization and new rules of the game. Peace Now leaders rejected comments that it was all a matter of cosmetic changes.[11] "Time for Peace" was launched with the active assistance of public relations experts. The new coalition was going to convince the public that peace was desirable by switching the emphasis from the price of peace to the dividends of peace. It sounded great but it didn't work.

Peace Now used the "Time for Peace" logo up to and including a major demonstration called by Peace Now on the eve of the Madrid Conference towards the end of October 1991. The difficulty was that, practically speaking, there were no other public forces on the Zionist left which joined Peace Now in "Time for Peace" activities. In fact, when Peace Now launched a major educational and information campaign against settlement activity during the spring and the summer of 1991, the campaign was carried out in the name of Peace Now and not in the name of the new and pretentious umbrella organization. The failure of the attempt to activate the party members and kibbutz members affiliated to the Zionist left seemed to indicate that Peace Now, in and of itself, despite its militant and somewhat "tarnished" image, was the one and only address for people who wanted to do something. Even in the most difficult of periods it was Peace Now, the seasoned protest force, which had the cadres and the resources to mount effective protest activity. People on the Zionist left who wanted to act were finding their way to Peace Now. It is reasonable to conclude that Peace Now decided, at a certain stage, that "Time for Peace" was simply more trouble than it was worth. "Time for Peace" disappeared without comment.

Back to Paris Square

During the missile attacks against Israel, Women In Black vigils were canceled, understandingly enough, all over the country. When the war ended, a series of discussions was held on whether and when to renew the vigil. One viewpoint called for an urgent return to the weekly vigil, whatever the expected turnout. Other activists suggested that it would be wiser to wait until it was clear that most of the previous participants were ready to return. After a few weeks' delay, the vigils were renewed and in approximately a month, the main Women In Black vigil in Jerusalem regained most, if not all, its previous strength. Smaller vigils reappeared in Tel Aviv, Haifa and at several key intersections in the countryside. But most of the thirty-odd vigils, which had demonstrated weekly all over the country during the first half of 1990, were permanent casualties. These vigils had been smaller from the start and disbanded as a result of their relative isolation and the chauvinist mood in the country.

Women In Black's experience paralleled that of most of the peace movement. The Gulf War inflicted serious damage on the movement, but a large core of activists, throughout the entire peace movement – which was, to borrow a metaphor, "battered but not bowed" – were convinced that, since the basic political problems remained unsolved, it was just a question of time until the political climate would enable them to gain lost ground and move forward.

Diplomatic activity in the region in the post-war period was dominated by a series of visits by the US Secretary of State, James Baker. After five visits to the relevant capitals, and intensive talks with the governments concerned and parallel discussions with a Palestinian delegation from the territories, acting with the approval of the PLO in Tunis, the United States issued an invitation to a Conference to discuss peace to be held in Madrid at the end of October, 1991.

It was not as if the Shamir government was interested in the Madrid Conference. The Shamir government was interested in continuing the occupation which allowed it to pour unprecedented resources into the settlement drive. On one occasion, James Baker exceeded the limits of protocol in order to inform the public that he was annoyed by the government's insistence on establishing a new settlement on the eve of each of his visits to Israel. Baker had painstakingly achieved the assent of all concerned to a very general set of formulations which served as the basis for the invitation issued by the co-sponsors, the United States and the Soviet Union. In the circumstances, Shamir could not have refused to attend the conference without risking a crisis in US-Israeli relations. All things considered, the conference created no new real obligations on the part of Israel.

Peace Now hesitated about calling a demonstration on the eve of the Madrid meeting. The slogan, Israel Wants Peace, was a bit ambiguous. There had not been a major demonstration since well before the Gulf crisis. There was more than the usual amount of pre-demonstration anxiety about the size of the turn out. The fears were proven unjustified when tens of thousands Israelis turned out in yet another massive expression of the deep widespread longing for an end to the conflict. The scenario was familiar: a right-wing Prime Minister was off on a diplomatic mission to a conference he was attending only because he had been unsuccessful in preventing it. Madrid might be the beginning of a new era in the diplomatic history of the region, but no one believed that this would be the last demonstration.

Afterword:
Measuring Success and Failure

Most of the work on this book was done during a grim period for the peace movement and hopes for the chances for Israeli-Arab peace. It wasn't long before the Madrid Conference, which convened in October 1991, appeared to have been a false-start. After the pomp and ceremony in Madrid, it seemed that nothing, even US diplomatic efforts, could wear down Shamir's obstinacy. The victory of the Labor party in Israel's national elections in June 1992 did provide a ray of light. The peace movement could see itself as a partner in the victory of Labor and felt a sense of satisfaction that MERETZ (the coalition of the left-Zionist parties composed of the Citizen's Rights Movement, MAPAM and Shinui) had done well electorally and become a major force in the emerging coalition.

Even before the final results were in, Rabin, who headed Labor's electoral list, announced that he, personally, would make all the important decisions and took pains to let everyone understand that his policies would be based on Israeli military might. Rabin's approach led, soon after he took office, to a series of measures against the Palestinians as draconic as anything the Likud ever dared to implement. These included the expulsion of 400 Palestinians in December 1992 and the rampant use of long-term closure and curfews against the entire Palestinian population in the occupied territories. The grounds for optimism based on the installation of a new government were dashed by Rabin's repeated resort to brutal repression against the Palestinians. The peace movement had to prepare to do battle against a government which it had helped vote into power.

These unhappy circumstances bracketed the emerging text. If forced to give this book a title back then, I might have opted for something like "Noble Try" or "Noble Failure." In the somber post-Madrid period, and during the first year of the Rabin premiership, it was impossible to prove that the intensive struggle waged by the Israeli peace movement during the first years of the Intifada had any permanent or lasting effects on the behavior of the government.

The work on the completion of the latter part of this book occurred in happier circumstances. The Declaration of Principles signed by Israel and the PLO in September 1993 was a historic breakthrough, though no one really believed that a just and lasting peace was just around the corner. However, from any point of view, the Declaration of Principles bore the deep imprint of the peace movement, which had been in essence a movement for mutual Israeli-Palestinian recognition. After the Oslo Accords and the Rabin–Arafat meeting on the South Lawn of the White House, one is tempted to present the peace movement as an unadulterated success story. Both characterizations of the Israeli peace movement's response to the Intifada – as either a failure or a success – are equally inadequate and misleading. The evaluation of the success or failure of a major protest movement is often no simple matter. It is true that, looking back over a quarter of a century, the peace movement in Israel can list several clear and unequivocal successes over the years. The most notable of these were the intensive campaign by the newly-established Peace Now which helped force Begin towards the Camp David Accords and the united anti-war efforts of both the militant left and the mainstream peace movement against the war in Lebanon in 1982. But even when it is most successful, the peace movement is only one of many forces operative in the political arena. The peace movement can shape the history of an epoch but it cannot shape its own history. The number of people who join its ranks, and their capacity for exerting effective political pressure, depend on circumstances that are inevitably far from being under its control.

If there is a lesson here, it is that it is unfair and unwise to evaluate the importance and success of the peace movement's efforts by a simple assessment – whether the goals of the movement were realized. Just as we should refrain from "blaming" the peace movement when its objectives remain unrealized, we must desist any temptation to exaggerate the role of the peace movement when those goals are attained. Having said all this, it is also true that most people in Israel consider the current peace process with all its limitations and complications as the crowning achievement of the Israeli peace movement.

There appears to be a remarkable deal of continuity and innovation in the Israeli peace movement over decades of activity. In this sense, the movement has accumulated a wealth of organizational tools and experience which enable it to respond to new crises. Moreover, each period has seen additional forms of struggle and new groupings of participants. The rise of an autonomous women's protest movement was one of these important innovations during the Intifada period. The plethora of protest groups, and among them the appearance and success of organization by profession, enabled the protest movement to tap the energy and the talents of wide sectors in the population. It can be said that the peace movement is constantly laying up treasures for future use.

The story of the Israeli response to the Intifada is a 'success story' in that so many Israelis understood that this was a challenge that they had to meet personally and politically. In doing so, they expanded the scope and the forms of protest which in turn added color and spectacle to the political scene. Protest is often fascinating and protest activity is often exciting. However, upon closer observation, it becomes clear that all the excitement and the commotion is the direct product of stubbornly determined, devoted and conscientious women and men who are ready to go to yet another meeting, to make another round of phone calls and, when this is needed, to stand alone passing out leaflets on a street corner.

The main motive for the book was to describe the goals, the successes and the limitations of the peace movement and to pay tribute to all the groups and individuals who felt a moral and political duty to respond positively to the Intifada. Israelis active in the peace movement hoped to convince their compatriots that Israel could never know peace and stability as long as the basic rights of the Palestinians were denied. At the same time, the peace movement believed, and was proven correct in this respect, that the enhanced prestige of the Palestinians, which resulted from the Intifada, would increase the chances for an historic compromise with Israel based on mutual recognition of the national rights of both peoples. In its battle for the recognition of Palestinian national rights, the Israeli peace movement operated on the basis of a universal principle common to peace activists everywhere, namely that internationalism is the highest form of patriotism.

Notes

Introduction: The Roots of Protest in Israel

1. Michael Wolffsohn, *Israel – Polity, Society, Economy, 1882–1986* (Humanities Press International, Atlantic Highlands, New Jersey, 1987) writes: "From the very beginning, polity and economy, society and culture – even the question of security – were . . . determined by party politics . . . Israel could be regarded as the model of the party state. Nothing was possible without the consent – not to mention against the will of the parties (p. xvii).

2. For a detailed summary of the work of the Israeli Peace Committee, see Tamar Herman, The Rise and Decline of the IPC, *Zionism*, XVII, pp. 245–82, Tel Aviv University, 1983 (Hebrew).

3. Tamar Herman in a fairly recent article, "Ihud," – A Peace Movement Under Fire, 1947–1949 (*State, Government and International Relations*, no. 33, Hebrew University, Spring 1991 – Heb.), bemoans the fact that Ihud's noble battle for peace is never mentioned by Israel's modern peace movements.

4. For further details of the "Lavon affair," see Susan Hattis Rolef, *Political Dictionary of Israel* (Jerusalem Publishing House, Jerusalem, 1993), pp. 192–3 and for the wider political impact of the crisis on *MAPAI*, see Joel Beinin, *Was The Red Flag Flying There?* (University of California Press, Los Angeles, 1990), pp. 12, 224.

5. Rodinson Maxime, *Israel, A Colonial-Settler State?* (Monad Press, New York, 1973) is a unique contribution to the discussion. The text first appeared in a special issue of Sartre's *Les Temps Moderns* in the summer of 1967. Rodinson supports the argument for the colonialist nature of Israel, but avoids facile conclusions negating the future of Israel and the possibilities of peacefully resolving the Israeli-Arab conflict.

6. Predictably, there were Maoist and Trotskyist trends, each of which underwent further splits, usually inspired by developments in sister organizations abroad. A third trend, centered in Tel Aviv, continued the original ideological tendency of Matzpen in Israel and steered clear of any international affiliation. The enervating effect of the splits

prevented any group from achieving the strength or prestige that the united movement commanded.

7. Yael Gvirtz, *Yediot Ahronot*, October 2, 1992. The article was occasioned by publication of a follow-up study of the signatories. The research found that none of the signers actually refused to serve. Interestingly their occupational profile was "irregular" in that a high proportion of the signers ended up in the creative arts, the media and the social services. The strongest line in the short letter read: "We have doubts about being able to fight in an endless war, with no prospects, while our government pursues policies that spoil chances for peace."

8. The Mo'ked (Focus) list ran in the 1973 elections and received one seat that went to Meir Pa'il. The list was based on a coalition composed of a section of SIAH headed by Ran Cohen, several Socialist-Zionist student groups and MAKI – which was actually the Jewish half of the CPI – which split back in 1965. MAKI was led by Ya'ir Tsahan, after the death of Moshe Sneh in 1972.

9. A satirical review authored by a rising playwright, Hanoch Levin, "Queen of the Bath" (Golda Meir!), had created a public storm during 1970. Most of the performances were successfully disrupted by right-wing activists and the Camerie Theater was forced to cancel the play.

10. The rise of the peace movement can be seen as a part of the overall transformation of Israeli politics: "An important change has occurred in the political culture of Israel starting in the early seventies. The age of protest arrived somewhat late to the country, but Israelis have adopted it with a vengeance." Gadi Wolfsfeld, *The Politics of Provocation: Participation and Protest in Israel* (State University of New York, Albany 1988).

1 From Miracle to Débâcle

1. "One prominent Israeli, it should be noted, dissented. Defense Minister Moshe Dayan, the most astute and influential member of Golda Meir's cabinet, argued that Israel should make an offer to Sadat to test his intentions. Dayan even presented the cabinet with a plan to draw the Israeli army back from the Canal . . . in order to persuade Egypt . . . " Milton Viorst, *Sands of Sorrow* (I .B. Tauris, London, 1987), p. 142.

2. Mordechai Bar-on, *Peace Now – Portrait of a Movement* (Kibbutz Ha'meuchad Publishing House, Tel Aviv, 1985), p. 16. While it is technically true, as Bar-on states, that the initiators of the letter were a small informal group in Jerusalem, many of those who drafted and disseminated the letter were associated with a student group centered at the Hebrew University, named the "Movement for a Different Kind of Zionism". The Movement's message was identical to the program

of "Peace and Security" – opposition on Zionist grounds to annexation or settlement of the occupied territories.

3. What is Peace Now? What Are its Goals and Functions? Peace Now pamphlet, August 1979 (English). I took the liberty of retranslating a number of key words which appeared to have lost some of their impact in the translation given there. It is unfortunate, though perfectly understandable, that many translations issued by peace groups in Israel do not always do full justice to the Hebrew original.

4. Ibid.

5. Mordechai Bar-On, *Peace Now, Portrait of a Movement*, p.18.

6. Ibid, pp. 44–45.

7. Peace Now publication, undated but circa March 1980.

8. There were Peace Now activists who felt that the movement was over cautious regarding the PLO. Dedi Zucker and Yael Tamir, acting on their own, met with Issam Sartawi in Europe in October 1980. The unofficial meeting caused one of the first crises in Peace Now. Zucker and Tamir's initiative met with so much suspicion and hostility in Peace Now that the two decided (or were forced) to leave the movement. Sartawi, who was Arafat's unofficial envoy to the Israeli peace camp, was assassinated in Lisbon by Palestinian adversaries, in September 1983, while attending a meeting of the Socialist International.

2 The Establishment of the Committee for Solidarity with Bir Zeit University

1. For an excellent summary of the contacts from the Palestinian side, see Salim Tamari, "Israeli-Palestinian Dialogue – Report from the West Bank" – MERIP Reports, January 1983, pp. 23–24.

2. Over the years, the above figure has been challenged from different sources, giving rise to a rather specious debate about how many demonstrators can occupy a square meter. No one has actually challenged the central fact that it was the biggest demonstration ever held in Israel and that it called for withdrawal from Lebanon. One of the speakers was, incidentally, Labor Party MK, Yitzhak Rabin.

3. Yesh Gvul has in Hebrew a double meaning. It means both "There is a border" and "there's a limit" as in "there is a limit to what I am ready to put up with . . . "

4. Gvul Ha'tsiut (The Limits of Obedience), published by Yesh Gvul, 1985, p. 175.

3 Intifada! – December 1987

1. Strictly speaking, the Israeli public is composed of two distinct components, the Israeli Jewish sector, and the Palestinian Arab sector, which comprises roughly a sixth of the population. However, in day

to day usage, concepts such as "Israeli public opinion" or the "mood of the Israeli electorate," refer to the Jewish Israeli sector. Political differences between the two sectors are so pronounced as to prevent any generalizations valid for the two groupings.

2. Robert Rosenberg, *Jerusalem Post*. The quote is from the first article – Peace Camp on the March – of an excellent four part series, February 22–25, 1988.

4 "End the Occupation" – The Militants Make a Comeback

1. Formal organizations with rules and regulations governing membership, election of governing bodies, etc., were and still are rare on the Israeli protest scene.

2. According to Israeli law, it is not necessary to obtain a permit for a demonstration, if the assembly is "stationary" and there are no speeches or loudspeakers, though placards and banners are permissible. For this reason, many protest activities assume the form of a vigil, whatever the time of day or night.

3. Dai La'kibush flyer (English) – February 1988.

4. Dai La'kibush flyer (undated).

5. *Ma'ariv*, March 29, 1988.

6. East for Peace was one of several important attempts to create a framework designed to attract sections of Israel's Mizrakhi population. East for Peace was the home base of a number of key figures such as Dr. Shlomo Elbaz and David Ish-Shalom, but the group never succeeded in building a permanent group of activists.

7. *Jerusalem Post*, June 5, 1988.

8. The reference is to the government of national unity, formed by the two main parties, Likud and Labor.

9. Dai La'kibush flyer, February 1988.

10. Yoram Harpaz, *Kol Hair*, February 19, 1988.

11. A good translation of the full text of the Covenant can be found in *Tikkun*, vol. 3, no. 3, (September–October, 1988). I have preferred to translate from the Hebrew text which is sharper and more direct in tone, *Ha'aretz*, March 4, 1988. The short passages in quotes are my translation from the Hebrew text, unless otherwise indicated.

12. The excerpts are based on the translation which appeared in *Tikkun*.

13. Ibid.

14. Yael G'virtz, *Hadashot*, February 19, 1988.

15. Ibid.

16. Hanan Hever, *Ha'aretz*, January 22, 1988.

17. "The 21st Year – Political Action," a flyer put out in English (the flyer is undated but must have come out in the late spring of 1988). The detailed list of activities and plans is the basis for a request for contributions.

18. Ibid.

19. Ibid.
20. On the basis of a plea bargain with the prosecution, the Nitzotz defendants admitted to membership in an "illegal terrorist organization" (the Democratic Front for the Liberation of Palestine). Though the prosecution never alleged the commission of any overt action against Israeli security, four defendants received prison sentences; the most severe was against the group leader, Ya'akov Ben Efrat – three years.
21. Newsletter of The Twenty-first Year, June 1988.
22. Ibid.
23. *Jerusalem Post* Supplement, December 16, 1988.
24. Eytan Rabin, *Ha'aretz*, November 30, 1988.
25. *Ha'aretz*, January 20, 1989.
26. Michal Sela, *Jerusalem Post*, February 3, 1989.
27. Amiram Cohen, *Hotam*, February 2, 1989.

5　Yesh Gvul – Selective Refusal Extended from Lebanon to the Occupied Territories

1. Yesh Gvul leaflet, March, 1986.
2. A Jewish terrorist organization based in the settlements in the occupied territories. Its members were convicted in July, 1985 of murder and terrorist activities which included car-bombing against three Palestinian mayors, murder of students at the Islamic College in the Gaza strip and conspiracy to blow up the Dome of the Rock on the Temple Mount. All enjoyed privileged conditions in prison and generous reductions in their sentences.
3. *Jerusalem Post*, January 1, 1988.
4. Advertisement, *Kol Hair*, June 3, 1988.
5. Pincas Sherut (Serviceman's Manual) Yesh Gvul publication, undated.
6. Gideon Alon, *Ha'aretz*, July 19, 1988.
7. ibid.
8. Gideon Alon, *Ha'aretz*, January 18, 1989.
9. Yesh Gvul press release – circa late January 1989.
10. ibid.
11. Larry Derfner, *Jerusalem Post*, May 16, 1989.
12. Ibid.
13. *Ha'aretz*, May 5, 1989.
14. Lily Galilee, *Ha'aretz*, October 29, 1989. The same account reports that 90 soldiers, reservists and conscripts, were jailed for refusal to serve in the territories since the beginning of the Intifada.
15. *Al Ha'mishmar*, June 1988. Grossman's step took the form of an expression of solidarity with Dov Yermiyah who supported Yesh Gvul openly and actively. Yermiyah, who had served as a high-ranking IDF officer in charge of alleviating the suffering of the civilian population in Lebanon after the Israeli invasion, was one of the leaders of Red

Line, a protest movement based in the north of Israel, which was prominent during the first months of the Intifada.

16. Yossi Sarid, *Ha'aretz*, June 16, 1988.
17. Mordechai Bar-on, *Peace Now – Portrait of a Movement* (Kibbutz Ha'Meuchad Publishing House, Tel Aviv, 1985), pp. 57–58.
18. The second demonstration of Peace Now, after the beginning of the Intifada on December 26, 1987 in Jerusalem, ended when police fired tear gas canisters at the crowd. The demonstrators believed that they had a perfect right to end the demonstration with a vigil outside Shamir's residence. The police, who thought otherwise, were tense and fired tear gas at an orderly and peaceful crowd.
19. Yesh Gvul published one book based on the Lebanon war period: *Gvul Ha'tsiut* (The Limits of Obedience), ed. Ishai and Dina Menuhin (Siman Kriah Books, 1985).
20. *Al Democratia v'Tsiut* (On Democracy and Obedience), ed. Ishai Menuhin (Siman Kriah Books, 1990).
21. *Na'aseh v'Nishmah*, (Obey First and Hear [the explanation] Later), Liat Kaplan and Michal Levin, educators for Democracy, 1989.

6 The Formation of an Independent Women's Peace Movement

1. "The women's peace movement, whose initiators and most active members are feminists, represents a departure from past feminist activity; prior to the outbreak of the Palestinian Intifada, most Jewish feminists in Israel did not view peace issues as legitimate feminist concerns." Swirsky and Sapir, *Calling the Equality Bluff* (Pergaon Press, New York, 1991). Members of the Feminist Movement played a key role in the establishment of the women's peace movement in Tel Aviv and Haifa, while in Jerusalem the initiative came from women associated with the left who had been active in the militant section of the peace movement (the Committee for Solidarity with Bir Zeit University and the Committee against the War in Lebanon.)
2. Randi Jo Land, *Jerusalem Post*, March 11, 1988.
3. *Jerusalem Post*, May 20, 1988.
4. Haim Baram, *Kol Ha'ir*, August 31, 1990. Hoffman spearheaded Women In Black's long, and relatively successful campaign to ensure police protection and impartiality.
5. *Ha'aretz*, June 26, 1988.
6. Women In Black leaflet, March 1990. Instead of presenting only the position of the majority as the position of the group, Women In Black preferred to publicize the existence of different approaches in the group.
7. Circular of Kibbutz Artzi, Political and Ideological Department, May 16, 1989.
8. *Jewish Women's Peace Bulletin*, no. 6–7, October 1990. The bulletin was issued by the Jewish Women's Committee to End the Occupation in

New York.
9. Circular letter, Women In Black, Jerusalem.
10. Circular letter, Women In Black, Jerusalem, April, 1990.
11. SHANI Press Release, March 8, 1988.
12. SHANI Statement, 1989.
13. SHANI, Open Letter, undated.
14. Randi Jo Land, "Peace is a Women's Issue, Too," *Jerusalem Post*, December 12, 1988.
15. Women's Organization for Women Political Prisoners was also known as Women for Support of Women Political Prisoners and other similar variations. These were variations on the Hebrew: "Nashim L'maan Asirot Politiot."
16. Edith Whitmen, "Simply Not to Become Thick-Skinned," *Hadashot*, November 13, 1988.
17. ibid.
18. Flyer, Women for Women Political Prisoners, undated, circa 1990.
19. Ibid.
20. Brochure, Women for Support for Women Political Prisoners, circa January 1990, p. 1.

7 Peace Now Back in Business

1. The more radical formations in the peace movement worked out a variety of tactics regarding Peace Now demonstrations. These included separate demonstrations preceeding the Peace Now demonstration, after which the militants would join the Peace Now rally as a group. This did not, as a rule, cause any particular tensions, unless banners and slogans raised by the militants were considered particularly provocative by the Peace Now organizers. It almost goes without saying that the Peace Now rallies were a natural spot for heavy leafleting by the more radical groups.
2. Peace Now advertisement, *Jerusalem Post*, December 18, 1987.
3. Yaron Zelig, *Al Ha'mishmar*, January 24, 1988. Crowd estimates in the media varied between 50,000 to 80,000. Assessing the number of participants in demonstrations of this size is difficult.
4. Peace Now flyer issued before demonstration January 23, 1988.
5. *Jerusalem Post*, February 12, 1988.
6. Betzalel Amicam, *Al Ha'mishmar*, February 28, 1988. Peace Now's support for United States policy and its insistence that the Palestinian leadership was just as culpable as the Israeli government for the stalemate alienated some of the newer activists who found their way to the more militant sections of the peace movement.
7. Shlomo Slutzky, *Al Ha'mishmar*, March 13, 1988. Reshef, from Jerusalem and a lawyer by profession, has been, over the years, the most important leader of Peace Now.
8. Ibid.

9. *Jerusalem Post*, July 25, 1988. Abu Sharif wrote that the PLO knows full well that the problem is not making peace with Peace Now, which would not be difficult, but with either a Likud or a Labor party government.

10. "My Darling Enemy", Sarah Leibowitz-Dar, *Hadashot* Supplement, April 30, 1993. The article published after Israeli agreement to permit Husseini to become an official member of the Palestinian delegation to the peace talks is an excellent summary of Husseini's single-minded fidelity to the principle of developing contact and understanding with the Israeli public.

11. *Ha'aretz*, August 1, 1988.

12. *Jerusalem Post*, August 5, 1988.

13. Peace Now publication – August 1988.

14. There were many polls which reflected a similar trend towards increased polarity in Israeli public opinion. The same polls which indicated increased support for direct talks with the PLO also showed increased support for "transfer", i.e. mass expulsion of the Palestinians.

15. Lily Galilee, *Ha'aretz*, November 23, 1999.

16. Advertisement, *Jerusalem Post*, November 23, 1988.

17. Dan Margalit, *Ha'aretz*, December 6, 1988. Margalit was so kind as to condone Peace Now's "understandable if unjustified" enthusiasm, as a reaction to the government's stubborn lack of interest.

18. The "forum-al" (literally, the highest forum) is the highest deliberative body of Peace Now. Theoretically, the body is composed of representatives from various Peace Now forums (or branches) all over the country. Usually, this meant leading figures from Jerusalem, Tel Aviv, the kibbutz sector and other individual members whose presence was considered important. The leadership of the movement was centered in Jerusalem and it was generally agreed that one of the major functions of the "forum al" was to counter-balance the limitations inherent in this situation.

19. This account of the meeting is based on reports by Gideon Levy, *Ha'aretz*, December 23, 1988 and Avi Ofer, Hotam (*Al Ha'mishamr*), December 23, 1988. Levy wrote as an invited journalist and Ofer as a Peace Now participant.

20. Andy Goldberg, *Jerusalem Post*, December 25, 1988.

21. Peace Now pamphlet (English), December 1988. I think this is the first Peace Now publication that carries an additional US address.

22. Ibid.

23. Ibid.

24. Aryeh Dayan, *Kol Ha'ir*, November 25, 1988.

25. Yossi Ben Artzi, *Ha'aretz*, February 6, 1989.

26. See Nahum Barnea, *Yediot Ahronot*, February 24, 1989 for this account of the meeting.

27. Michal Yudelman, *Jerusalem Post*, March 3, 1989. Shamir did not

consider it necessary to explain how "an element that cannot influence anything" could sabotage Israel's fight for its very existence.

28. Marda Dunsky, *Jerusalem Post*, April 4, 1989.
29. Involved participants in the political process tend, naturally enough, to pounce on favorable polls and to ignore, as far as possible, negative findings. There is a good summary of public opinion shifts during the Intifada in "The Intifada and Israeli Public Opinion", by Goldberg, Barzilai and Inbar, *Policy Studies* no. 43, Leonard Davis Institute, Hebrew University, Jerusalem, February, 1991: "The Intifada had two major effects on Israeli public opinion: bipolarization and a growing dovishness . . . the main obstacle in identifying that [dove] lay in overemphasizing the importance of voting patterns." This summary predates the Gulf War and a rise of anti-Palestinian sentiment.
30. Joel Greenberg and Larry Derfner, *Jerusalem Post*, May 28, 1989.
31. Ibid.
32. Tuvia Baskind, *Al Ha'mishmar*, December 18, 1989.

8 The Demise of the Militants

1. Advertisement, *Hadashot*, November 18, 1989.
2. Orly Toren, *Jerusalem Post*, June 2, 1989.
3. Gideon Levi, *Ha'aretz*, June 2, 1989. The member of the group explained afterwards that he made the sign so that the local Palestinians would understand that the 27 were not settlers. He also insisted that the "V" sign when made palm turned inward means "peace" and not "victory" which is expressed by a "V" sign with the palm outward.
4. The letter appears in *Walking the Red Line – Israelis in Search of Justice for Palestine*, ed. Deena Hurwitz (New Society Publishers, Philadelphia, PA, 1992). The book is one of the first in English to deal with the thinking of activists in Israel and contains much valuable information.
5. Ibid. p. 103.
6. Ibid. pp. 104–5.
7. Ibid. pp. 104–5.

9 Taking Protest Personally

1. Paid advertisement, *Ha'aretz*, November 3, 1989.
2. *Al Ha'mishmar*, March 4, 1990.
3. The kibbutz "refusenick" had less economic worries than his urban counterpart. Even so the city-dweller doesn't have to deal with a common complaint aimed at the kibbutz "refusenick" such as "Who do you think you are? While you were sitting in jail, we had to support your family." Quoted from *Kibbutz, United Kibbutz Movement Weekly*, March 28, 1990.

4. Ibid.
5. *Ha'aretz*, July 26, 1990.
6. *Ha'aretz*, July 27, 1990.
7. Dan Margalit, *Ha'aretz*, July 29, 1990.
8. *Ha'aretz*, July 30, 1990.
9. Ibid.
10. *Jerusalem Post*, July 30, 1990.
11. Tali Tamir, "Faces of the Intifada," *Kol Ha'ir*, August 12, 1988.
12. Ibid.
13. Yizhar Be'er, *Kol Ha'ir*, June 17, 1988.
14. Ibid.
15. *Hadashot*, February 5, 1988.
16. Berman's article in *Politika*, February, 1988 is quoted from Shlomo Slutsky, *Al Ha'mishmar*, June 17, 1988. Slutsky, who describes himself as "someone who monitored developments among mental health workers and their limited social involvement," published a glowing account of the conference. Slutsky mentions three antecedents: historical research by psychologists dealing with the particularly high stress level in Israeli society. During the 1981 elections there was an initiative to publish a petition dealing with the state of Prime Minister Menahem Begin's mental health. The initiative was cancelled on "ethical grounds" and instead a group of psychologists published an analysis of the manipulative elements in the right-wing Likud election propaganda. An initiative during the first half of 1982 to convene mental health professionals dealt with the deterioration of the situation in the territories was cancelled with the outbreak of the war in Lebanon at the beginning of June 1982.
17. Ibid.
18. Imut announcement on the formation of the organization, its goals, contact people in the main cities and additional organizational information, including membership voucher. (In Hebrew and Arabic – undated).
19. Joachim Stein, The Uneasy Conqueror, *Ha'aretz*, April 25, 1989.
20. Shosh Avigal, *Hadashot*, June 6, 1989.
21. This and other quotations on Cohen's analysis are from a manuscript of his lecture, "PsycholgicaL Barriers to Peace," given at the IMUT Conference on May 24, 1989.
22. Advertisement, *Jerusalem Post*, February 5, 1988.
23. *Yediot Ahronot*, March 27, 1988.
24. *Hotam*, April 1, 1988.
25. *Al Ha'mishmar*, May 31, 1988.
26. A literal translation of the phrase, "Ad Kan" would be, "Up to here," but the translation, based on the connotation, i.e., "No Further," is, indeed, much better.
27. Publication of the AIPPHR, June 15, 1988 and circular letter of the AIPPHR, February 1989.

28. Yitzhak Peterberg, *Jerusalem Post*, August 31, 1989. Peterberg is responding to a report by Michal Sela, on the Association's findings which appeared in the *Jerusalem Post*, August 15, 1989.
29. Ibid.
30. Advertisement, Rabbinic Human Rights Watch, *Jerusalem Post*, March 21, 1993.
31. *Jerusalem Post*, February 2, 1990.

10   Dismal Deadlock

1. *Yediot Ahronot*, December 8, 1989.
2. *Jerusalem Post*, December 6, 1989. The article, by Wolf Blitzer, is based on a *New York Times* interview with Rabin published the previous day.
3. B'Tselem, Israeli Information Center for Human Rights in the Occupied Territories. Annual Report 1989.
4. *Ha'aretz*, Lead editorial, December 5, 1989.
5. *Hotam*, Weekly Supplement *Al Ha'mishmar*, May 1989, provides us with a fascinating account of the difficulties encountered by a Women In Black vigil in the organizing stage with the local kibbutz authorities and the Kibbutz Artzi Federation. The big problem was fitting the Women In Black phenomenon into the standard classifications, e.g. whether or not Women In Black were a Zionist group or unwittingly subversive. Soon after the incidents described there, which included refusal to use the kibbutz bulletin board, the Kibbutz Federation endorsed Women In Black activity.
6. Neri Livneh, *Hadashot*, December 10, 1989.
7. Jean-Paul Chagnollaud, "The European Community and the Middle East Conflict," in *Intifada*, ed. Nassar and Heacock (Praeger, New York, 1990), pp. 257–67.
8. Michal Sela, *Jerusalem Post*, May 29, 1989.
9. All quotes are from an identical pamphlet issued separately by SHANI and the Reshet which includes both the Brussels Declaration and the petition based on the three principles.
10. Information Sheet, Israel Women's Peace Net, undated.
11. Dan Izenberg, *Jerusalem Post*, July 15, 1990.
12. *Ha'aretz*, February 8, 1990. The Jewish leadership was simply much closer to the Labor Party positions and the liberal approaches that guided its thinking were sufficient to land it close to the dove wing of Labor.
13. *Jerusalem Post*, February 23, 1990.
14. *Jerusalem Post*, December 10, 1989. Many militants were angered by Peace Now's equating the fate of hundreds of Palestinian victims with that of a handful of Jewish victims, but Peace Now felt that this was an effective way to counter charges that the peace movement was insensitive to the fate of victims of violence on the Israeli side.

15. Peace Now flyer (undated), entitled "Two Years of Intifada and Political Paralysis – Till When?

16. Rolly Rosen, *Kol Ha'ir*, December 29, 1989.

17. *Jerusalem Post*, December 27, 1989.

18. *Jerusalem Post*, December 29, 1989.

19. The most comprehensive descriptions of the events are to be found in Harriet Lewis, *New Outlook*, January/February 1990, and *News From Within*, January 10, 1990. The daily press devoted tremendous coverage to the Peace Now, Human Chain and the clash between the police and demonstrators, but hardly mentioned the activities on Women's Day.

20. Avi Katzsman, "Facing the Water Cannon, the Truncheons and the Rubber Bullets," *Ha'aretz* Supplement, January 5, 1990. The article contains a detailed account of the El-Kawati clash by Docca Valent, Italian member of the European Parliament.

21. Lead editorial, *Hadashot*, December 31, 1989. Police conduct was criticized, though not in the same sweeping terms, in editorials in the *Ha'aretz* (January 1, 1990) and the *Jerusalem Post* (January 1, 1990).

22. *Jerusalem Post*, January 1, 1990.

23. *Ha'aretz*, January 15, 1990.

24. *Jerusalem Post*, January 18, 1990.

25. "Shalom Achshav," May 1990. A two page summary of the 17 page report submitted to the Chief Commissioner of Police is given in a movement bulletin which appeared every few months.

26. *Yediot Ahronot*, April 15, 1990.

11 Crisis at the Top

1. Leon Shelef, *Ha'aretz*, April 13, 1990. Shelef is a professor of Law and Sociology at Tel Aviv University.

2. Ibid.

3. *Jerusalem Post*, March 11, 1990.

4. *Ha'aretz*, May 27, 1990.

5. B'Tselem is Hebrew for "in the image of" from Genesis 1,27: "And God created man in His image. In the image of God did He create him. Man and women He created them."

6. What Is B'tselem? – Statement B'Tselem (January 25, 1990).

7. Ibid.

8. What is B'tselem, January 25, 1990.

9. B'tselem folder, undated.

10. *New York Times*, International, January 19, 1990.

11. The Intifada and the protest movement usually received fairly balanced treatment in the Israeli media. IDF and government "sources" had full access to the media and pushed their own versions intensively. However, there were a number of favorable factors in play: many media people were simply shocked that many of the actions

by the IDF were unprecedented in terms of brutality and cruelty; the international media were usually in hot pursuit after newsworthy items (including protest activity in Israel) and this set the professional standards for their Israeli colleagues; finally, there was a large core of journalists who covered the territories with professional dedication and many progressive columnists ready to expose official hypocrisy.

12. Stanley Cohen, Torture in Israel: Defining the Issues, *New Outlook*, September 1990 (vol. 33, no. 9). Cohen refers to a series of articles that appeared in the London *Sunday Times* in 1975–76. Almost all observers agree that Menahem Begin personally ordered restraints on the use of torture when he became Prime Minister in 1977.

13. Ibid.

14. The Public Committee Against Torture in Israel – Founding Statement, January 1990.

15. Ibid.

16. Stanley Cohen, Summary of Comments at Press Conference of the Public Committee Against Torture in Israel, April 4, 1990.

17. The Report is summarized in a follow-up to the March 1991 Report issued by B'Tselem in March 1992. The description on the 1991 Report given here, as well as the Israeli and international media responses, are based on the B'tselem follow-up study and presented as given therein.

18. The Follow-Up Report is quoting Vered Lamm, "It Does Bother Them," *Ha'aretz* Supplement, May 6, 1991.

19. *Yediot Ahronot*, May 3, 1991.

20. Adi Ophir, *Davar*, "Objective Description of Moderate Physical Pressure," May 31, 1991; "Torture Montage," June 7, 1991; "Collage of Evil," June 14, 1991.

21. "Poets Will Not Write Poems," ed. Ilana Hammerman.

22. Stanley Cohen, *Davar*, July 5, 1991.

23. Kav La'Oved Newsletter, June 1992. The figures relate to the employment figures for autumn, 1990.

24. Who We Are and What We Do – Kav La'Oved, Workers' Hotline, undated but c. 1991.

25. Kav La'oved Newsletter, December 1992. MK Ya'ir Tsahan (Mapam) was quoted in the January–February 1991 Newsletter of Kav La'oved as saying, at a symposium in Tel Aviv in December 1990, that the Treasury had received, over the years, the equivalent of two billion dollars from this source.

26. Thousands of Palestinian Workers Laid Off, Kav La'oved, September–October 1990.

12   The Gulf Crisis and the Peace Movement

1. Yizhar Be'er, *Ha'aretz*, August 6, 1990.

2. Ibid.

3. Ibid.
4. In the interest of historical accuracy it should be said that Yaron London, a prominent media figure, responded similarly to Sarid, a few days earlier, to the Palestinian support for Sadaam Hussein. In a column (*Yediot Ahronot*, August 14, 1990), London bid farewell to the Palestinians and blamed himself for being duped into believing that the Palestinians really want peace. Sarid's article which appeared a few days later had, of course, infinitely greater impact.
5. Yossi Sarid, *Ha'aretz*, August 8, 1993.
6. The personal disappointment motif was prominent in the aforementioned article by Yaron London. London wrote: "Now I know, the vast majority of the Palestinians support a modern leader who will unite all the Arabs and expel all the non-Arabs from the Near East."
7. "Do Not Come Looking for Me," Yossi Sarid, *Ha'aretz*, August 17, 1990.
8. Ibid.
9. This generalization may be less accurate regarding human rights issues. Leaders, like Shulamit Aloni, have shown a high degree of consistency and loyalty to human rights principles.
10. Yael Dayan, *Yediot Ahronot*, August 21, 1990.
11. Zev Sternhal, "Buck Up, Friends," *Hadashot*, August 24, 1990.
12. Ibid.
13. Dedi Zucker, "We Are Back to 1987," *Ha'aretz*, August 21, 1990.
14. Interview with Tom Segev, *Ha'aretz*, August 24, 1990.
15. Amiram Goldblum, Peace Now spokesperson, *Ha'aretz*, August 28, 1990.
16. Open Letter to the Palestinian Leadership in the Occupied Territories, Advertisement, *Jerusalem Post*, August 17, 1990.
17. Amiram Goldblum, the Peace Now spokesperson, characterized Peace Now's position on the Gulf War in the following terms: "As a non-party movement, Peace Now can not reach unanimity about the war and its consequences. Some of us were for the war, hoping that it would accelerate the peace process in the Middle East . . . Others stated that the war is, in any case, a terrible gamble . . . that the lives of thousands of people are at stake, and if we can solve the conflict by negotiation, combined with economic and military pressures, this would be preferable."
18. Zev Sternhal, *Hadashot*, August 31, 1990.
19. *Ha'aretz*, September 7, 1990.
20. News From Within, September 5, 1990.
21. Yael Gvirtz, *Hadashot*, December 6, 1990.
22. Rolli Rosen, *Kol Ha'ir*, January 18, 1991.
23. *Yediot Ahronot*, October 14, 1990.
24. *Jerusalem Post*, October 15, 1990.
25. *Jerusalem Post*, November 2, 1990.
26. Tsali Reshef, *Ha'aretz*, October 29, 1990.

27. Dan Izenberg, "Left and Right: the Twain Have Met," *Jerusalem Post*, November 2, 1990.
28. Ibid.
29. *Ha'aretz*, October 29, 1990.
30. Ibid.
31. *Jerusalem Post*, November 2, 1990.
32. This is the title of the Peace Now leaflet calling for demonstration near Shamir's residence on December 8, 1990.
33. Ibid.

13   The War and its Aftermath

1. *Ma'ariv*, January 29, 1991.
2. *Ha'aretz*, January 30, 1991. The Peace Now letter concentrated on explaining its own position and avoided the condemnatory tone used by the writers and other sections of the peace movement towards their colleagues in Europe and the United States.
3. Advertisement, *Ha'aretz*, February 15, 1991.
4. Dan Margalit, *Ha'aretz*, February 1, 1991.
5. Lily Galilee, *Ha'aretz*, February 10, 1991.
6. News From Within, September 5, 1990. News From Within tries to present a spectrum of views, but generally ends up giving prominence to the views of Israeli and Palestinian "rejectionists" who oppose the two-state solution in principle.
7. Dr. Azmi Bashara, Yesh G'vul, December 1990.
8. Stanley Cohen, Voices From the Sealed Room, The Israeli Peace Movement During the Gulf War. From a reprint and expanded version of an article which appeared in *Il Manifesto*, March 1991.
9. Gideon Levi, Interview with Tsali Reshef, *Ha'aretz*, February 8, 1991.
10. Zev Zachor, *Al Ha'mishmar*, March 8, 1991.
11. For a detailed analysis of the Time for Peace initiative see Sarah Honig, Peace Now – Looking for Alternative Strategies, *Jerusalem Post*, June 21, 1991.

Bibliography

Periodicals

Al Hamishmar; *B'tselem Reports*; *Challenge*; *Davar*; *Hadashot*; *Ha'aretz*; *Hotam – Al Hamishmar Supplement*; *Jerusalem Post*; *Kibbutz*; *Kol Ha'ir – Jerusalem*; *Ma'ariv*; *MERIP, Middle East Reports*; *New Outlook*; *News From Within, State, Government and International Relations*, Hebrew University; *Tikkun*; *Yedioth Ahronoth*; *Zionism*, Tel Aviv University

Books and Articles

Avneri, Uri. *My Friend, the Enemy*. London, Zed Books, 1986.

Alonso, Harriet Hyman. *Peace as a Women's Issue*. Syracuse, Syracuse University Press, 1993.

Aranoff, Myron J. *Israel, Visions and Divisions*. Transaction Publishers, 1989.

Back, Aharon and Fellman, Gordon. *Peace Soon? Israel Protest Politics and the Intifada*. Unpublished manuscript, August, 1988.

Bar-on, Mordechai. *Peace Now, Portrait of a Movement*. Tel Aviv, Kibbutz Ha'meuhad Publishing House, 1985.

Beinin, Joel. *Was the Red Flag Flying There?* Los Angeles, California University Press, 1990.

Chagnollaud, Jean-Paul. *The European Community and the Middle East Conflict-Intifada*. New York, Praeger, 1990.

Cohen, Stanley. *Torture in Israel: Defining the Issues*. Tel Aviv, *New Outlook*, Vol. 33, No. 9, 1990.

Cohen, Stanley. *Voices from the Sealed Room, the Israeli Peace Movement during the Gulf War*. Rome, Il Manifesto, March 1991.

Cohen, Stanley. *The Intifada in Israel: Portents and Precarious Balance*. *Middle East Report*, May–August 1990.

Fellman, Gordon. *Peace Forces in Israel*. New York, *Jewish Currents*, June, 1988.

Fernea, Elizabeth Warnock and Hocking, Mary Evelyn, Editors. *The Struggle for Peace: Israelis and Palestinians*. Austin, University of Texas Press, 1992.

Freedman, Robert O., Ed. *The Intifada, Its Impact on Israel, the Arab World and the Superpowers.* Florida International Press, 1991.

Goldberg, Barzilai and Inbar. *The Impact of Intercommunal Conflict; the Intifada and Israeli Public Opinion. Policy Studies* No. 43. Jerusalem, Davis Institute, 1991.

Hall-Cathala, D. *The Peace Movement in Israel, 1967–1987.* London, Macmillan Press, 1990.

Hattis Rolef, Susan. *Political Dictionary of Israel,* Jerusalem, Jerusalem Press 1993.

Herman, Tamar. *Ihud – A Peace Movement Under Fire, 1947–1949. State, Government and International Relations* #33 Jerusalem, Hebrew University, 1991 (Hebrew).

Herman, Tamar. *The Rise and the Decline of the Israeli Peace Committee, Zionism* XVII, Tel Aviv University, 1983 (Hebrew).

Horowitz, Dan and Lissak Moshe. *Trouble in Utopia.* State University of New York Press, 1989.

Hurwitz, Deena. *Walking the Red Line – Israelis in Search of Justice for Palestine.* Philadelphia, New Society Publishers, 1992.

Kaplan, Liat and Levin, Michal. *Obey First and Ask Questions Later.* Educators for Democracy, 1989 (Hebrew).

Kedar, Aharon. *Brith Shalom. The Jerusalem Quarterly,* Number 18, 1981.

Langfur, Stephen. *Confessions from a Jericho Jail.* Grove Press 1992.

Lockman, Zachary and Beinin, Joel, Editors. *Intifada – The Palestinian Uprising Against Israeli Occupation.* Boston, South End Press, 1989.

Menuhin, Y. Editor. *On Democracy and Obedience.* Siman Kriah Books, 1990 (Hebrew).

Menuhin, Y. and Menuhin, Dina, Editors. *The Limits of Obedience.* Siman Kriah Books, 1985 (Hebrew).

Nassar and Heacock, Editors. *Intifada.* New York, Praeger 1990.

Rigby, Andrew. *Living the Intifada.* London, Zed Books Ltd., 1991.

Rodinson, Maxime. *Israel, A Colonial-Settler State?* New York, Monad Press, 1973.

Rosenwasser, Penny. *Voices From a 'Promised Land'.* Conn., Curbstone Press, 1992.

Sasson-Levy, Orna. *The Problem of Gender in Israeli Protest Movements.* Paper presented to Association for Israel Studies, Milwaukee, Wisconsin, May 1993.

Schiff, Ze'ev and Ya'ari, Ehud. *Intifada – The Palestinian Uprising – Israel's Third Front.* New York, Simon and Schuster, 1989.

Schnall, D. *Radical Dissent in Israeli Politics.* New York, Praeger, 1979.

Shalev, Aryeh. *The Intifada Causes and Effects.* Tel Aviv, Papyrus, 1990 (Hebrew).

Shindler, Colin. *Ploughshares into Swords? Israelis and Jews in the Shadow of the Intifada.* London, I.B. Tauris, 1991.

Shultz, George. *Turmoil and Triumph: My Years as Secretary of State.* New York. Charles Scribner's Son's, 1993.

Swirsky and Saphir, Editors. *Calling the Equality Bluff*. New York, Pergamon Press, 1991.

Tamari, Salim. *Israeli-Palestinian Dialogue – Report from the West Bank. MERIP*, January 1989.

Viorst, Milton. *Sands of Sorrow*. London, I.B. Tauris, 1987.

Wolffsohn, Michael. *Israel – Polity, Society, Economy, 1882–1986*, New Jersey, Humanities Press International, 1987.

Yishai, Yael. *Land or Peace?* California, Hoover Press, 1987.

Index

Index